# AMERICA'S PUBLIC LANDS:
## Politics, Economics and Administration

# AMERICA'S PUBLIC LANDS:
## Politics, Economics and Administration

Conference on the Public Land Law
Review Commission Report, December 1970

HARRIET NATHAN, Editor

Institute of Governmental Studies
University of California, Berkeley • 1972

5·23·73

Library of Congress Cataloging in Publication Data

Conference on the Public Land Law Review Commission
    Report, San Francisco, 1970.
    America's public lands.

    Bibliography:  p.
    1.   United States, Public Land Law Review Commission.
One third of the Nation's land. 2. United States--
Public lands. I. Nathan, Harriet, ed. II. California.
University. Institute of Governmental Studies. III. Title
KF5605.A2C6   1970       333.1'0973          72-4850
ISBN 0-87772-084-3

$7.00

Milton A. Pearl (1914-1971)

Director
Public Land Law Review Commission


With a background in law and real estate,
Milton Pearl served for a number of years as a
civilian employee of the Corps of Engineers and
more recently held important staff posts with
the House Committee on Interior and Insular
Affairs. As Director of the Public Land Law
Review Commission, he completed his work with
the commission after launching the San Francisco Conference on the report.

Mr. Pearl then rejoined the staff of the
House Committee as Special Counsel on Public
Lands. Congressman Wayne N. Aspinall, Chairman
of the Committee, indicated that Mr. Pearl had
been at work preparing legislation to implement
the commission's recommendations until his
untimely death on April 30, 1971.

Both his mastery of the material and his
appreciation of its significance were evident
to conference participants, and can be recognized as well in his comments as a discussant
and devoted advocate.

# Contents

PART TWO:   ECONOMICS AND THE PUBLIC LANDS

PART THREE:   POLICIES FOR THE USE OF THE PUBLIC LANDS

PART SIX:  POLITICS AND THE PUBLIC LANDS

# Foreword

Demands made upon the land--for housing, business and industry, for recreation and open space, for roads and highways, for farming and ranching, for mining and logging, and for the many other requirements of a mature society--have greatly increased pressures for intensified exploitation and development. Simultaneously, an awareness has been growing that virgin land is a precious and perishable resource, because the processes of land use modification are almost always irreversible. Consequently it is imperative to think carefully about the needs of a long-term future in arriving at decisions on major transfers of ownership or alterations of land use.

This is especially true of the federal public lands, which total 755.3 million acres, or one-third of the nation's entire territory. Unanswered questions concerning the future of federal lands prompted a 1964 act establishing the Public Land Law Review Commission. The commission reported in the Summer of 1970 on a program for the future, including long-range goals, objectives and guidelines.

As the report emphasizes, most of the nation's public lands are situated in the western United States and Alaska. Alaska alone has nearly half the total. And 90 percent of the remaining lands are in the western area's eleven contiguous continental states.

Accordingly it seemed essential that a western regional conference focus attention on the commission's report and findings, in the light of conditions and needs in this area. The Institute of Governmental Studies was asked to sponsor the conference, which was held in San Francisco in December, 1970. The Institute is now pleased to publish this report of the meeting. The insights of distinguished conferees and discussion leaders should contribute significantly to better understanding of the needs confronting us in the west, and of the alternatives and options available. The report also outlines the prerequisites that must be met if what is left of America's vast, varied and still-beautiful heritage is to be transmitted to our successors reasonably intact, with an optimal balance between desirable uses and wholesome preservation.

Many individuals and organizations provided invaluable help during the process of organizing and conducting the conference. Only a few can be acknowledged here, but thanks are due to them all. The Institute's Director, Eugene C. Lee, presided as chairman of the conference sessions. An advisory committee of University of California faculty members also served as moderators for the panel discussions: J. Herbert Snyder (Davis), John A. Zivnuska (Berkeley), A. Starker Leopold (Berkeley), Ira M. Heyman (Berkeley), and Grant McConnell (Santa Cruz). Mrs. Ruth Majdrakoff, University Extension, carried major responsibilities as conference coordinator. She was aided by Stephen Zwerling, Berkeley campus graduate student in political science. Louise Howe contributed significantly to the editing of the conference proceedings. Nancy Maslin was responsible for the typing.

Finally, the cooperation of the Public Land Law Review Commission, extended through its Director, the late Milton A. Pearl, facilitated both the conference sessions and publication of this report.

Stanley Scott
Assistant Director

# PART ONE

# Background and Purpose
# of the Conference

# WELCOME AND INTRODUCTION

## Eugene C. Lee

*Program Chairman*
*Director, Institute of Governmental Studies*

On behalf of the Institute of Governmental Studies
and the University Extension of the University of California at Berkeley, let me welcome you to this working
conference on the public lands of the United States. We
are here to discuss an important aspect of our future:
our public lands of 724.4 million acres or, in the words
of the report of the Public Land Law Review Commission,
"One Third of the Nation's Land."[1]

When we learned about this important report a year
ago, we approached the commission's staff and asked in
what manner the University could contribute to a discussion, in the broadest sense of the term, of this document. It was agreed that the University would organize
and conduct a conference. With great credit to the
commission and Mr. Pearl we were delegated complete
responsibility to organize the conference, plan the
program, choose the speakers and panelists and invite
you, the audience. So any criticisms of the conference
should be directed entirely at the University and, more
specifically, at the Institute of Governmental Studies.


## A Working Conference

The prospects for this meeting are exciting. The
papers, which I have had a chance to read ahead of time,
are all of high quality. They are provocative and constructive, and they will provide the basis for stimulating discussion.

3

But above all we have designed this meeting to be a *working* conference. That is why we are meeting in a small room with an audience smaller than it might have been. We want each of you to participate in the proceedings.

## The Real Theme

Every conference should have a theme. Upon first reading the title of ours, "One Third of a Nation," I thought it didn't seem quite adequate to the topic. So I tried to recall once again the words of Supervisor McSheehy, a man who lived in San Francisco in the 'twenties and had a way of coming up with themes for conferences such as this.

For example, after looking at a new city building that was going up, McSheehy said: "This proposed building has all the earmarks of an eyesore." Or after hearing a proposal that the city purchase a dozen gondolas for Golden Gate Park: "Why spend all the money? Let's just buy two and let nature take its course." Or in a comment that could be the keynote for almost any conference: "Along the invisible path to the future, I see the footprints of a hidden hand."

But then, to be serious, I saw in the first few pages of the commission's report a text that should really guide our discussion. I refer to John Ruskin's quotation:

> God has lent us the earth for our life;
> it is a great entail. It belongs as
> much to those who are to come after us...
> as to us; and we have no right, by any-
> thing we do or neglect, to involve them
> in any unnecessary penalties, or to
> deprive them of benefits which it was
> in our power to bequeath.

Or in the same vein a professor at the Berkeley campus, C. West Churchman, has said:

> Of all the principles or ethics that
> men have been able to devise, none is
> so fundamental as an ethical postulate
> as that we are morally obliged to meet
> the demand that coming generations
> would have imposed upon us, were they
> able to speak to us today.

It strikes me that here is the real theme for our conference. We are morally obliged to meet the demands that coming generations would have imposed upon us were they able to speak to us today.

## NOTE

[1] The figure of 724.4 million acres excludes 30.9 million acres of Indian reservations.

# THE REPORT OF THE PUBLIC LAND LAW REVIEW
## COMMISSION: AN OVERVIEW

Milton A. Pearl

*Director, Public Land Law Review Commission*

Since most of you are already familiar with the organization of the commission, I will not go into the details of how it was formed. But I would like to mention that it was the function of the commission:

1. to examine all the land uses and policies underlying them;

2. to review the regulations, rules and practices involved in their administration; and

3. to seek modifications if any were necessary and make recommendations concerning those modifications to the President and the Congress as may be required to insure, in the words of our mandate, "that public lands of the United States are either retained and managed or disposed of...in a manner to provide the maximum benefit to the general public."

That was the charge of the commission. That was what we set out to do and we hope, have done.

Supporting the 19-member commission was an advisory council composed of representatives from all interested groups outside of government, plus nine departments and agencies of the federal government. In addition each of the 50 governors appointed liaisons to work with us, and these 50 representatives, along with members of the advisory council, were called upon continuously to provide us with their comments on every stage of our work. Many of these people are here today.

## FACT-FINDING THROUGH RESEARCH AND MEETINGS

To provide the commission with the information needed as a basis for making decisions and recommendations, we developed two different programs to develop factual and legal data. One was a research program, involving the preparation of separate manuscripts on 33 different subjects. The second was a series of meetings across the country--north, south, east, west--during which we heard from over 900 witnesses as we carried the message to these parts of the nation that the Public Land Law Review Commission was interested in the problems people were having on our public lands. We heard from all shades of opinion as we did this. In addition we had literally thousands of pieces of correspondence coming into our offices offering suggestions and making inquiries.

## History of Public Lands

In the research program, I think a few of the results are outstanding, and I would like to refer to them in part. The first paper we contracted for was a history of public land law development. This history has been published and is available from the Government Printing Office. We think this document is every bit as important as the final report of the commission because we believe we can learn from the mistakes of the past. So we urge you, even if you don't read any of the other manuscripts, even if you don't grapple with the in-depth analysis of the individual subjects, read the history.

Other outstanding results of the research showed us that there were no statutory goals or directives for the use or management of public lands. For example, there is nothing in the statutes to indicate who is responsible for damage to the environment of the public lands either currently or in the future.

Our research program also disclosed something that we should have known had we stopped to think about it.

The Multiple Use Act, applying to both the Forest Service
and the Bureau of Land Management lands, are only autho-
rizations. They offer no guidelines for resolving the
inevitable conflicts, and land managers, we learned, are
in search of such guidelines.

## Categories of Problems

We found that the problems of public lands fall
into three general categories: (1) legislative-executive
relationships--and I might say that in my opinion it was
this relationship that gave the greatest impetus to the
creation of the commission; (2) intergovernmental
relationships--relationships between the federal government and state and local governments; and (3) user
relationships--relationships between the federal government and the users, among the users themselves and
between users and potential users and the public.

## The Testimony

In the testimony there were of course those who suggested that all of the public lands of the United States
should be retained just because we own them. Then there
were others who suggested that all of the public lands
should be disposed of and that it was not intended for
the federal government to remain the owner of any public
domain lands that were not dedicated to a specific purpose, such as a national park. Some went even further
and said that the federal government was not authorized
by the Constitution to retain lands for park purposes and
that it should retain lands for only those purposes
specified in the Constitution.

On the other side there were those who advocated
that the land base of the United States be expanded.
They believed we should buy more lands as well as hold
on to what we have because, in their view, we don't
have enough lands in the areas where we need them, particularly for recreation.

Finally, since the report has come out, there has been a tendency among some people to say: "Well, one third of the nation's land is enough. Keep it at that level, but don't buy any more."

## FINDING THE PURPOSE

The commission considered all of these arguments and came up with its first conclusion early in the game. This was that the United States should not retain all of the land simply because it now owns it; nor should it dispose of all the land; nor should it simply go out and buy additional land. The question, which we built into every piece of our research, was, *for what particular purpose* was the land to be acquired or disposed of?

In other words the commission made a decision that a public interest test had to be applied as to whether land should be kept in federal ownership. There had to be a scrutiny of the circumstances of the need.

In the commission's view very little public land would at the present time serve the public interest in private ownership and therefore the bulk of the public land should remain in federal hands. But that is a matter for discussion later in the conference. The point for now is that the commission did not automatically set out with the idea of disposing of all of the land or of holding on to all of it either. The public interest was the sole rule of thumb.

# POLICY IMPLICATIONS OF THE COMMISSION REPORT

Maurice K. Goddard

*Member of the Commission*
*Secretary of Forests and Waters,*
*State of Pennsylvania*

I first want to congratulate all who are attending this conference because I sincerely believe the work of the commission has been well done and the impact on the American people will be very substantial *if* we can explain our recommendations and develop the necessary tools to carry them out. The commission has carried out its assignment. Now you, the American people, must see that the recommendations are implemented.

I enthusiastically endorse the report. In spite of what some conservation organizations have stated, I believe it is well organized and thoroughly thought out. It is the product of a great deal of conscientious and thoughful work by a group of experienced, intelligent workers and advisers under excellent leadership.

## THE DISTRIBUTION OF LAND

Let me be more specific. If one looks at the present distribution of federal public lands, one finds that over 90 percent of those lands outside of Alaska are located in the 11 contiguous western states, and that about one-half of all public lands are located in Alaska. If one then attempts to measure or compare on that basis alone the impact that implementing the Public Land Law Review Commission report would have on the eastern and western areas of the country, one might easily conclude that the major effect would be in the West where the bulk of the land is located.

10

But that conclusion would be dead wrong. The relative impact on the two areas simply cannot be assessed on that one factor. There are many other factors involved.

## East and West

Easterners have made and will continue to make heavy use of western public lands for recreation and for the resources that come from those lands. In my opinion, therefore, it would be in the East's interest to agree with and support the basic underlying principles designed to guide future policy concerning public lands as outlined in the 17 broad recommendations contained in the introductory summary of the report, "A Program for the Future."

Indeed I believe very strongly that these recommendations, if carried out, would result in improved administration and management of public lands for the benefit of both eastern and western citizens. While all are far reaching and of great importance, I will only attempt to give the East's viewpoint on a few of the recommendations at this time.

## Against Large-Scale Disposal

The first recommendation for example, urges reversal of the present policy of large-scale disposal of public lands. Instead it proposes that future disposal be restricted and that lands be held in federal ownership where "values must be preserved so that they may be used and enjoyed by all Americans."

This recommendation is totally in accord with eastern thinking--we simply do not want western public land disposed of. The East has learned a lesson in this respect. Early in the history of this country, as you know, most eastern public lands passed from public to private ownership and today the eastern states are hard

pressed to provide lands for urgently needed public use
and recreation.

My own state of Pennsylvania is no exception. For
us the lesson has been very costly. To fill our needs--
indeed to stay just barely ahead of them--we have had to
buy back two million acres of state forest lands and one
million acres of game lands. By the end of December we
will have spent $70 million since June 22, 1964 for the
acquisition of an additional 179,000 acres for state,
regional and local parks and wildlife lands.

For this reason I strongly support the first recommendation and emphasize that wholesale disposal of
federal public lands is certainly not in our interest.
I therefore endorse the recommendation to bring the
present basic disposal policies to an end--the old Homestead Act, the Desert Land Act and all the others.

I also agree that the public lands are so important
for the use of the general public that they should no
longer be made available under lease or permit for private residential and vacation purposes and that such
existing uses should be phased out. (Recommendation 95)[1]

I understand of course that this is another case of
too much and too little--too much public land in the West
and too little in the East. But it is also true that if
western lands are retained in public ownership to help
meet eastern needs, the eastern taxpayer must help foot
the bill.


IN LIEU OF TAXES

It is quite obvious that you can't consider the
first recommendation without coupling it with the recommendation regarding tax payments. (Recommendation 102)
As the report states, "A system of payments in lieu of
taxes provides a better standard for determining the
level of payments than does a system of sharing revenue."

It is not fair to expect a state, such as the State of Nevada where 86 percent of the land is owned by the federal government, to bear the entire burden when the public lands in that state receive nationwide use and their retention in federal ownership would be beneficial to all citizens of the country.

In short, if the policy is reversed I believe that payments in lieu of taxes should be provided to the state and local governments where the public lands happen to be situated.

It would be expensive. As I remember the facts, we now pay about $93 million per year because of revenue sharing on the public lands. If we paid in lieu of taxes, the total would be about $193 million, roughly $100 million more. Nevertheless I think this is the price the American people must pay if we want these lands retained in public ownership. And it is not a lot of money at a time when we talk about a national budget of $225 billion.

An in-lieu-of-taxes system is the finest recommendation the commission has made. It would be my hope that it is one of the first to be implemented. I sincerely believe that if we can't implement this recommendation we are not going to succeed with any other recommendation, because in my opinion this is the one for which there is unanimity all over the nation.

## ENVIRONMENTAL STANDARDS

I believe too that the recommendations designed to provide statutory guidelines to protect and enhance the environment both on and off public lands are of prime importance. These are to be found in Chapter Four on "Public Land Policy and the Environment." While all the recommendations in that chapter are important and far reaching, I would like to stress three in particular.

I agree that federal standards for environmental control should be established for public lands, but

contend that where state standards have been adopted
under federal law the state standards should be utilized.
In short, the federal government should set minimum
acceptable standards, but if the states set more stringent standards, the latter should prevail.

Many of you are familiar with the case of the *State
of Minnesota v. the Atomic Energy Commission*, in which
Minnesota seeks to establish stronger standards than
those of the AEC. I am glad to report that the State of
Pennsylvania has joined with Minnesota in this action.
As an example we licensed the shipping port plant of
the Duquesne Light Company on the Ohio River about five
years ago; the standards we drew up are about 10 times
as severe as those of the Atomic Energy Commission. So
I believe if a state wants to have more stringent standards than the federal government, it should have that
right.

## How to Deter Pollution

The second recommendation in Chapter Four that I
would like to stress is the one stating that "Congress
should authorize and require the public land agencies to
condition the granting of rights or privileges to the
public lands or their resources on compliance with applicable environmental control measures governing operations
of public lands which are closely related to the right or
privilege granted." (Recommendation 23)

This recommendation, if carried out and enforced,
could be one of the strongest deterrents to the pollution
of our environment. Remember we are talking about the
resources coming from almost a third of the land of the
nation. If this recommendation to control the use of our
raw materials were implemented it could be one of the
best tools imaginable to bring reluctant industries into
line.

For example, if you were cutting pulp wood from the
United States Forest Service lands and that wood was to

be sold to a mill or processor that was not meeting
established water and air pollution control standards,
the sale could be stopped. You could not sell materials
from public lands to a processor polluting the environment.

If it is in the national interest to say there will
be no more air pollution, no more water pollution, no
more desecration of the landscape, then it is also in the
public interest to withhold raw material from the
pollution-making processor.

The State of Pennsylvania this summer adopted this
principle by executive order of the governor. As an
example of how it worked, a small steel company on
Brandywine Creek in the southern part of the state builds
guardrails and other structures for the highway system.
They were in violation of the state sanitary water laws.
With the new principle in operation, the Highway Department lifted all of their contracts; two weeks later they
were in compliance with the Sanitary Water Board requirements.

So I believe this is a great recommendation. It
should be implemented at the federal level.

## A Model for Reform

The third recommendation in Chapter Four of the
report is the one to require by statute that users of
public lands and resources conduct their activities in
such a manner as to avoid or minimize adverse environmental impact and to make these users responsible for
restoring areas to an acceptable standard. (Recommendation 25)

Most of the environmental degradation that has
already taken place in this country has occurred in the
highly industrialized and urbanized areas of the East.
This degradation was once thought to be a necessary price

for progress and industrial growth. Today the price has become too high; indeed this past desecration is stifling our economic growth.

While we in our state are working hard to restore our environment, our wounds--inflicted by over a century of unrestricted coal extraction--will take a long time to heal. Pennsylvania has probably the strongest mining laws in the country--laws, such as proposed in this recommendation, designed to rectify the damage done on public lands and to prevent new damage to our land and water resources on a statewide basis.

Unfortunately these Pennsylvania laws were passed only after we finally recognized that the environmental quality of the land affected had to be restored and that every effort had to be made to assure that our land, both public and private, would suffer no further desecration.

Other states in the East are of course suffering from this problem too, but many do not yet have the legislative controls to do an adequate job. Acceptance of this recommendation and passage of a federal statute to bring these requirements into being on federal lands would serve as a model for many of the eastern states and go a long way toward bringing necessary legislative reforms.

I should point out that the rehabilitation job in most of the East is on lands in the nonfederal and private sector. Nevertheless the federal government should learn from our past mistakes and not allow its lands to be mutilated.

## MINORITY OPINIONS

It is amazing to me that there are only a few minority opinions expressed by the commissioners in a report of this magnitude, one covering such a myriad of subjects. As Commissioner Clark pointed out however, the report is a consensus effort and must be read against nearly 200 years of history.

I will discuss only one of the cases where divergent views were expressed, and this case is found in Chapter Seven, entitled "Mineral Resources."

A majority of the commissioners held that the Mining Law of 1872 would still be adequate if major surgery were applied to correct deficiencies and weaknesses. The most important changes recommended are:

1. Require an exploration permit whenever equipment that would be damaging to the environment is being used.

2. Permit the land management agencies to improve conditions in such permits in order to protect environmental values.

3. Impose royalty charges on production of minerals.

4. Subject minerals to competitive bidding whenever competitive interest can reasonably be expected.

5. Permit the miner to obtain patent only to the mineral deposit and such surface area as is necessary for production.

At a meeting in Boston last week, Dr. Perry Hagenstein discussed these recommendations in a paper, stating that:

> This proposal would correct many of
> the defects in the General Mining
> Law identified by conservation and
> other non-mineral interests. It
> would provide for some control over
> environmental factors and for pay-
> ment to the federal government of
> the value of the mineral body and
> of such surface area as is needed.
> At the same time, it would leave

the existing rights of the miner to
unrestricted entry on the public lands
largely unchanged, and would thus
continue the priority afforded hard
rock minerals over other public land
resources.

In spite of the excellent recommendations to modify
the existing mineral law, Commissioners Clark, Hoff,
Udall and I recommended instead that a general leasing
system for all minerals, except those made available for
outright sale by law, should be adopted. However if a
general leasing system cannot be adopted, it is essential that the commission's recommendations as outlined
in Chapter Seven be implemented.

I am frankly convinced that these are *minimal*
acceptable changes to the Mining Law of 1872. In fact I
think a lot of people looked at the report, saw that the
commission did not recommend repeal of the Law of 1872,
and decided immediately that the report was no good without reading any further. That's how strongly some people
feel about this law.


## PLANNING LAND USE

I also want to stress the importance of Chapter
Three of the report, entitled "Planning Future Public
Land Use." The commission is not satisfied with the way
land use planning is currently being carried out. We
find that many of the individual problems that led to
the creation of the commission and which emerged from
our study had their roots in an inadequate planning process.

The commission believes that public land agencies
must be required to plan uses to obtain the greatest net
public benefits. (This is Recommendation 2.)

It now appears that one of our most controversial
proposals is the one (Recommendation 4) stating that

"Management of public lands should recognize the highest and best use of particular areas of land as dominant over other authorized uses." In short, call this the "dominant land use concept." Frankly I am amazed at the outcry against this philosophy. Isn't this the very concept of our national parks system, wilderness preservation system, riverways and scenic rivers system, among many others I could name if our time weren't limited? Under this recommendation, areas of national forest and unreserved public domain lands would be classified to locate those areas that have a clearly identifiable highest use. These would be specified as "dominant use" areas; however, other uses would also be allowed where compatible.

As a practical matter all public lands will not be placed in one dominant use zone or another. Only those areas that have an identifiable highest primary use at the time of classification would be placed in a dominant use category. The remaining lands would remain in a category where all uses are considered equal until such time as a dominant use becomes apparent.

Such an approach would provide an excellent guide for investment of federal funds in management practices. For example, investments in timber management should be directed primarily to timber dominant areas; on the other hand, land investments in recreation should be directed primarily to recreation dominant areas. Wildlife the same way; grazing, and other uses. If you carefully study the planning chapters and pages 48 through 51, I am confident you will have a much better understanding of this concept and not find it as unreasonable as some have reported.


A SINGLE DEPARTMENT

As I conclude, may I emphasize one additional recommendation (Recommendation 131): "The Forest Service should be merged with the Department of the Interior into a new Department of Natural Resources."

I feel particularly qualified to discuss such a subject because the Pennsylvania General Assembly recently
created a new Environmental Resources Department and
abolished the Department of Forests and Waters, which I
had headed for the past 16 years. Frankly I am not happy
about this action as I believe regulatory agencies and
management should not be housed in the same agency. The
Nixon Administration's action to create an Environmental
Protection Agency is a more logical procedure than that
taken in Pennsylvania.

To me it is perfectly logical to combine the major
public land management agencies into a single department.
Why should the one major public land agency not now in
the Department of Interior be left by itself? I suggest
that you study the reasons for the commission's recommendation on pages 282 through 283. The actual uses of the
lands of the Forest Service and the Bureau of Land
Management are for example, almost identical. I can see
no difference in timber that is harvested on national
forests or on BLM lands.

I firmly believe in the commission's recommendation
that the major part of the remaining unappropriated public domain lands be retained in federal ownership.
Forest Service programs should be under the same policy
direction as the other major classes of public lands and
vice versa. Policies and practices for the management
and use of public lands should be the same for all lands
and agencies. And the easiest way to obtain such consistency is to have a single Department of Natural
Resources.

## A CAUTION FOR CRITICS

The fairest assessment of the Public Land Review
Commission report that I have seen to date is contained
in a short editorial by James B. Craig. In the August
1970 issue of *American Forests*, published by the American
Forestry Association, he emphasizes the joint statement
by Congressman Aspinall, Vice Chairman Mock and Director

Pearl that "no one part of the report can or should be read or considered by itself."

Mr. Craig points out that most people studying the report will find things in it that do not meet their approval, but "people who challenge it had better do their homework before throwing a monkey wrench into any given part."

He concludes that "no one can digest this interlocking, legalistic mechanism in just a few days.... Anyone who chooses to go up the Hill to attack any one or more of the parts therein had better go clad in belt and suspenders of complete preparedness lest he depart naked."

So let me again congratulate you for participating in this conference so that you can speak intelligently about the recommendations of the Public Land Law Review Commission. Please remember if any good comes from the time and money spent on the report--and there has been an awful lot of both--it will be because of your dedicated efforts to understand it and to help us try to implement the important recommendations.

## NOTE

[1]See the Appendix, "Summary of Commission Recommendations," this volume, pp. 365ff. Speakers' references to chapters and page numbers relate to *One Third of the Nation's Land*, the commission report.

# A FURTHER WORD

Milton A. Pearl

I would like to expand on a few of the things that
Dr. Goddard said.  In the first place, in connection with
his latter remarks about criticism of the report, we
found that nobody likes this report and we regard that as
a rather healthy sign.

Something must be good about it if everybody finds
something wrong, and no group that I know of has embraced
it in its entirety.  At the same time only one group has
attempted to criticize it in its entirety--to say that
it is completely worthless and ought to be completely
shelved.  That group is the Sierra Club and I would like
to take a moment or two to let you know what the basis
of its opposition is.

The Sierra Club opposes the entire report because
the report is based on the archaic assumptions that the
twin evils of population growth and economic growth will
continue.  Now I guess I am as responsible as anyone for
the adoption of these assumptions, because we structured
our research in response to a charge by the statute creating the commission that we compile data to understand
the demands on the public lands within the present and
the foreseeable future.  And the commission decided--we
all decided--that we could not see beyond the year 2000.

## ASSUMPTIONS AND PROJECTIONS

On the one hand, the year 2000 is only 30 years
away.  On the other hand, look back 30 years and try to
think how many of the things that have since happened
you would have been able to predict at that time.

It's always hazardous to make predictions, but we went ahead. We said we would look forward to the year 2000, and to do this we consulted with demographers and economists and we retained a firm to make our initial projects for consumption of all products producible on the public lands in the year 2000. And since population is directly related to these questions, projections were also made of the population for the year 2000.

The Bureau of the Census provides high, medium and low population projections, showing what could happen under different circumstances. The high projections at the time of our research went much higher, but the medium projections, which were adopted by the commission, indicated that there might be as many as 100 million additional people by the year 2000, or a total of 300 million. We now concede that it might only total 275 million, but that's a slight difference.

## A Growing Population

The facts are that every person who will be 30 years of age in the year 2000 is now here with us, and most of the people who will be of childbearing age by that time are also with us. So patterns are already adopted and, unless we were to have an overnight reversal and somehow achieve a zero population growth, our population is going to grow whether we like it or not.

Indeed estimates show that if we were to immediately slow the population growth rate to two persons per family from now on, we still would not get a stabilized population until the year 2075. So we are going to have a growing population, and we are going to need the goods and services to take care of that growing population.

In addition, we now have 55 million Americans who are classified as either below, at or just above the poverty level. The latest figures that we have show that 48 percent of our population--much more than 55 million--does not earn $8,000 a year. And $8,000 a year is hardly part of the affluent society.

If we are going to carry out our obligations to these 55 million Americans who are barely getting along at or below the level of poverty, and the millions more who are aspiring to a higher standard of living, we must have increased economic growth. We can't deny to these Americans the goods and services to which they are entitled.

For example, we have in the statute books a policy to construct 26 million homes between the years 1969 and 1979, a 10-year period. If we want to provide decent housing for most Americans, then we must provide additional timber resources. These are the things the commission is talking about when it says we are going to have an added demand.

Even if each member of the affluent society would say today that he has had enough and wants no more, we would still have to provide for those who have not had enough. And that is all that the commission has said.

## New Cities and Workers

We can see that if we were to establish immediately a zero population growth (a question that the commission never considered as part of its function), then some of the commission's recommendations would be invalid. Some, but far from all.

As an example, it is said that if we don't have the additional people and the additional economy, we won't need the new cities that are mentioned in the report. Well, that is true, but we have been told by other groups that have studied the problem that we are going to need new cities, 100 new cities, between now and 2000. And all the commission has said is that public lands could be made available--where it is ecologically and environmentally feasible--as sites for these new cities. But, yes, if we are not going to have the new people and the added economic growth, then these new cities will not be needed.

Statistics show that because of the number of Americans already born, our labor force will grow by 55 million persons between now and the year 2000. We have a choice of what these additional 55 million people will be doing. Are we to say that they must become unemployed? Or are we going to let them become producers? If they become producers, our GNP (gross national product) will automatically grow.

## A Continued Trend

Thus all the indications are that the assumptions we started with are correct: the trends of the past will continue. We did ask our researchers to take into account all of the variables that could impinge on these trends. Nevertheless we think that forces are now in motion that will result in increased population and increased economic growth through the year 2000 and shortly beyond.

None of us--I think I can speak for each member of the commission--favors a wasteful society. But that does not mean that those who are now part of the affluent society are going to give up overnight that which they have been enjoying and accruing for themselves over the past several years.

GUIDELINES FOR PLANNING PUBLIC LAND POLICY

One of the main recommendations of the commission is that we get away from the case-by-case method of establishing public land policy. The commission proposes that policy be established in advance: first, by guidelines from Congress, and secondly, through the planning procedure that has been described for you by Commissioner Goddard, where everybody has an opportunity to take part. We need to know in advance what the rules of the road are and what we can expect, and this includes anticipated changes in administrative procedures as well.

## Outer Continental Shelf

Because of the particular interest of the states represented at this meeting, I would like to mention the Outer Continental Shelf. One of the most significant recommendations of the commission has been given very little attention outside of the trade press. But I was very pleased to read in the newspaper yesterday that the President has directed the Secretary of the Interior to proceed with an action recommended by the commission--that is, for the Department of the Interior to impose federal conservation and production controls on the Outer Continental Shelf.

## Domestic Supplies

Other recommendations of the commission concerning the Outer Continental Shelf involve environmental control particularly. Here again, the commission took the position that we are going to need additional sources of domestic supplies to meet increased demands of the future, and that because of the environmental danger we should not cut that domestic supply off, but rather find ways of making certain that there will be no damage in the future.

## THE STATE OF ALASKA AND REGIONAL COMMISSIONS

With regard to Alaska, the commission made a basic conclusion: that once Alaska has achieved its equality with other states, it should be subjected to the same land laws that the other public land states are subjected to. The same procedure should be available and the same policies applicable.

But the commisson made another significant recommendation as well. It said that between now and the time that the Alaskans complete land selection, we have an unprecedented opportunity to help the state plan its own destiny. We should coordinate very closely with the

State of Alaska as it selects which lands will go into
state ownership, or stay in state ownership or go from
the state into private ownership, so that the pattern
of development will be one desired by the Alaskans and
in accordance with planning procedures.

While the commission recommends that regional commissions be established throughout the United States, it
makes a special point of the need for an immediate
regional commission in Alaska to provide coordination
between the federal government and the state government
with all elements of the state government involved.

## EDUCATION AND LEGISLATION

The commission has completed its work. Its report
was submitted in June, and we are now engaged in bringing the report to the people. We are engaged in a two-
pronged educational process: (1) to educate the public
through the opinion makers, the people who have constitu-
encies of their own, and (2) to hear from those who come
to these meetings what the people think about the recommendations, how they might be improved upon and which
ones could be immediately implemented and which could
not.

The educational process will be a necessary input
for the next step, which is the legislative step. About
80 percent of the recommendations, we believe, require
legislative implementation.

When Congress meets in January, it will be in a
position to start taking up legislation for a meaningful
revision of the public land laws. We have spent five
years and $7 million, and now we are ready to go to work
to get these laws that have been needed for some time on
the books so that we can have the best use of the public
lands, whether in federal ownership or nonfederal ownership, for the benefit of the American people.

# DISCUSSION WITH THE AUDIENCE

## PUBLIC DOMAIN OR NATIVE AMERICAN RIGHTS?

*Cornelius:* Mr. Pearl, I heard you and Dr. Goddard say you want to hear the opinions of people. And then I heard you talk about public domain while you were discussing my ancestors' land. I can see now why you have taken so much from us.

My name is Mary Cornelius. I am an Ojibwa Indian from the State of North Dakota where I live on a tiny reservation that is 6 miles wide and 12 miles long. We have 14,730 people residing on this tiny reservation.

I have received over a thousand certificates from the government that say: "This is to certify that Mary Rose Peletier Cornelius, an Indian of the Turtle Mountain Ojibwa Tribe, is eligible as an Indian to receive land on a public domain, either in a national forest or a public domain." This is the Act of June 25, 1910.

Now, Mr. Pearl, when we Indians from North Dakota come up to you and say we want part of this land, what are you going to say to us? We have our certificate from the government. It is dated 1966.

## Exclusion of Indian Reservations

*Pearl:* Well, first of all, as you probably know Indian reservations were excluded from the purview of the commission's review. The law establishing the commission specifically excluded the consideration of the Indian reservations. And I am sure you are aware that an entirely different body of law has arisen. It has been developed concerning...

28

*Cornelius:* Correct. I am not speaking of only Indian reservations; I am speaking of public domain and national forests.

*Pearl:* I will come to that. So that the problems of the Indians--your problems--to which we are all very sympathetic...

*Cornelius:* Which doesn't help. You have been giving us sympathy since 1872, and we are still existing in poverty. Our Indian kids are still being beaten, their faces and their hands still freeze and all we can get from you is sympathy. Sympathy doesn't do anything to me.

*Pearl:* I know that there are problems, but the problems --your problems--are not land problems.

*Cornelius:* Our problem *is* the land problem. A reservation that is 6 miles wide and 12 miles long, a poverty-stricken area, with a population of 14,730--some of whom are starving--trying to live off this tiny little island, and you don't call that a problem? You created the problem for us. We once owned 10 million acres in the State of North Dakota. I did research, too.

## No Special Consideration

*Pearl:* As I was saying, the problems of Indian reservations were specifically excluded from the commission's consideration.

In considering the question of the public domain generally, the commission came to the conclusion, as described by Dr. Goddard, that there should be a continuous examination of the public lands to see whether they would be more useful to the maximum benefit of the general public in nonfederal ownership for all Americans, regardless of whether they are Indians or otherwise; and that no American should be given a special call on any part of the public domain. It would be impossible to do careful future planning if there were

that type of special call by any group of Americans.
Therefore the commission came up with recommendations
calling for a public interest test before any lands
are transferred out of federal ownership.

In that regard, the commission says that you and
all other Americans have the opportunity of influencing
your Congress, and if you can find the means of developing for congressional approval a special consideration
for the public interest test, then there should be some
given. But in the absence of such a public interest
test, the commission believes that most of the public
land in the United States would serve the public interest best by remaining in federal ownership. This means
that there would be only selected disposals as indicated
by Commissioner Goddard, reading from the recommendation
that appears on page one of the report.

In other words, in answer to your question, there is
nothing in this report that provides anything special
for you or any other Indians.

## Who Was Consulted?

*Cornelius:* In your report and your research, how many
Indians were consulted? How come you always excluded
us?

*Pearl:* We never excluded anybody, and as a matter of
fact, representatives of various Indian tribes...

*Cornelius:* May I have a list of these Indian tribes'
names when we have a recess?

*Pearl:* Well, I don't have them with me. They are in the
files.

*Cornelius:* I would like to have a copy.

*Pearl:* I can tell you that the Navajos, for example,
were very active. In addition to sending people to
testify at the meetings, representatives of the Navajos

met on several occasions with me in our office in Washington, and they met also with the chairman of the commission and presented their particular problems and their particular views. The same avenue was open to all other Indians. Your representatives in Congress presented views as they saw fit to the commission, and we held hearings, as I said, and meetings throughout the country. We tried to...

*Cornelius:* I don't recall ever being invited to any of your meetings. I have been quite active for five years, but I don't recall any time the record showing that we were invited to your meetings from the State of North Dakota.

*Pearl:* Well, I don't know that we sent the specific invitation to anyone...

*Cornelius:* I would like to have a complete copy of the Indians that attended your meetings.

*Pearl:* Thank you very much. Yes, ma'am.


BEYOND THE YEAR 2000

*Edmisten:* My name is Buela Edmisten. Regarding the frame of reference, I concur thoroughly with John Ruskin and the commission that we must act so that coming generations might be counted in with our decisions, but I would like to say that my son, who will very soon be starting law school, is one member of these coming generations who shares my concern. In fact, he is dead scared that you look ahead only to 2000, because in that case probably no one will look much further ahead in our nation. My time line may end before 2000, but let us hope that the time line for a healthy America does not, and our public lands will be a vital factor in that.

We wonder at your assumptions that either labor will be unemployed or we will just continue snowballing the way we have done. I wish your contractor had considered a shorter workweek or a shorter workday. It

is not irregular to think that we could change our population trends or that we could change our accent from
GNP to net national quality.

Many of the recommendations seem to indicate the
frame of reference for the same old snowball down the
hill at the expense of our public lands. Many others do
not. But I would like to simply say that many of us are
dead scared at looking ahead only to 2000. Let's raise
our sights.

*Pearl:* Anybody else? Yes.

## AUTHORITY TO WITHDRAW LAND

*Jackman:* I'm David Jackman from the Stanford Law School
Environmental Law Society. I would like to ask a question with reference to one of the earlier recommendations included in the report.

If the kind of comprehensive land use planning you
recommend is adopted and dominant use zoning is applied,
would Recommendation 7, which says that Congress should
give the agencies power to suspend the operation of certain of the public land laws, mean that agencies could
exclude zones set aside for recreation, fish and wildlife purposes for the mining laws?

*Pearl:* As the wording of that recommendation shows, the
idea is that if some emergency requires an immediate
withdrawal in order to protect some important public
interest, the executive should have the authority to do
it.

*Jackman:* In Recommendation 7 it was unclear to me who
would have that authority.

*Pearl:* It wouldn't contrast at all with the present
authority, but it would limit it because in the future
the commission recommends that large-scale withdrawal be
accomplished only by Congress and that executive withdrawal be limited. But this particular type of withdrawal would be done the same as now.

## Geological Resources

*Jackman:* Fine. I notice in the research program bro-
chure you let us have today a reference to a manuscript
to be published, entitled "Geothermal Steam Resources on
the Public Land," which is being prepared by the commission staff. As you know, in Alaska and California we
probably have the most promising geological prospects in
the country for the development of these resources.
Could you give us any insight or information as to what
this manuscript will say?

*Pearl:* The manuscript is available now for those who
want it. Most people who are interested have had an
opportunity to look at it. It's on deposit, as indicated in that reference, in the National Archives and in
selected centers throughout the country. It's just a
factual and legal document. It makes no recommendations
of any kind. None of our reports are supposed to make
recommendations. The recommendations are in the commission's report.

## Mechanics for Development

*Jackman:* Well, it's my understanding that in the current
session of Congress, Senator Bible of Nevada will introduce a bill he has been shepherding lo these many years,
Senate Bill 468, which has a good chance of passing. If
it does, it will open up to the Department of Interior
some million acres of land for competitive bidding for
the development of these resources. Has the commission
staff or the Department of Interior, to your knowledge,
operated on that yet?

*Pearl:* Operated on what?

*Jackman:* On setting up the mechanics of how this would
work.

*Pearl:* The commission wouldn't have anything to do with
that. That's something you would have to investigate
with the Secretary of the Interior. The legislation

has been pending for some time. I'm glad to hear from you that it stands a good chance of being enacted at the next session of Congress, because we have needed this legislation for some time.

## PROPERTY RIGHTS: PUBLIC AND PRIVATE

*Di Vita:* Mr. Pearl, I am Mrs. Di Vita and I have 10 acres of land in Tahoe National Forest.

One year ago plans were drawn up to take 120 acres of lumber from down in the canyon in the forest and they picked 800 feet that went through my property. Now, I wasn't notified. No consideration whatsoever was given to how I would feel about this until about three or four months ago when communications started.

I was then presented with the idea that their decision was just to take out the lumber. On investigation of my own, I found out that they wanted it as a permanent right to go through the property in the future for the purpose of opening up a recreational venture.

Now, I am against this. Taking 800 feet through the heart of my 10 acres leaves me nothing. Yet I seem to have no say about this whatsoever. What are my rights?

*Pearl:* You do have a say about it, but from the facts that you have given, it's impossible for me to draw any conclusions. Obviously, you should have been notified.

*Di Vita:* That's right.

*Pearl:* I know that the Forest Service procedures provide for that. If that wasn't done in your case, it's unfortunate, and the commission recommends that the one instance where acquisition of property is needed is when acquisition is required to cross private property in order to obtain the use of public lands that have important public values. So that if it is necessary to cross your land to reach some hunting and fishing land, it would be within the purview of the commission's recommendation to do that. Of course, it needs to be done in accordance with law. It needs to be done in accordance with procedures that bring you into the planning stage so that you can explore together the alternative routes. Of course you have the right to just compensation in the end, before they can...

Eminent Domain                    1793447

*Di Vita:* You talk about the right of just compensation. It took me five years to find this piece of property. It has water on it. They are going within 10 feet of the water.

All right, let me finish. Suppose they exercise the right of eminent domain. Where do I stand? No money can buy this. This is what I have looked for. This is what I want.

*Pearl:* You know, it's impossible for me to give a complete answer because I don't know the situation.

*Di Vita:* You don't know the particulars of it, but I have tried to explain it as far as I can.

*Pearl:* As far as the principles are concerned, let me make a couple of observations. Number one, the United States has the right of eminent domain and must have the right of eminent domain.

*Di Vita:* I have the right of my property. This is what's wrong. We are in a phase of revolution, whether we know it or not. A person has a right to own property. Why can the government come in? The government is the working class that we elect and pay and employ. In a case like this, why can't we have the right to stand up and say something? Then you exercise the right of eminent domain and that puts us where?

# PART TWO

# Economics and the Public Lands

# ECONOMIC ASPECTS OF PUBLIC LANDS

Marion Clawson

*Resources for the Future*
*Washington, D.C.*

This is a conference on public lands. In context, but not in explicit statement, "public" in this case means federal--in other words, a conference about federally owned lands. I shall conform to this interpretation in most of my comments.

I should like to emphasize at the beginning however, that a considerable area of important land in the United States is owned by units of government other than the federal government. All states own some land; some own quite large areas. In 1950 states (not including Alaska, which was then not yet a state) owned about 80 million acres, or about 4 percent of the area of the 48 contiguous states.

Most counties own some land, although often relatively small areas; all cities own land, if nothing more than their streets. City and county land is mostly used for transportation (streets and roads) or for recreation (parks) and not as forests or grazing areas. Interestingly enough, public land ownership within cities, including the largest cities, is about a third of their total area--the same as federal land in comparison with national land area.

The management of the federal lands has had less attention than many of us think desirable; that is one reason why we welcome the report of the Public Land Law Review Commission. But the management of state, county and city land has had almost no attention by the general public, by researchers and by analysts generally. The

uses of these lands involve virtually all citizens and
the economic values concerned are substantial.

Among persons familiar with land management, there
is a widespread belief which I share, that the management
of public lands other than federal has generally been
incompetent, marked with favoritism and sometimes cor-
rupt. I doubt if there is any state, except possibly the
new State of Alaska, where there has not been one or more
major political scandals over the management of state
lands. Repeatedly, city and county lands are used for
purposes other than those authorized when the lands were
acquired--diversion of park lands to other purposes being
especially common.

It would lead us afield from our purpose here today
to consider the management of state, county and city
lands; and in any case we do not have the necessary data
to do so. But I think everyone here today should realize
that there is a major public land management problem a
great deal closer to where he lives than are most federal
lands. I do not mean to divert attention from federal
land management; on the contrary I have tried to call
attention to it over the years. But I would urge that
more consideration be given to the management of other
public lands; the necessary facts are usually not readily
available, and public interest has rarely been focused on
them except at times of political controversy.

## THE COMMISSION'S TASK AND ITS
## TERMS OF REFERENCE

It may help to focus our discussion here today and
to avoid a dispersion of our time and effort, if we
review briefly the task assigned to the commission and
its terms of reference. In Section 4 of the Act creating
the commission (Public Law 88-606), it was directed to
study existing statutes and regulations applicable to
public lands, review the policies and procedures of the
federal agencies, determine the demands now made and
likely to exist for public lands and recommend such

modifications in laws, regulations, policies, and practices as would, in the commission's judgment, best serve
the policy set forth earlier in the act.  Elsewhere, public lands were defined.

In addition to thus briefly stating the commission's
duties, it may be helpful to list some of the things the
commission was neither authorized nor directed to do.  It
was clearly:

*not authorized* to consider and recommend a national
land policy for private lands nor for lands in cities;

*not authorized* to deal with national water policy;

*not authorized* to consider the optimum land settlement pattern of the United States, including population
distribution as between cities and countryside;

*not authorized* to formulate a national resources
policy in general; and

*not authorized* to recommend a national population
policy or a national policy about economic growth.

Some of these subjects have been assigned to other
national commissions; pending legislative proposals would
deal with others.  These are extremely important matters;
they are related in varying degrees to the management of
the public lands and they must be taken into account, as
the commission did to a considerable degree, in formulat-
ing proposals.  But it was not the commission's task to
deal with these subjects directly, and it is inappropriate to criticize the commission for not doing so.
Just because you do not like the tune, don't shoot the
piano player.

The commission explicitly or implicitly made assumptions about future population and future economic growth,
as a basis for the demands on the federal land "likely
to exist within the foreseeable future," to use the language of the act.  By and large, its assumptions were

conventional ones--about 300 million people in 2000 and a larger but not strictly specified national output in the same year.  The population estimate may be a little high, according to recent analyses of population growth; if trends in the birthrate of the past 10 years continue for another 10 years, then in 40 or 50 years the United States would have a constant population of 240 to 250 million.

Past projections of population growth have been notoriously inaccurate; in the late 1920s and early 1930s most demographers were predicting a stationary population long before now, and at a much lower level than present population.  But the difference between 250 and 300 million is not overwhelming as far as demands on public land are concerned.

There is a virtually unanimous consensus among economists that economic growth will continue; the makeup of the national output may change and special measures to reduce the impact of economic activity on the environment may slow down the rate of growth, but no reputable economist that I know of projects zero economic growth as probable in the foreseeable future.  Unanimity does not guarantee accuracy, of course; but the commission is in the mainstream of economic discourse when it assumes continued economic growth.

## WHERE ARE THE FEDERAL LANDS?

By any one of the several tests the federally owned lands are important nationally, regionally and in many localities.  The title of the report we are considering here today, *One Third of the Nation's Land*, pithily suggests their national role in an area sense.  As the report points out, the acreage of federal land ranges from one percent or less in five states, to a high of 95 percent in Alaska.  The overwhelming proportion of the federal lands (94 percent) are in the 11 western states plus Alaska, and here they constitute 63 percent of the total land area.  It was this western regional concentration of federal land ownership that so long led people in other regions to think they had no great interest in federal land management. As the report of the commission makes clear however, every state has some federal land within its borders and often has quite strategically located tracts of such land.

Colorado has 36 percent of its area federally owned, and California 44 percent. In extensive parts of each state nearly all the land is privately owned, while in other parts the percentage of federal land is much greater and for large areas approaches 100 percent. Thus, locally within states, federal land ownership is dominant.

The acreage figures exaggerate the importance of the federal land, however one wishes to measure "importance." Because of the long process of selective disposition of federal lands, by means of which individuals and corporations acquired the "best" lands as they saw them at the time, the land left in federal ownership has been that which was the least valuable at the time it was reserved for permanent federal ownership. Some of these lands have come to acquire much greater value, compared to private lands, in the succeeding decades. In the United States, there has long been a philosophic or political conviction that lands in certain uses should be in private or local governmental ownership; virtually all cropland, land used for industrial, commercial, residential, and other urban purposes and some other kinds and uses of land have been in private ownership. Public ownership--both federal and state--has been primarily of forest, grazing and park land.

## Spotlight on Timber and Oil

The importance of the federal lands can be measured in other ways than by their area. The commission report states: "...the Federal Government now owns some 20 percent of all the country's commercial forest land, nearly 40 percent of merchantable timber and over 60 percent of its softwood sawtimber." As the cutting of timber has

reduced the stock on privately owned lands, the federal
timber has come to have greater and greater importance.

For some types and grades of timber, the importance
is greater than these figures suggest. Although national
forests and other federal timber have always been important, their importance has risen in the last two decades,
and is likely to increase much further in the decades
ahead. One result has been to focus a spotlight of public attention on federal timber management, to make it
controversial and "political" in a sense that earlier
foresters did not envision.

The federal lands, including offshore areas as
"land," are an important source of oil and gas. Between
6 and 7 percent of the national oil and gas output comes
from federal lands; and additional amounts from the submerged areas; the proportion is likely to rise in the
future. Consequently, federal policies in oil and gas
leasing are important and likely to become more so. A
most important field of concern, looming on the horizon,
is the leasing of oil shale lands.

For a great many years, to my personal knowledge,
oil shale has been looked to as a future source of oil.
When I was a boy 50 years ago, there were two experimental oil shale extraction plants, one federal and one
private, in our town, in an area which no longer is considered a likely place for oil shale development.
Throughout my years of involvement and concern with public land management, commercial development of oil shale
seemed imminent.

There is an immense volume of oil in the federal oil
shale lands; it will almost certainly come into use some
day. Spent shale and other wastes will create extremely
difficult problems of environmental degradation; and the
financial terms on which the federal lands will be leased
will surely provoke political debate and controversy--
indeed, have already done so. Some persons are concerned
that a "giveaway" of billions of dollars of public wealth
is in the making; others point to the fact that one
recent offer of leases on federal land produced no

serious bids from any organization with the capital and knowhow to exploit these shales.

## Livestock, Recreation and Revenue

The federal lands are also an important source of forage for range livestock. Nationally only about 3 percent of the total forage requirements for roughage-consuming livestock are produced on federal land; within the 11 western states the proportion rises to about 12 percent; within the portions of those states where the federal lands are concentrated the proportion is far higher. But these comparisons understate the role of federal grazing land.

Most federal grazing land is seasonally useful; the livestock that graze on it in one season find their feed on private lands during the rest of the year. In some cases, the federal range is a major portion of the forage available at some season. For many ranchers, the forage from the federal land is critical; his investment and use of his private land is dependent upon the availability of federal forage. Federal grazing land management has attracted a considerable amount of attention in the past; in particular, controversy has been frequent over grazing fees. I have often thought that grazing and the fee question have attracted attention out of proportion to their importance, at least as compared with federal land management for other purposes.

The federal lands are particularly important as a resource for outdoor recreation. The national parks and parts of the national forests are world famous for their beauty and recreational value; some federal wildlife refuges have birds or other wildlife of international importance. Total numbers of recreation visits to federal lands are about equal to total visits to all the state parks. In some parts of the country, the federal areas must involve far more visitors than do the state parks.

I have not looked at the detailed data, but I would
expect that in many western states the total numbers of
visitors to federal lands would far exceed the totals to
state parks. There is considerable difference in types
of areas and in use, between the federal and state areas
The federal areas, or at least some of them, are unique
and outstanding by national standards, and draw people
from considerable distances while many of the state park
provide mass outdoor recreation, primarily to people
within comparatively short distances.

The importance of the federal lands may also be
measured in terms of the monetary expenditures on them,
and the monetary receipts from them. As I have pointed
out several times in my writings, the federal lands are
big business in the American sense of that term. Total
receipts from federal lands (including submerged areas)
are now in the general range of $400 to $500 million
annually (if one somewhat normalizes the episodic
receipts from sales of leases on submerged areas), and
total expenditures are somewhat higher. Receipts of
this magnitude would put the federal lands well up
(slightly above the middle) on *Fortune's* list of the 500
largest industrial concerns; the Forest Service and the
Bureau of Land Management would each make this list on
the basis of their receipts.

## A Conservation Viewpoint

The federal lands have never been managed for maximum profit in the private sense of that word. Various
public purposes, such as preservation of unique natural
areas, or provision of a continuous supply of timber, or
protection of vital watershed areas, have been dominant.
The management of the federal lands has been dominated
by a "conservation" viewpoint, not by a business orienta
tion. In a number of ways and for a number of reasons
the management has differed materially from that which a
consideration of business aspects would suggest.

I do not propose that federal lands, or any part of
them, be managed solely for monetary returns; I do agree

that there are public purposes in federal land ownership. If there are not, then there is little or no reason for such ownership. But I have argued, and later in this paper I will develop the point further, that the management of federal lands should include more consideration of the economic benefits and costs than has been traditionally done. Any enterprise that produces some hundreds of millions of cash revenue annually has major economic aspects that should be faced directly. In my view a more explicit consideration of such economic aspects would strengthen rather than weaken the conservation management of the federal lands.

## In the Right Direction

If the area of federal lands overstates their importance, the revenue from them understates it, in part because many goods and services in the past have been available at much less than commercial prices. The commission recommends (in Recommendations 44, 48, 65, 81 and 136) various steps away from this past policy, in the direction of charging full market value or a reasonable approximation, for the goods and services provided by these lands. The commission does not extend this principle to all such goods and services; most notably, it omits consideration of the value of water flowing off federal lands, including the value of water produced by special watershed management programs. But the commission's recommendations are a notable step in the right direction in my view and, if adopted, will lead to larger revenues from the federal lands in the future.

The commission report states (page one), "While there may be some modest disposals [of land], we conclude that at this time most public lands would not serve the maximum public interest in private ownership." Other parts of the report raise some doubts as to the meaning of "modest" and "most" in that sentence; not only law but administrative practice is involved. The commission report does not go quite as far as Burnell Held and I did in 1958 when we stated in *The Federal Lands* (page 5), "for an indefinite period into the future the acreage of land in federal ownership will show no major change from the present." We contemplated some disposals, perhaps less than does the commission report. But it does seem clear that the idea held for many decades--that the federal lands should ultimately be disposed of--has been finally interred.

## BENEFICIARIES OF FEDERAL LANDS

A great many people in the United States benefit from the management of the federal lands. The most obvious beneficiaries are the users--the millions of people who enjoy recreation on these lands, the thousands of timber purchasers, owners of livestock that graze there, lessees of mineral rights, holders of mining claims and many others. The commission report gives some information on this point.

There are some aspects of use about which we know relatively little. For instance, we know the number of recreation visits to federal land, but we do not know how many individuals this represents; it would be difficult to find out. There is no reliable information on the number of mining claims that have been filed on federal lands, much less upon the number of these that are valid. Although the number of outstanding mineral leases is known, we do not know how many individuals are involved as original lessees, and still less how many possess such leases by assignment.

## A Measure of Importance

In any case, mere numbers of primary users of federal lands would not include an important dimension of the benefits of this land--how important is the use to the individual who enjoys it? At one extreme is the person who once a year picnics in a federal area or someone who hunts a day or two on federal land; at the other extreme are the timber processor all of whose logs come from federal land, the rancher all of whose livestock find seasonal forage on federal land, and the mineral processor whose source of supply is entirely from federal land. To some, the federal lands are critical to their entire operation; to others, they are helpful but not vital.

The indirect beneficiaries of federal land are more numerous and harder to identify. The timber processor, who buys federal timber employs a labor force, and his operation may be a major part of the economic base of his town. The lumber, plywood and other products from his mill enter the channels of trade and become the basis for a substantial part of the construction industry. With federal timber such a major part of the national supply, the supply of new housing is heavily dependent upon timber grown on federal land.

A generally similar situation exists for the other commercial operations based upon products from federal land. The recreationists who use federal land spend several billion dollars for equipment, supplies and travel which help to support employment in many parts of the country. I have sometimes said, only half in jest, that if the national parks did not exist it would pay the manufacturers of film to invent them; certainly a substantial expenditure on cameras and film owes its inspiration to the federal scenic areas.

## The Flow of Products

In the interregional trade possible in a large country like the United States, some parts are producers of raw materials, and for them an adequate resource base is essential. The federal forest, mineral and grazing resources play this role. The recreation opportunity cannot be exported as such, but people from other regions can travel to the areas where the federal lands are located.

Even when purchasers of products from federal land pay a full market price for the commodities or services they get, the assurance of a resource supply is important. The purchaser does not have to invest his capital in a source of raw material supply.

Many observers have concluded that ranchers get substantial economic advantage from grazing fees less than a market price, or that other users get similar advantage if the commodities or services they get from federal land are available at less than full market prices. There are many arguments in favor of selling products from federal land at full market prices; the commission report states some of them, and many of us economists have dwelt upon them. But sometimes the purchaser does not benefit as much as a superficial analysis would suggest; sometimes the federal regulations, procedures and delays largely offset the lower cash price; sometimes the value of the lower price on federal resources gets capitalized into private property values so that the purchaser of a ranch or other property really pays the full market price for the federal resources, but in another form.

## HINDRANCES TO ECONOMIC MANAGEMENT

Economic management of the federal lands has been hampered in the past, and is hampered now, by a number of situations or relationships.

The whole process of budget making, appropriations and expenditures of federal funds is ill adapted to natural resource management. The process concentrates upon the expenditure of funds; it is primarily concerned with public programs that benefit citizens but cost the public treasury money.

In the typical federal program there are no significant revenues, and the budget-appropriation-expenditure process takes little account of revenues. A budget examiner or an appropriation subcommittee may question a resource management agency at length about its proposals to spend money, yet accept almost without question the whole receipt side of the operation. In particular there is never an explicit consideration of net revenue, of the balancing of outlays against income; the process never employs the marginal-cost marginal-revenue analysis so basic to economic analysis. In the language of business, there is never a consideration that the best way to achieve a greater net return may be to spend more money.

## Budgets Based Upon the Past

Federal budgeting places great emphasis upon past expenditures; the analysis and the appropriations make marginal changes from the past, but do not establish levels of expenditures *de novo* each year. There are great advantages to this process, especially for public service programs; continuity of program and of its level are more nearly achieved in this way. But it may be too slow to adjust to changing times in resource management. When the demand for some resource from federal lands changes sharply the appropriation change may lag substantially. Increases in appropriations are likely to be looked at more carefully and more critically than continuances of past items. Every good bureaucrat seeks to get appropriations in his "base," because in this way similar amounts are more likely to be forthcoming in future years.

The federal budget process is too slow and time-consuming for good resource management. The budget for a fiscal year is largely determined 18 months in advance of the beginning of the fiscal year or 30 months before the end of the year, yet the final appropriation may not be known until the year is well under way. While supplemental appropriations are theoretically feasible, practically they are almost unavailable, being surrounded with difficulties and delays.

If the requirements of good resource management change sharply during the period a particular budget is under consideration, or change during a fiscal year, there is often little the federal administrator can do to change his program, regardless of the advantages that might accrue from doing so. When I was a federal land manager, I envied private land managing firms that could deal with a board of directors on a few weeks notice--a board whose concern was profits and measures to achieve them, and whose reverence for the past was minimal.

In the federal budgeting-appropriation-expenditure process, there are many actors who can react negatively and make their action stick, but who cannot assure a positive action by endorsement. For example, the budget examiner may prevent an item from being submitted to the Congress, but he cannot assure that the item he approves will be accepted by the Congress.

## A Further Hindrance: Revenue Sharing

The revenue sharing feature of many federal resource programs has been a further major hindrance to economic management of the federal lands. Revenue sharing is a form of gross income tax; the agency must share a part of its total revenues with states or counties. The businessman who finds a federal tax on net income repressive should consider what a gross income tax would do. Economists and others have shown the difficulties a gross turnover tax, or a sales tax on intermediate production goods, would create; sharing of gross revenues is similar in principle but greater in amount. For instance, the Forest Service or BLM builds a timber access road; the value of the road is reflected in the value of the timber sold, but the counties get from 25 percent to 50 percent of this revenue, and the income to the U.S. Treasury may be less than the outlay. The Forest Service found a way around this with Knutson-Vandenburg funds and by requiring timber buyers to build roads. BLM has found a way around this by agreements with O & C* counties in Oregon

---

*O & C refers to Oregon and California revested lands. These are alternate sections along the railroad right of way, originally granted by the federal government as a stimulus to the building of the railroads. The O & C lands were eventually absorbed by the Southern Pacific Railroad. See Marion Clawson, *Uncle Sam's Acres* (New York: Dodd, Mead & Co., 1951).

that the cost of roads and other improvements were to be
financed out of the counties' shares of the receipts.
But these devices have had their critics, including the
commission's report. If a federal forest manager makes
a timber sale to salvage dead timber so as to reduce his
fire hazard and the value of the timber sold just matches
the cost of making the sale, a careful analyst would say
that this was good forest management, but when he has to
pay 25 percent of the sale receipts to the county he
winds up in the hole.

## Setting the Price

The outputs from federal land have frequently been
priced below a fair level by laws that set prices at
which land should be sold, by administrative actions that
accept customary rather than market prices, by lack of
competition in the nominally competitive sales and by
other means. This has further reduced the incentive to
good economic management of the federal lands.

Although almost every major class of users of
federal land has received some services or products at
less than a full competitive price, the disparity, both
relatively and absolutely, has been greatest for recreation. For a long time there were virtually no charges
for recreation use of most federal land; even today,
charges are far below a maximum revenue level. There may
be sound arguments in favor of subsidizing outdoor recreation, although I have elsewhere argued that the usual
argument of helping poor people visit national parks and
other federal areas is nonsense--really poor people never
get there anyway. If we seriously advocate charges for
use of federal land at about the level a fully competitive market would require, then we cannot escape a reex-
amination of the charges for outdoor recreation.

In the administration of federal land, there has
been a notable hiatus between the legislative and the
appropriation committees of the Congress. The acquisition of a new unit of the national part system is authorized, but the appropriations are forthcoming so slowly

that the ultimate cost is twice what it need have been. The legislative committee, after hearings and careful consideration, authorizes a program of tree planting, or range reseeding or some other type of improvement which the appropriation committee ignores in its action on budget requests, and so on. A federal agency and the supporters of a program must fight for legislative authorization, but this is often only the beginning of their struggle. The fact that this relationship may be worse in some other federal programs is not much comfort to the manager of federal lands.

## RECOMMENDATIONS FOR CHANGE

The report of the Public Land Law Review Commission touches on those issues, but not as directly or forcefully as I would have liked. First of all, its impressive congressional membership was almost wholly on the legislative side, not from appropriations. Based on past experience, the recommendations of the commission will have some, but perhaps very limited, influence on the appropriations committees.

The commission strongly urges, and I agree, that the agencies develop long-range plans for management of their areas, but will the budget-appropriation process provide the agencies with manpower to do this? The commission report makes a number of excellent recommendations about preservation or improvement of environmental conditions on federal lands; many of these will cost money. Will the budget-appropriation process provide the necessary funds? If I were a federal land manager, I would welcome the commission's report on these and other matters, but I would not start to carry out their recommendations until I saw what the Office of Management and Budget and the appropriations committees were going to do.

## Ending Revenue Sharing

The commission makes recommendations on payments to counties and states in lieu of taxes to end the revenue-sharing arrangements. While the commission's proposals differ somewhat from proposals I made as early as 1958, in general I go along with the commission. Something of this kind is indispensable to a really economic management of the federal lands. But I suspect that even the prestigious congressional members of the commission will have some difficulty getting these proposals adopted by the Congress; and the problem of appropriations will come later. In this case I would judge that, if the enabling legislation is passed, the appropriations will be forthcoming. Too many congressmen would feel the heat from back home for there to be much reneging on arrangements provided in the basic law.

## Selling at Market Price

The commission makes recommendations about selling products from federal lands at fair market prices, as noted earlier. They seem equivocal in their treatment of outdoor recreation, and they do not mention water originating from federal land. Nevertheless their recommendations on this point are a notable step forward. Selling products at fair market prices will greatly simplify administrative problems. It is far harder to dispose of something at less than its value than it is to sell it for full value, especially if one wishes to avoid charges of favoritism. Simplification in administration will be particularly notable in the case of mining claims, where it is proposed (recommendation on page 128) that purchasers of surface resources on their claims be required to pay a full value for all such resources. Most of the the very troublesome and controversial mining claim applications of the past would never have arisen had the "miner" been required to pay for the surface resources he was really after. But the implementation of these recommendations will also encounter some opposition, I predict.

At various places, the commission's report skirts the edge of the difficult problem of balancing outlays with results, or of expenditures with income, but I feel that it does not adequately deal with this matter. The most specific recommendation it made (Recommendation 29) on the financing of management on the "timber production units" will surely stir up a hornet's nest of controversy, in part because it so closely resembles proposals made by the timber processing industry that were shot down by conservation groups.

## ASSUMPTIONS AND PROCEDURES IN ECONOMIC MANAGEMENT

I have made several references to the economic management of the federal lands, and I wish to conclude this paper with a brief outline of what I think such management includes and to suggest how the commission's report fits into such a program. In this section, I make certain assumptions which should be stated explicitly:

1. Federal land ownership is permanent. While there may be some modifications of total area and will surely be changes in specific tracts, by and large the lands now in federal ownership will stay there and, by and large, there will not be major additions to the federal ownership of land;

2. The federal lands are now important in the economy of the nation, of the West and of some localities; their importance is likely to increase in the future, especially in timber, recreation and some minerals; and

3. Any program of federal land management, whether or not it includes more consideration of the economic aspects of such management, must in the future give greater attention to the maintenance of good environmental situations where these now exist and to the restoration of better environmental situations where this is practical. More concern for the production from federal lands should not be at the expense of the integrity of those lands.

If these assumptions are reasonably accurate, then the nation, many states and many localities have a major stake in the best attainable management of the federal lands. In a country where citizen opinion can and does have an effect upon government, the residents of many areas have both an opportunity and a responsibility to influence federal land management in directions they think desirable.

## The First Step: Evaluation of Outputs

The first step of a number that are all necessary in the economic management of federal lands is a careful evaluation of all the output or annual benefits from such land, valued as closely as possible at a full market price where one exists or at the closest approximation thereto when such prices are unavailable. This is fairly obvious and not too difficult for the products such as timber, grazing and leasable minerals which are now sold or leased for a cash sum. Some of these do not now return their full market value, but could be made to do so. But an evaluation of the benefits from federal land management must reach into the services for which little or no charge is made today. Notable among these is recreation. I have long advocated substantially higher charges to recreationists, but even if present charges remained the same, an estimate could be made of the full value of such recreation opportunity.

The matter of evaluating the water that flows off federal land is both difficult and politically touchy. Some will argue that the owner of the watershed has no claim upon the value of the water that flows from it. Do they think he has any obligation to maintain either the quantity or the quality of that water? And what about programs at federal expense that increase water flow beyond that which exists in a natural state of the watershed? Should this water be free to any appropriator? As with recreation, so with water; the problem of evaluating the output of the federal lands is separate from the issue of charging for the output, although of

course the two are related. In any event, increasing
inventory value of federal timber and of improvements to
land is one output that should be measured and included
among the annual flow of output.

## Costs and Willingness to Pay

At this point, I can hear park lovers asking if I
think we can or should put a value on a beautiful sunset,
any more than we can or should put a value on a mother's
love. The answer is: One need not evaluate either the
sunset or the mother's love, as such, but he can measure
what people are willing to pay for the sunset, at least.
Provision of opportunity for outdoor recreation, whether
on federal, other public or private lands costs money,
both to the owner of the land and to the whole society.
Costs include both actual expenditures and income foregone.

The question must be asked: Are the benefits worth
the costs? Is there another way of getting the same
benefits more cheaply? I do not see how recreationists
can expect a blank check from society to provide outdoor
recreation opportunity without limit and without charge.
Recreationists are a very large interest group concerned
with federal lands, but they are only one group, and far
from the totality of the population.

## Accounting and Analysis

A second essential step is to establish an investment or capital account for federal lands. As it now
stands, cash expenditures for capital improvements are
treated as annual outlays, thus exaggerating the latter.
But no depreciation or interest charge is made for past
capital investments, thus minimizing the annual costs of
management. The federal government follows an accounting
practice and a system of analysis that would be condemned
strongly if used by any private firm, and in some cases
would be illegal. Expenditures for roads, replanting of

trees and grasses, forest stand improvement, improvements for recreation areas and other outlays are clearly a form of capital investment and should be treated as such. Likewise, use of these capital items should involve an annual charge. This is established practice for private resource management; it should become standard for federal land management. Increased value of timber stands is clearly part of income from federal lands.

A third essential step in economic management of the federal lands is a full accounting of all the costs of annual management. This obviously includes the annual appropriations for administration, but also excludes the annual appropriations for capital improvements. But it should also include some interest allowance on the value of the federal lands. Difficult as it may be to evaluate these lands accurately, there is no doubt they have a very large value--something to be measured in billions rather than millions of dollars. The acquisition cost of these lands is meaningless today. Sums of money equal to the capital value of the federal lands could be invested elsewhere, at the most conservative financial management, and produce some hundreds of millions of interest annually. No private owner can afford to neglect the investment value of his land, and when the federal government tries to do so it reveals an economic illiteracy. The true cost of a visit to a national park is not merely the annual cash expenditure divided by the number of visits, but must include some allowance for interest on the capital value of the park. Likewise, when mature timber is held back for later harvesting, one element of cost is interest on the realizable values of the harvestable timber. The estimate of full annual cost of management should include some depreciation charge for past investment in depreciable items; this is a corollary of establishing a capital account.

## Costs and Returns

A fourth essential step in economic management of the federal lands is to substitute some form of in-lieu tax payments for the present revenue sharing. The latter is a form of gross income tax as we have noted; regardless of its equity with respect to the units of state government (and it has serious deficiencies in this regard), it is a major obstacle to intensive economic management of the federal land. If a federal agency must give counties or other units of government a fourth or more of gross revenue resulting from any land management practice, then a great many otherwise highly desirable programs simply become uneconomic. If the in-lieu tax payment is largely fixed, irrespective of particular management practices, then this obstacle to economic management of federal lands has been removed.

Last, an essential step is a careful marginal-cost marginal-revenue analysis, in total and by specific management practices or programs. Does a program, or a proposed program, produce more value than it costs? Would additional "units" or steps in such a program cost more or less than the additional values created? I have used the word "value" rather than "income" to connote that one should consider values not now realized in cash terms. The old rule of efficiency in management is to increase outputs in each program or line of output until marginal net returns are equal from each. If the cost of capital is included in the costs, as it should be, inputs should be increased until the net return from each reaches zero. This is not only conventional economic theory, it is standard business practice. There may be some difficulties in estimating marginal costs and returns and one may have to be satisfied with approximations, but the general idea should be clear enough.

## A Rough Budget

What I have in mind may be illustrated by a rough budget for federal lands, which I published some years ago (Table, p. 62). There is a capital account, showing values, additions, depreciation charge and interest charge. The income is shown separately for the cash actually received, for income in kind (such as Knutson-Vandenburg funds), and for the additional value of products and services sold at less than market prices. The latter does not include anything for water, which I would now be inclined to include. Operating expenses are shown in cash, in kind, in depreciation, in interest and in payments to states and counties. In-lieu tax payments should be substituted for the latter, if my suggestions made here are followed.

This is an extremely rough calculation; for a number of items I lacked accurate data. It is "in the ball park" for 1963, the year to which it applies, but accurate figures might shift the small negative balance substantially. It does not attempt a marginal analysis; this was simply beyond my capacity, given the data available to me. It was originally intended to be, and I offer it today as, illustrative only.

The Table shows major types of federal land separately; this separation should be preserved in a more sophisticated economic analysis. In addition, a similar analysis should be made by major management areas of each kind of land--for each national forest, national park or grazing district and in some cases by districts or parts of these units. It should also be made, in at least an approximate way, for each major output from federal lands, such as forage, timber and recreation opportunities.

One need not allocate overhead management costs to various outputs in order to apply marginal-cost marginal-value analysis. One is concerned only to know if more input brings proportionately more or less output. Federal administrators may object that this would be prohibitively costly or prohibitively time consuming, but if it is as vital as I think it is, the time and money would be well spent.

Moreover, I know that many federal land managers have intuitively or approximately made similar calculations; they regard some programs as worthwhile in some situations, and others as impractical. My suggestion would merely make this process explicit within the agencies and would make it the basis for appropriations or

TABLE

FINANCIAL STATEMENT, FEDERAL LANDS, 1963[1]

*(in millions of dollars)*

| Item | Total | National forests | Public domain, etc. | National park system | National wildlife refuges |
|---|---|---|---|---|---|
| *Capital account:* | | | | | |
| Value of land and resources[2] | (12,000) | (6,000) | (4,000) | (1,500) | (500) |
| Undepreciated value of past investments[3] | (1,720) | 1,160 | (50) | (500) | (20) |
| Total assets | (13,720) | (7,160) | (4,050) | (2,000) | (520) |
| Cash investment made during year | 189 | 111 | 6 | 58 | 14 |
| Investment in kind, during year[4] | 61 | 55 | 6 | 0 | 0 |
| Increased value of property[5] | (156) | (100) | (10) | (40) | (6) |
| Annual depreciation charge[6] | (94) | (60) | (3) | (30) | (1) |
| Annual interest charge[7] | (686) | (358) | (202) | (100) | (26) |
| *Income, cash:* | | | | | |
| Forest products | 146 | 112[9] | 34 | - | - |
| Mineral leases | 319 | 9 | 318[11] | - | 1 |
| Grazing | 9 | 4[10] | 4[10] | - | - |
| Recreation | 6 | | 8 | 6 | 0 |
| Other | 14 | 5 | 8 | - | 1 |
| Total | 494 | 122 | 364 | 6 | 2 |
| *Income, in kind:* | 31 | 27 | 4 | 0 | 0 |
| *Additional value of products and services provided at less than full market price:* | | | | | |
| Forest products | (11) | (10)[9] | (1) | 0 | - |
| Mineral leases | (35) | | (35) | 0 | - |
| Grazing | (12) | (4) | (8) | 0 | - |
| Recreation | (330) | (125) | (5) | (180) | (20) |
| Total | (388) | (139) | (49) | (180) | (20) |
| *Total annual output*[8] | (1,069) | (388) | (427) | (226) | (28) |

| | | | | | |
|---|---|---|---|---|---|
| Cash | 274 | 163 | 54 | 47 | 10 |
| In kind | 31 | 27 | 4 | 0 | 0 |
| Depreciation of capital assets | (94) | (60) | (3) | (30) | (1) |
| Payments to states & counties | 93 | 31 | 61 | - | 1 |
| Interest on assets | (686) | (358) | (202) | (100) | (26) |
| Total | (1,178) | (639) | (324) | (177) | (38) |

[1] This table is intended to be suggestive, not definitive. The best readily available data have been used, but some do not conform to desired definitions. Where no reasonable data existed, the author has made illustrative estimates; these are bracketed (100, etc.). Except as noted data are drawn from appendix tables [in *The Federal Lands...*].

[2] These are obviously only the roughest kind of estimates. General Services Administration, in its *Inventory Report on Real Property Owned by the United States Throughout the World*, lists land at *cost*; for all BLM lands, this was $1 million as of June 30, 1958--an absurd figure for present value.

[3] Roads, buildings and other improvements. Land, trees, grass, etc., included in "land."

[4] Author's estimate of value of roads built as part of timber sales contracts ($5 per 1,000 board feet of timber).

[5] From investment exceeding depreciation, or from growth of timber, etc. Does not include possible increased price per acre unrelated to such changes.

[6] On past investment in buildings, roads, etc.; approximate order of magnitude, at best.

[7] At 5 percent.

[8] Cash income, income in kind, additional value of products and services provided at less than full market price, plus increased value of property. Does not include any value for water originating from federal lands.

[9] Included in public domain.

[10] Not recorded separately.

[11] Includes only $200 million from submerged areas, as an approximately normal annual receipt from these areas.

*Source: The Federal Lands Since 1956* (Washington: Resources for the Future, 1968), p. 54.

expenditures and for congressional and other action to determine such appropriations or expenditures.

## Economic Analysis

There will be little gain from any such analysis unless there are real prospects that the necessary congressional and executive action will be guided by such economic considerations. If economic analysis determines that an expanded program of forest planting is profitable but the money is not forthcoming to carry it out, then there has been limited gain from the economic analysis. Such economic analysis has been notably lacking in the past, and only scant attention has been paid in the appropriation process to the analyses that were made. Unless or until the federal government as a whole is willing to put its money where its mouth is, the value of additional oratory is low.

## A FEDERAL LAND MANAGEMENT CORPORATION

I am convinced that existing forms and procedures for budgeting and appropriating federal funds will not produce an economically sound management of the federal lands. The solution is not simple. Some years ago I advanced the idea of a federal land management corporation, which would to some degree shortcut the tortuous path of federal appropriations and whereby some of the revenues could be plowed back into management.

I think this idea deserves serious consideration today. I know that many conservationists will oppose it because they think it will put undue emphasis upon those aspects of federal land management that produce cash revenue. But it would be possible to recognize noncash income, as well as to recognize noncash expenditures. If something such as I proposed in 1957 had been in effect these past 15 years, I believe that outdoor recreation, preservation of the environment and other programs not now yielding much or any cash would have fared better at the hands of federal administrators than they have in fact fared at the hands of the Bureau of the Budget and the appropriations committees. In federal land management, as in other public programs, the choices often have to be made between actual alternatives, not between one of them and some ideal.

## FORMS AND KINDS OF MANAGEMENT

Other speakers today have the responsibility of dealing with administration of the federal lands, and possibly they will get further into this subject. I simply argue that the form of administration goes a long way to limiting the kind of management that will actually be forthcoming, and further, that the past budgeting-appropriating-expending process has led to serious under-utilization of the productive capacities of the federal lands.

The commission report goes some distance toward the objectives I have outlined. It offers (a) Recommendation 136, pricing output from federal lands at full market prices, although it seems to waver on this in some important instances; (b) Recommendation 101, a form of in-lieu tax payments instead of revenue sharing; (c) Recommendation 134, "a consolidated budget for public land programs that shows the relationship between costs and benefits of each program." Elsewhere it either endorses or implicitly accepts some of the proposals I have made here today. It does not explicitly recommend a capital budget or account, nor does it discuss depreciation and interest charges.

On some matters it is not as explicit as I think is necessary, but perhaps that can come later. It does propose Recommendation 29, a revolving fund for timber development on those lands classified as dominantly for timber purposes. This recommendation is similar to one the forest industry made some months ago, which aroused so much opposition from the conservation interests.

Applied only to timber management, with the implication that only timber values are to be considered, this does have disturbing possibilities. Applied to all outputs of the federal lands, with nonmonetary as well as monetary values and costs included, it might have quite different possibilities. The matter of administrative organization for federal land management enters here also: a form of handling large sums of money that would be desirable under one form or organization might be unacceptable under another.

My biggest skepticism about the commission's proposals is that they do not commit the chief actors in the budget-appropriation-expenditure process. Whether we like the commission recommendations or oppose them, there is a substantial likelihood that they will not be carried out, especially on those aspects which call for federal appropriations--which includes a great deal of the commission's proposals.

# PANEL DISCUSSION ON ECONOMICS OF THE PUBLIC LANDS

Moderator:  J. Herbert Snyder, *Chairman,*
*Division of Resource Sciences*
*University of California, Davis*

Panelists:  James Crutchfield, *Professor of Economics,*
*University of Washington, Seattle*

Carl Newport, *Management Consultant,*
*Portland, Oregon*

Norman B. Livermore, Jr., *Secretary,*
*The Resources Agency of California*

*Snyder:*  In sending instructions to our panelists, we
posed several questions relating both to the commission's report and to Dr. Clawson's paper. We asked them
to consider the assumptions used by the commission and
by Dr. Clawson regarding the economic dimensions of
federal lands and the economic management or levels of
management that have been allied to these lands in the
past. And we asked that the panelists consider these
questions from their particular vantage points and areas
of responsibility and then to speak briefly. We will
give them a chance to enter into discussion with Dr.
Clawson and the audience.

First on our list of panelists, then: Professor
James Crutchfield of the University of Washington,
Seattle.

*Crutchfield:*  Thank you. I am particularly grateful that
you mentioned the list of questions we were supposed to
direct attention to and our limited time. As a former
sufferer on the Marine Science Commission, my sympathies
are very strong with the commission members. One important point is that you simply cannot read the commission
report, which is inevitably something of a mish-mash,

67

and get a full view of what the commission really considered and the depth of its recommendations. So with full apologies for my failure to read very many thousands of the 30,000 words of the backup document, I may be a bit off target in a few places.

Like Marion Clawson, I will not waste time on the ayes. The commission did a fine job in many areas. It is bound to have come up with needed suggestions. So instead of saying further nice words about the good things that are in the report, let me settle on some weaknesses to be corrected.

## THE MISSING FRAMEWORK

The most important, I think, is that the commission had an opportunity to lay out a framework for social choice; that is, a framework in which the tools of social analysis are directed at goals that also involve expensive resources and choices, but are not quantifiable in conventional economic terms. I think some of the criticism that the report is excessively focused on economics ignores a vitally important consideration that economics is, after all, one very important, although certainly not exclusive, mechanism of social choice. You may not want to rely entirely on economic analysis for decisionmaking, but you ignore it at your peril as a conservationist. Nevertheless, I think the commission somehow missed its opportunity to establish a framework for the analytical work needed.

There are different objectives. Reconciling economic outputs is an objective. Defending environmental considerations is an objective. Economic redistribution of income or opportunity is an objective. Let me give you an illustration of the things that concern me.

For example, the commission's statement, as Marion has indicated, with regard to pricing the outputs from public lands at fair market value is excellent. Yet in the same section in which this statement is made, there is a complete denial with respect to outdoor recreation and a reversion to an earlier--and I think nonoperational--view that somehow access to outdoor recreation must be viewed as a part of an antipoverty program. I don't imagine that's too strong a statement. It gives us very little opportunity to distinguish qualitatively between aspects of outdoor recreation that are crucially important.

I also find little justification, though there may be excellent justification for it in a number of other areas, for transfers of lands to state and local governments at less than market value. If the justification exists, it certainly is not clearly spelled out in the general report.

## Areas of Perversion

With regard to specifics, there seem to be areas of perversion of economic concepts and that worries me greatly. One is a statement on page 46 of the commission's report about the use of benefit-cost analysis to the effect that primary and secondary benefits and costs should be weighed carefully in making the land management decisions.

I had thought that economists had laid to rest the ghost of secondary benefits as a legislative device. It is now being revived under another name, but the fact remains that if one wishes to use benefit-cost analysis, there is in the water resources field, for example, a far more sophisticated and analytically far more correct set of views as to both the uses and the limitations of this technique than appears in the commission's report. Again, the backup documents may well do a better job, but not everybody is going to get to them.

Then there is a statement on page 122 that mineral deposits have economic value, are relatively rare and therefore there is little opportunity to choose between available sites for mineral production as there often is in allocating lands for other types of use. Moreover,

it is stated that the development of a productive
mineral deposit is ordinarily the highest economic use
of land. I don't know what backup there is for that
statement, but it needs a lot. It is not sensible
economics, and it opens doors that worry me very
severely.

## Astounding Omissions

With regard to the economic framework I think the
commission might have erected, I am astounded to find
no reference to international trade policy as it relates
to some of the crucial outputs of the land and water
system with which the commission was dealing. Surely
you cannot make any sensible statements at all with
respect to demands for oil, gas and many types of minerals without setting them within a framework of an
international trade policy of some sort.

There is almost the implication of a kind of economic self-sufficiency argument in the report's discussion of minerals. Certainly there is no clear recognition of the fact that an enormously large and significant reduction in the environmental impact of oil and
gas and the problems associated with exploration and
development could be achieved by the simple process of
eliminating a nonsense system of quota restrictions on
imports.

Finally, while I realize that the commission could
not do a study of water resources as well as land
resources, the use of agricultural land under irrigation
for intensive cultivation (which is a strong point in
the commission's recommendation that some disposition
of land take place), cannot be discussed in the 11 western states without reference to the deliberate policy of
selling water for far less than it is worth. The demand
for agricultural land and the pattern of agricultural
output in the West is intimately related to that water
policy, and this is clearly a part of the framework that
needs to be considered.

## The Maximum Contribution

I would like to add a point or two to Marion's argument, not by way of disagreement but as reinforcement. In stressing the desirability of maximizing economic return from the public lands we have the implication of a federal government version of Scrooge squeezing the last ounce of rent out of some poor tenant. Let me just turn the thing upside down and point out that the significance of our arguing that the public extract the market value for the uses to which its land is being put is a way of saying that we guarantee that those lands can be used only by those--and only with those specific techniques--that use them efficiently. This is another way of stating that the public lands make their maximum economic and noneconomic contribution, and it's a vitally important one. The underpricing of land, as well as the underpricing of water, is at the root of many of our disposition problems, as well as many of the grosser instances of unfairness.

## Environmental Quality

With respect to the environmental impact, there are other people better qualified than I to discuss it, and other sections in this conference devoted to that question. I would simply stress the point that no economic analysis of public lands can ignore the fact that it is vastly easier to assure environmental protection and enhancement starting from a base of federal ownership than it is from any other. And as Marion Clawson himself and many others have pointed out, there are very few substitutes for environmental quality. With a growing population increasingly insistent on environmental quality as one of the things it wants to buy along with economic products, we can be sure that the economic value or, if you like, the social value of the demand for land-water systems will rise over time. This is implicit in the commission report, but it is not integrated fully in the way I think it might have been.

With regard to the recommendations for disposal
policy, I share the uncertainty I am sure many must feel
about what that policy really implies. You could be un-
friendly and say it implies that we will dispose of only
relatively small lots of the relatively good stuff, and
that could be very disturbing, to say the least. On the
other hand, there is definite progress in the overall
attitude that the commission report indicates.

## Making Decisions

One final point. I want to reinforce what Marion
laid out explicitly in his paper. The current decision-
making process within the federal government is totally
inadequate to live up to the standards and the challenges imposed by the commission. One of the major
reasons for turning to a pricing system that makes sense
on the public lands is to remove some of that intoler-
able burden of decisionmaking by making it unnecessary.
But even after you have done that, you need to consider
the idea of the public corporation or some similar
approach. Techniques that have worked so well in
improving efficiency in the private sector are going to
be urgently needed in the public sector as well.

*Snyder:* Thank you very much. Next on our list of
panelists is Dr. Carl Newport of Mason, Bruce & Girard,
Portland, Oregon.

*Newport:* Thank you.


ECONOMIC ANALYSIS AND ECONOMIC GOALS

One of the main points I want to emphasize with
respect to the commission report is what I feel to be
the difference between *economic analysis* and *economic
goals*. I think a lot of criticism has been leveled at
the report because it puts heavy emphasis on economic
goals--economic in the sense that they are dollar goals
or the kinds of goals that we associate with growth

rates, GNP and those things. I want to distinguish those from economic analysis, because I feel that such analysis has a great deal to contribute to the management of the public lands and that it is a tool for achieving efficiency in accomplishing goals, regardless of whether they are the traditional economic growth type of goals or the social or environmental type of goals.

## Setting the Goal

This brings me to the question of goals. I agree with the commission report that goals need to be clarified and specified in order for public land management to be more effective. However I disagree that it is necessary for us to specify or change these goals statutorily.

I also disagree that it is necessary for Congress to pass laws or revise the laws that we have. I feel that the basic laws are necessarily broad and that they permit the flexibility over time that's required to suit any type of situation. I feel that what is really needed is a system under which the agencies in charge of managing these various kinds of lands are required, as the first step in their process, to specify and clarify the goals that they are seeking.

Now this may sound like I am saying the agencies should set the goals, but this is not the case. I would only require that they specify the goals for congressional review and also make clear to the public what these goals are so that there could be participation by the public in deciding whether or not these are the proper ones.

Having gone through this goal-setting procedure, there would then be a much better climate for using economic analysis. It's not the entire answer, but it's one of the best tools we have for deciding objectively which of various kinds of procedures would most efficiently achieve a specific group of goals and objectives.

## Specifying the Goal

One of the situations we have had in the past is that some goals have been very clearly specified while others have not. For example, we quantify our goal for timber, but we leave our goals for recreation and water, among other areas, loose and unquantified. As a consequence we have a situation in which we force the public agencies to make decisions regarding wilderness areas and parks and recreational developments without ever having any measure of how much of the total need or goal has been satisfied already by their efforts in that direction, or will be satisfied by proposed programs.

I have another illustration of this. Some of you may be familiar with "The Douglas Fir Supply Study," made by the Forest Service. It was primarily concerned with the potential for timber production from the public lands. That study started out by trying to establish a framework in which a choice could be made among management programs based on as full as possible a quantification of the timber output as well as the specific effects on water, recreation and wildlife. But in the process of working it out and presenting a published report, those things other than timber were only included in a qualitative sense, and therefore there was no sound basis for weighing among the alternatives. In this particular case only broad, general statements were made that could influence decisions one way or the other without providing any basis in fact or in quantification.

## DOMINANT USE v. BALANCED GOALS

An item that I disagree with in the report is the one related to the dominant use zoning for a commercial timber production. I really feel that the commission's proposals in this regard are out of line. I think that we need a framework in which you try to maximize some group of uses for a given area rather than trying to set up the areas on a dominant use or zoning basis.

This is related to the need in each one of the
areas, each national forest or each unit of land, to
have goals and objectives specified and made clear.  If
that were the case, it would be much easier for the
manager to come to a decision regarding the proper balancing of these goals.

The matter of incentives for efficient management is
also important.  The performances of agencies and their
managers are currently measured by picayune performance
standards that relate to conformance to regulations or
procedures, rather than to the achievement of some
assigned goals and objectives.

For example, we have stated in the law and in the
regulations the objective of community stability goals
with respect to some of the public lands.  But as far as
I know, there has been no measure of the performance of
a forest supervisor or a public land manager in terms of
how well he has helped to stabilize the local community.

## Revenue Sharing Defended

I take issue with Dr. Clawson's proposal that a
change from revenue sharing to in-lieu tax payments
would remove something that has been a disincentive to
management.  Dr. Clawson objects to revenue sharing on
the basis of the bad effect it has had on the incentive
of an agency or manager.  That was not among the reasons
given by the commission report.  The commission's reasons were obscure, but seemed to be based on some need
for uniformity with respect to payments to the local
units of government, and the need somehow or other to
compensate the state and local governments for tax immunity of public lands.  But the commission's criteria for
what should be done were not clear.  I don't believe
that either Dr. Clawson or the commission carefully considered the suitability of the alternative they were
suggesting.  In-lieu tax payment  means, in effect, that
public lands are going to pay on the basis of the ad
valorem property tax as levied on private owners.  Thus
public lands would help support state and local government.

## Against the Property Tax

When you just say in-lieu taxes, it's not clear just
what taxes you are talking about paying. But I think
it's fairly clear when you read the report completely,
and on the basis of what Dr. Clawson said, that you are
talking about property taxes. The recommendation then
seems to be predicated on the assumption that the property tax is a suitable tax for financing state and local
government. And I, for one, think that this is not the
case.

Experts in taxation have long expressed concern over
the inadequacies of the general property tax for financing local government. The property tax fails on all the
important criteria that are used to judge the suitability of a tax. The ability to pay, the benefits received
equity, ease of collection--property taxes have been
notoriously bad in this regard--as well as on the criteria of ability to provide an adequate revenue to the
taxing body.

One of the current most pressing problems in local
government throughout the nation is an inadequate source
of funds. There have been proposals for trying to assist in this problem by having the federal government
share income tax revenues with the local units. The
dependency of local governments on the property tax has
been declining. Of necessity, they have been seeking
other sources of funds, and this trend is expected to
continue.

Now this being the case, there is serious question
about the advisability of using the property tax as a
suitable measure of payments to counties for federally
held lands. Tax equivalency for public lands is likely
to worsen an already existing problem.

Dr. Clawson has said that it is not an incentive to
good management to share the revenue. He gave the illustration that by building a road at federal expense
and thereby enhancing the value of the timber to be
sold, the agency's extra timber income would have to be

shared with the local unit of government. But look into the situation under ad valorem tax on forest land and timber. In all those places where it is an important source of tax revenue, accessibility of timberland is a primary criterion in determining the ad valorem value of the land and timber. So the construction of this federal road that he alludes to would also increase the value of the land and timber and increase the ad valorem taxes due on not just that timber which is cut but on the growing stock as well.

I don't think that particular example was a very effective one for convincing people that we should change to a different system of having the federal lands pay their share. I contend that the current system of revenue sharing doesn't influence agency management efficiency at all. Agency receipts of all kinds go to the federal treasury. The agency itself does not benefit from the receipts. Recent attempts to have the agency benefit through special funds or expenditures to manage more intensively have failed.

## Summary

To summarize, I think a number of things are needed: incentives for better management; charting of goals for each of the kinds of lands; and economic analysis in determining how best to achieve these sets of goals and objectives. Finally, we need a system of dollar revenue sharing that would provide some revenue to the treasury, some to the agency for expenditures and for increasing the intensity of management and some to the local units of government, basing the amount on criteria that are more reasonable with respect to the needs in each of these categories.

*Snyder:* Thank you very much, Carl. To complete the Pacific Coast triumvirate of Washington, Oregon and California, let me introduce Norman Livermore of The Resources Agency, Sacramento, California.

## FIVE ASPECTS OF THE CLAWSON PAPER

*Livermore:* I am privileged to be here. Dr. Snyder gave
me the choice of commenting on the commission report or
on Marion Clawson's paper. As you know the report has
137 recommendations and there are 97 footnotes in the
Sierra Club's comments alone. So, adding 97 to 137, I
would much prefer to talk to the five major points in
Marion's paper, and that is what I intend to do.

## A Startling Statistic

The five topics I have chosen are of particular
interest to me. Far the most interesting one--in fact,
a bombshell to me--was Marion's statistics on the amount
of public land ownership in cities: about one-third of
the public lands in metropolitan areas is publicly
owned. That is mainly the streets, of course, but the
fact still struck me very forcefully because I believe
that many of our environmental types--and I include
myself among them--are more concerned with country open
space than city open space. This startling statistic
makes one realize how huge are the problems of closing
the streets and eliminating automobiles.

## Overlooked Revenue

The second problem I would like to mention is the
lack of consideration of the net revenue in public land
programs. I certainly heartily agree with Marion's
criticism of this failing. I know at the state level,
for instance, that income produced from our state lands
tends to be overlooked by our legislators and appears to
be given little consideration during the budget-making
process. It is partly with the end in view of hopefully
helping to correct this procedure that our California
Resources Agency recently produced an illustrated pamph-
let of its operations. I would be glad to send one to
you. It shows a very substantial income of some $74
million this year produced by units of the California
Resources Agency.

## For Greater Efficiency

The next topic I would like to comment on is the greater efficiency of private land management. And I would like to quote from Dr. Clawson's paper where he says:

"When I was a federal land manager, I envied private land managing firms that could deal with a board of directors on a few weeks notice--a board whose concern was profits and measures to achieve them, and whose reverence for the past was minimal."

I like that quote. I know it might be misinterpreted, but it simply means more efficiency in land management and land purchases.

Speaking solely to the purchasing side, I think all hands present will agree that the intermediary purchasing procedure of the Nature Conservancy, for instance, has been very helpful and definitely more efficient than public land purchase procedures.

## In-Lieu Taxes

The fourth topic I would like to mention is in-lieu taxes. Dr. Clawson touches a point that is particularly sensitive to local governments and citizens. As a specific California case, in my opinion conservationists were not nearly insistent enough in attempting to deal with this problem in Del Norte County in connection with the Redwood National Park purchase. You might not all know that the purchase of the Redwood Park has resulted in a reduction of tax income to Humboldt County of some $400,000, which amounts to 2 percent of their total county tax, putting a substantial burden on the local people and one that does not sit well with local citizens. I sometimes use the illustration--I think it's at least arithmetically apt--that if the same percentage were deducted from the State of California, instead of $400,000 it would amount to $120 million, which is quite a substantial sum.

## The Price of Recreation

My last topic is recreation fees in relation to poor people and parks. I like very much Marion's statement-- and I quote:

> I do not see how recreationists can
> expect a blank check from society
> to provide outdoor recreation oppor-
> tunity without limit and without
> charge. Recreationists are a very
> large interest group concerned with
> federal lands, but they are only one
> group and far from the totality of
> the population.

And again in his paper he said:

> There may be sound arguments in favor
> in subsidizing outdoor recreation,
> although I have elsewhere argued that
> the usual argument of helping poor
> people visit national parks and other
> federal areas is nonsense. Really
> poor people never get there anyway.
> If we seriously advocate charges for
> use of federal lands at about the
> level a fully competitive market
> would require, then we cannot escape
> a reexamination of the charges for
> outdoor recreation.

It appears to me that more realistic recreation fees, plus emphasis on the charitable level of providing parks and open spaces closer to population centers, is a must in our society. Pertinent to this are the remarks in the talk to the Sierra Club by United States Senator Thomas Kuchel on May 4, 1968, and I quote a portion of them:

> All of us need to realize that decent
> housing is as important to humanity as
> is the majesty of a public park, that

clear air and clear water are as important to mankind as is the beauty of a
protected waterfall and that adequate
transportation is as important to our
well-being as is a primitive trail in
the wilderness area.

Mr. Chairman, I think these five topics have used
up my time.

## DISCUSSION WITH THE AUDIENCE

*Snyder:* We would like very much to have your questions
or your comments that pertain to the topic of this particular session--economics and the public lands. We
would like you to be brief and to the point, and I will
do my best to direct the traffic either to Marion Clawson, the principal speaker or to the three panelists.

## SUPPLIES FROM PRIVATE LANDS

*Whitehead:* My name is Carleton Whitehead, and I would
like to echo a remark that was brought up here, and that
is the fact that the Public Land Law Review Commission's
study seemed to be done, in substantial part, in a
vacuum, without taking into real consideration the other
elements that could contribute: the fibers, the minerals that society needs. Repeated forestry studies have
shown that some of the greatest potential for growth,
for increased timber yield, lies on private lands not
on public lands, and that what may well be needed is
some kind of private land timber resupply law rather
than simply a federal timber act. I wonder to what
extent the Land Law Review Commission felt that it
should consider, and did consider, these external con-
tributors.

*Snyder:* Carl, I think you perhaps had some contact with
this historically. Would you like to comment on this?

*Newport:* I am not sure that I had any contact with this, but I am familiar with the situation you are reporting. You are in effect saying that if the Land Law Review Commission were really concerned with the satisfaction of timber goals from these lands, the study should have been done in the context of where else we can also obtain timber, and I think that's true. The commission can always fall back on the premise that that context wasn't specified in the directions it received as to how to proceed.

But one comment that I have in this regard is that within the directions that were given, after having evaluated the contributions that the public lands could make, the commission might have put this into the context of the nation's needs and then reevaluated its emphasis on what I call economic goals and come to a better recognition of the fact that the nation may be turning away from economic growth in these areas and turning more toward social goals and the desirability of environmental improvement. There might not have been any different recommendations.

## RESIDENTS AND NONRESIDENTS

*Snyder:* Yes?

*Lutz:* My name is Loren Lutz. My question has to do with Recommendation 13: "State and local governments should be given an effective role in federal agency land use planning. Federal land use plans should be developed in consultation with these governments, circulated to them for comments, and should conform to state or local zoning to the maximum extent feasible." At the bottom it says, "As a general rule, no use of public land should be permitted which is prohibited by state or local zoning."

Now, if you go over to Recommendation 67, it says: "State policies which unduly discriminate against nonresident hunters and fishermen in the use of public

lands through license fee differentials and various
forms of nonfee regulations should be discouraged."
And it says in a later paragraph: "Implementation of
our recommendations in Chapter 14 for equitable payment
in lieu of taxes should eliminate the need for further
reliance on this practice." And this has to do of
course, with the discriminatory practice of some of the
western states with respect to nonresidents.

Now, my question is: Aren't these mutually antago-
nistic statements and recommendations? And if you followed the line of reasoning in this report, is the commission advocating that conservation agencies in the
states go to a general fund for their money instead of
the fund that generally is handled by the fish and game
departments?

*Snyder:* Perhaps Mr. Pearl would like to respond briefly
to this one.

*Pearl:* Well, in the first place, the recommendations are
not inconsistent. They are very compatible. The first
recommendation deals with the zoning of land use. The
second recommendation you referred to deals with the use
of the public lands by all the citizens of the United
States. It was the commission's view that federal public lands should be opened equally to all of the citizens of the United States, regardless of where these
federal public lands are when the people go there for
such accepted activities as hunting and fishing. The
lands are zoned for that use.

## The Need for Differentials

It is recognized by the commission that there are
some instances where there need to be differentials made
between resident and nonresident hunters and fishermen,
particularly hunters. Therefore, the report's emphasis
is on *undue* discrimination against the nonresident.

The two recommendations are in harmony, because you
don't use lands that are not open for hunting and

fishing. You only use those that are zoned for that
purpose, but all the citizens of the United States
should have equal rights to go on those lands which are
owned by all the people of the United States.

*Lutz:* And how about the second part of the question?
Are you advocating that these in-lieu taxes go to the
state government in the general fund?

*Pearl:* Yes, but the commission specifically says that
the management and the question of control should follow
traditional patterns so that state licensing would
still continue and the funds that are collected by state
agencies for hunting and fishing licenses would still
continue. The only thing the commission objects to--
and I do personally--is having discriminatory practices
so that a citizen of the United States can't go on land
that he owns unless he pays an awful lot more, either
in dollars or some other way, for the privilege of using
his land.

## The Economics of Pricing

*Snyder:* Some of Dr. Crutchfield's research has taken
him into the area of the economics of pricing and the
use of recreation and other public use facilities. Jim,
would you like to comment on this one?

*Crutchfield:* Just one additional comment. We tend to
forget that if you deliberately underprice an important
type of outdoor recreation, then as the commission has
indicated, you have got to find some other rationing
device, because there simply isn't going to be enough
to go around. In fact, if that rationing does not take
place, it will not take place effectively under the commission's proposed alterations either. The rationing
that really is effective is the process of putting too
many people into a given type of recreational activity
and eventually producing a situation bad enough so that
the amount supplied and the amount demanded are roughly
equated.

I think that the process of using discriminatory
fees within a state is probably more narrowly defined
as a way of tapping outsiders to permit you to enjoy
subsidized access to public facilities. And I know as
well as anyone that that is not a proper way of pricing.

*Pearl:* May I ask both Dr. Crutchfield and Dr. Clawson
whether they are recommending the pricing of outdoor
recreation--for example entrance to Yosemite Park--on
what the traffic will bear or on a basic market value
approach?

*Crutchfield:* Let me answer first. I think Marion
Clawson's point--he can react to this as he chooses--is
that the value in the recreational service may well be
calculated on that market basis. Now, you can make your
own decision as to how you distribute that value. You
can charge less than this, which would actually maximize
the real recreational value of the service.

Your own report has a horrendous picture of an enor-
mous line of automobiles backed up from Yosemite, and I
suspect that they have not yet found--and you have not
found--some way of rationing access to outdoor recreation so that you do not ration by simple destruction of
quality.

No, I don't think you have to charge the full
amount, but we need to go a lot farther now than we are
able to go in telling which are the best kinds of outdoor recreation, which ones are most in demand, which
groups of people are going to enjoy it the most.


## Social Goals Cost Money

*Clawson:* I think sometimes Jim Crutchfield and I disagree, but on this point I think we are pretty well
together. There are, as I tried to say, two issues.
One is: What is our estimate of its worth? The other
is: What are we going to charge for it?

Now I am going to be blunt about this, although I may be misunderstood. I think there has been an awful lot said about social goals. Social goals cost money. The whole process of economic analysis and economizing in the true sense of the word--how you best realize social goals at minimum costs, minimum real costs--is very, very appropriate irrespective of these goals and not necessarily in conflict with the realization of more revenue at the same time.

I wrote much too long a paper. I struggled and kept the paper down. It would have been easier to have written 200 pages. After all, I have been involved in some of this for a long, long time. Some of what I said about in-lieu tax payments I have said in greater detail at other times and other places. The charging of entrance fees, as I say, is a somewhat separate issue from the question of evaluations. But I don't know why we should continue to subsidize certain kinds of outdoor recreation.

## Local Parks in Poor Areas

We are in this country today very largely subsidizing the groups that need it least. If we are going to really subsidize outdoor recreation, the two ends of the spectrum, as I see it, need have the best claim. One is the local park in the poor area. If you are really serious about doing something for low-income people, do something where they can easily have access to it. And I think, Dr. Goddard, you made this same point.

I also feel--and this is a personal bias--that we should have some subsidization of the more remote areas, the wilderness areas, if you will, the areas where we deliberately want to keep use down, where management's objective--or, if you want to call it the social goal-- is in conflict with the maximization of income or even the maximization of economic output.

But the great bulk of the people who use outdoor recreation are not poor. The crisis in our recreation, if I can use the word, arises because middle- to upper-income people are flooding into parks way beyond the capacity of those parks. These people have the capacity to pay. The fact that we do not require payment is certainly one of the factors that has created the problems we have to cope with.

Now, how high the charges should be is another issue. You have a very wide range in which you can make decisions based on other criteria than maximum revenue.

## LAND AND IN-LIEU TAXES

*Nelson:* My name is Edith Nelson. I was wondering if there were any plans to assess the in-lieu taxes in accordance with the burden to the community. For example, the mining industry might bring in 100 families with children needing education and police protection and the land wouldn't be taxed for that, and yet wilderness areas will not require the same services as the local service area.

*Clawson:* This gives me an opportunity to make another speech. The property tax is still an important tax. It's not the only way out, but it's got a long way to go. It does produce a lot of revenue. It is a basic source of revenue for many local governments, and it's likely to continue so for a long, long time. It is highly variable in different parts of the country. The tax base is variable and the rate is variable and the demands are variable.

Now, the proposal that I first made on this was that the local government has the right to receive a tax benefit from the federal agencies. It should be based upon the proportionate amount that the federal lands would have paid if they had been in private ownership, minus whatever the federal agencies were spending on those lands, expenses that otherwise the local government would have had to assume.

There is a precedent for this legislation. Similar arrangements have existed in the past for various federal programs, and what I suggested could be enormously flexible to meet different local situations. Of course the federal lands would not voluntarily pay in-lieu tax payments higher than the private lands would be taxed. There would have to be some form of arbitration, because the local tax assessor might say, "I think you owe me a million dollars," and the forest supervisor might say, "I think we owe you a thousand dollars."

There would be disagreements, but I think it would be perfectly possible to work out flexible arrangements. It's true that revenue sharing has not impeded economically the administration of the federal lands in the past, but that's because we didn't really have it anyway. If you are going down the street and all the traffic is blocked up at the first traffic light, the second traffic light really has nothing to do with the traffic stoppage. But if you somehow unblock the first one, then the second one may be quite an important bottleneck in traffic flow. I would certainly say that up until now the revenue sharing has been only incidentally important.

If we were to take new steps to bring the administration of the federal lands under a much more intensive and economic base, I feel quite confident that the revenue sharing would be a major obstacle.

## FEDERAL WATER IN METROPOLITAN AREAS

*Rogers:* My name is Michael Rogers, and my concern is that the commission missed the fattest cow in the pasture in regard to water. That's the metropolitan areas where use of water is without regulation.

The pollution from the metropolitan areas is going out into the ocean, destroying ocean life and also damaging the beaches. It seems as though there is an opportunity here for regulations on the amount of federal water or water from federal lands being used by the metropolitan areas. This would serve also as a regulator to control their pollution, because they would then have to clean up and perhaps reuse some of their waste rather than just merely turning it out like the mining industry has done, as Dr. Goddard pointed out.

## Some Hidden Recommendations

The other situation that we are concerned about is the hidden recommendations of the commission. Mr. Pearl pointed out that it didn't have a section on Indian people or Indian lands, but yet it made the recommendation in regard to the appeal of the Indian Allotment Act and also the study of regulations regarding Indian reservations.

Now, if these are hidden recommendations of the commission, it would be rather interesting to know how many other hidden recommendations there are for the recommendations that we have taken at face value here. This certainly, in my own opinion, justifies the fears of the Sierra Club.

*Snyder:* I have the feeling that the points you make are important, but I think in terms of the particular topic of this panel that they are somewhat like the quotation that Gene Lee made about the invisible path and the footprints on the sands of time. I think we will move on to another question.

## The Price of Water

*Crutchfield:* One quick point of correction about the pricing of federally produced water. The big villain with respect to excessive water use and the resulting impact on pollution is not the metropolitan areas. The proper criticism of federal water policy is that it charges discriminatory prices, excessively low for agricultural use and in comparison excessively high for metropolitan M and I uses (meaning municipal and indus-trial).

So while it is perfectly true that bad pricing of water contributes to significant pollution, it is much more evident in agriculture than it is in industry.

*Rogers:* Well, the situation in our area is that the Los Angeles Department of Water and Power has introduced legislation into Congress to pump water without liability to federal lands. They are asking Congress for simply the right to pump, and it seems to me that this would be important for the future, because this method of using water could turn many areas into biological areas.

*Crutchfield:* That's a much bigger problem.

*Pearl:* I would like to add one comment. About the time the commission started its work there was legislation in the Congress, which ultimately was passed, to establish a National Water Commission. Therefore the Public Land Law Review Commission did not consider many of the aspects of water that it might have, leaving these for the National Water Commission study, which is now under way.

## TAXES AND INVESTMENTS

*Tollenaar:* My name is Ken Tollenaar, University of Oregon. I'd like to return to the in-lieu-of-taxes problem for just a minute. It should be evident from what Carl Newport said that there is not unanimous agreement on this question around the country, as was indicated by Dr. Goddard. In fact, it is much more complicated than the commission's report would indicate.

The National Association of Counties for example, is on record with a position that is inconsistent with the commission's report. This position was taken a year ago before the commission's report came out, but it is now being reevaluated in terms of the commission's report. It is my understanding that there has been no particular agreement reached on behalf of the county associations, which of course represent some of the major interests involved in this question.

The third report is a step in the right direction, in that it recognizes that there is a federal obligation on behalf of all public lands and not just on behalf of the few that have been haphazardly singled out over the years. But as Carl Newport indicated, it only views the problem in the context of the property tax. It does not consider the total impact of federal ownership on the total state and local government revenue system. If it were to do that, it would have to consider the impact on state income taxes and local property taxes and perhaps other types of revenues and charges that are received by governments.

I would like to end up with a question to Dr. Clawson whose position on this matter has been consistent over the years and has a lot of merit. In view of the concern you have, Dr. Clawson, for the inadequate level of investment on the public lands, and in view of the difficulties in the approach of a separate land management corporation, would it not be something worth considering to continue and in fact liberalize the shared revenue system in order to encourage local governments and state governments to supply the investments that probably will not be forthcoming from Congress?

*Clawson:* I am personally very much opposed to this, and I think there will be a great deal of opposition in the Congress. Congress may be unwilling to give you the money, but I think it also would be unwilling to surrender the jurisdiction and that would inevitably follow if the states made the investments, even if the corporation idea is dim.

I have long felt that the Bureau of the Budget was largely wasting its time on examinations of such matters as why you need three new clerks instead of two. I speak with experience. If you need $2 million for a new program, your chances of getting it are much better than if you wanted three new clerks instead of two.

It would be possible to initiate some of the kinds
of review I am talking about without the corporation
idea, and it would be possible to introduce considerable
flexibility in management.

Revenue sharing is extremely spotty today. I have
not examined the figures in the last five years, but
certainly at one stage the Oregon counties were getting
very substantially more from O & C lands than from Coos
Bay lands, although both are federally owned and both
are administered by the Bureau of Land Management.

The oil royalty business has shifted enormously from
state to state. As I have pointed out, there are places
in southern Oregon where you can have three Douglas fir
trees in a space less than the size of this room, and
on one of them the state gets 75 percent of the revenue,
on one it gets 25 percent and on one it gets 5 percent.
Now, it's a little difficult for me to understand this,
except on the basis of history.

If you think tax laws are inconsistent and bad, then
revenue sharing is enormously more complicated and less
defensible. It is perfectly true that you could have
revenue sharing that would be better than what we now
have, but I think that there are great advantages to
in-lieu tax rates. Revenue sharing is distinctly disad-
vantageous to good management of the federal lands.

## Switching Taxes

*Snyder:* Carl Newport also wanted to comment on this.

*Newport:* Wanted to comment? I could hardly sit still.
I can't see any reason why we should switch from revenue sharing to in-lieu tax payments for the reasons that
you have given.

Take the reason that the revenue sharing differs
from one type of land to another. To me this is not a
basically sound reason for changing. Anybody who has

been even a very superficial student of ad valorem property taxes in the United States will recognize that. If you think revenue sharing on the public lands varies, take a look at ad valorem property taxes throughout the nation, which range from an assessed value about 6 percent of the true market value in some places to about 7 percent of market value in other areas.

Compound this with the fact that taxing districts may have a uniform assessed value as a proportion of market value, but also have different levies. These levies are a result of a determination of what local government needs to support the kinds of interior activities you are speaking of here, in which local citizens vote for an assessment upon themselves to pay for something they want.

It seems ridiculous to me that we lack the depth perception to see that the correction suggested here is for the removal of an appendix to cure an ailment that's in an entirely different part of the body. I would like to suggest to Dr. Clawson that if he envisions the corporation manager as being most able to reach the board of directors quickly, he should try functioning as a manager of one of these forest properties and timberlands and dealing with the tax agencies. He doesn't have to have a very big property to find out that he may have half a dozen different tax lots, with each one of them being appraised by a different assessor and having different levies on it. I think it's very Pollyanna to think it would correct anything to change over to permitting the local taxing body to submit a bill to the public agency and let it then have the power to determine what to do.

So I am critical of this business of not identifying what problem we do have. If it's a difference in the levels of revenue sharing, why not then correct that problem by an adjustment in revenue sharing instead of jumping off to an in-lieu tax basis.

## WHAT ECONOMICS CAN'T DO

*Wood:* I am Sam Wood. I want to direct a fairly quick question to Mr. Newport.

I have been sympathetic to the economic analysis and feasibility study approach. But I get suspicious when economists try--and I have done this--to quantify recreation values and, in the process, decide between competing recreation or competing land uses on public lands. Now, do you think it's feasible to do that, Mr. Newport?

*Newport:* Well, I should develop my thoughts on how you should apply economic analysis. I think Dr. Clawson was very clear that he wanted to establish a value in terms of dollars on specific uses and commodities, such as recreation. I am not in agreement with doing this, because that is saying we want to put dollar values on all these things--the scenery, the recreation and so on--and then reach the decision only by economic analysis.

I make a distinction here. I say that you use economic analysis in the process of reaching a decision, but that's not your only basis. If you think of it in those terms, then you can use economic analysis to evaluate the most efficient way to produce a benefit that has nondollar value.

Now, this may seem rather strange to you, but it is possible and, in that Douglas fir supply study that I recommended to you, there was a rather crude technique suggested for weighing the alternatives. There have been others who have been concerned with the social choice among social ends, or the mixture of social and what we call dollar or economic ends.

There have been some models and techniques designed that would be very helpful in making such a choice, but they would only be helpful if we are specific regarding our goals and objectives. They aren't helpful when the public is inclined, and even some of the managers, to equate a reduction in the allowable timber harvest with an improvement in the environment. This is a very poor method of making a choice. For example, in the recent Six Rivers management plan in California, the total allowable cut went up and many people felt that this was poor for the environment. But if you look and see what was actually done there, the cutting of the type that people have objected to was reduced and the kind of cutting that ended up in increasing the timber output was the kind that we have found to be environmentally much more acceptable.

So this is the kind of thing I am talking about. I am not trying to set artificial dollar values because that implies that the entire decision can be made by economic analysis, and I don't believe it can.

## WHAT ECONOMICS CAN DO

*Crutchfield:* Just one point, if I may. It is that economic analysis can be of tremendous benefit in many cases where recreation is in potential conflict with other uses. By simply flipping the coin you can measure with some degree of accuracy the cost of providing for a particular exclusive type of use. It may be outdoor recreation or preservation, whatever combination you may want.

For example, nobody I know would seriously contend that an economic evaluation of the benefits of reserving the middle fork of the Salmon as a wild river would be particularly meaningful. But it would be meaningful if you could pinpoint accurately how much you would have to give up over time to make such a reservation.

The need to do this, I think, was pinpointed by the kind of so-called economic analyses that underlie the justification for the North Cascades Park. It's a magnificent area. I am delighted that it is going into park status, but the economic analysis was so poor that had it been subjected to any kind of careful scrutiny, it would have been shot down immediately.

Outdoor recreation people must bear this in mind. If you take the position that outdoor recreation and wilderness are priceless, then you must face the fact that some are more priceless than others. You still have to make decisions and choices, and we don't want to get caught on that hook.

*Snyder:* If I am to fulfill my obligations and avoid getting a rap on the knuckles, I must close at this point. I leave those of you who have questions yet unanswered with perhaps a motto for the day: Take a panelist to lunch.

# PART THREE

# Policies for the Use of the Public Lands

# PUBLIC LAND POLICIES AND NATURAL RESOURCES

Walter J. Mead

*Professor of Economics*
*University of California, Santa Barbara*

## FOCUS ON TIMBER AND MINERAL RESOURCES

The purpose of this paper is to review some of the recommendations made by the Public Land Law Review Commission regarding development of resources contained on or in the public lands. Special attention will be given to timber and mineral resources since these are the most important revenue-producing resources. Due to the time limitation, relatively little attention will be given to such important problem areas as recreation, grazing and environmental policies.

Where natural resources are in public ownership but processing of such resources is delegated to the private sector, the government trustee must answer the following questions: (1) Should resources be allocated among interested parties by competitive or noncompetitive methods? (2) How should the price of the resource be determined? (3) How should the processor be selected from among several interested parties? (4) If competitive bidding is to be employed, what should be the object of bidding--a royalty, a cash bonus, a combination of the above or some other variable? (5) What restrictions, if any, should be imposed on the processor on behalf of resource conservation, environmental protection or other objectives? The commission has received studies on each of these problems and has made policy recommendations concerning them.

## The Extent of Public Ownership

Although the federal government has used natural
resources for nearly two centuries as a means of buying
economic development and paying veterans for war service,
there are still vast and valuable resources remaining in
public ownership. About 56 percent of the net volume of
sawtimber remaining in the United States is in public
ownership. The federal government still retains ownership of 34 percent of the nation's land area. Most of
the federal land is in the mineral-rich western states.
At present, 9 percent of the federal lands are under
lease to private enterprise for oil and gas exploration
or production. The remaining public lands constitute
potential oil, gas, coal and other mineral reserves.

In addition, immense new areas under government control have become available for mineral resource development. The coastal states control submerged lands three
miles beyond the mean high tide line on their shores.[1]
The 1958 Geneva Convention on the Law of the Sea confirmed national sovereignty over the continental shelf
area. Article I of the convention defines the continental shelf as the seabed and subsoil adjacent to the coast
to a depth of 200 meters or "beyond that limit, to where
the depth of the super-adjacent waters admits of the
exploitation of the natural resources...." Thus, the
federal government may lease minerals for private exploitation beyond state jurisdiction to the limit of opera-
bility. An active program of sulfur, sodium and especially oil and gas leasing by the federal government in
the Gulf of Mexico has been under way since 1954. In
1969, 269 million barrels of oil were produced from the
U.S. Outer Continental Shelf, accounting for 8 percent of
total U.S. petroleum production.

## Oil Reserves

Oil reserves in the form of oil shale, about 85 percent owned by the federal government, are so vast that
their magnitude and value can best be understood when
compared to worldwide reserves of crude petroleum and to

the value of the national debt. Oil shale reserves
located in Colorado, Utah and Wyoming contain at least 2
trillion barrels of oil. The Bureau of Mines estimates
that this shale is in formations "thick enough to be considered mineable in the future."[2] This volume of known
oil reserves is equal to 6.7 times the known world
recoverable reserves of liquid petroleum. The Secretary
of the Interior has indicated that high-grade reserves
of oil shale amount to about 600 billion barrels, or
about twice the known world reserves of crude petroleum.
If the 2 trillion mineable barrels have an average net
value in place of 20 cents per barrel, then its total
value is $400 billion, slightly more than the present
national debt. While an oil shale industry is still in
the pilot plant stage, the Department of Interior view
is that eventually it will dominate the oil market.[3]

Oil shale resources, in addition, are intermixed
with other minerals, the most important being Dawsonite.
This is a sodium aluminum carbonate, a source of aluminum bauxite. Since the United States aluminum industry
is currently dependent upon foreign sources for more than
85 percent of its aluminum bauxite requirements, the
presence of Dawsonite intermixed in oil shale resources
is of added importance.

## Problems of Pricing

It is obvious from the above partial listing that
important natural resources remain in public ownership.
By tradition if not rational decision, publicly owned
resources have been transferred to private ownership for
processing. Transferral raises several difficult pricing
problems. First, the product to be sold is heterogeneous
by reason of its location, accessibility or quality.
Second, there is no "going market" to indicate a "fair
price." Third, the markets for timber and oil and gas
resources tend to be narrow and are characterized as
oligopsony markets. For example, in the Douglas fir
region, 70 percent of the timber sold from national forests is purchased by buyers located within 50 miles of
the sale location and 92 percent of such volume is

limited to a 70-mile radius.[4] The average number of
bidders expressing some interest as buyers of national
forest timber was 4.2 bidders per sale. For oil and gas
leases offered by the federal government in the Gulf of
Mexico in the period 1954 through 1964 there was an
average of 1.45 bidders contesting for leases. Fourth,
the bidding for the natural resources discussed above
involves great uncertainty. This is particularly true
with respect to oil and gas resources where there are
doubts concerning the presence of any petroleum resources
in the area subject to bidding and also about the quality
and quantity of resources that might be present. In
bidding for oil shale resources offered for lease there
will be great uncertainty concerning technology as well
as markets. Since costs and revenues are subject to wide
estimating errors, the residual value of the resource is
largely speculative.

## COMPETITIVE v. NONCOMPETITIVE TRANSFERS

Currently, the publicly owned mineral and timber
resources are transferred under three different systems:
(1) leasing, which may be either competitive or noncompetitive, (2) location, followed by patent at the option
of the locator and (3) sale. All onshore mineral deposits on acquired lands, plus oil, gas, coal, phosphate,
potash, sodium, oil shale, bituminous minerals and sulfur (in Louisiana and New Mexico) on the public domain
are leasable minerals.

## Leasing

Oil and gas resources on a "known geological structure" (as designated by the U.S. Geological Survey) must
be leased competitively. Minerals listed above other
than oil and gas are subject to competitive leasing if
the deposit is known to be of sufficient quality and
quantity to warrant development. If not, a prospecting
permit may be issued which includes a preference right to
a noncompetitive lease if a mineral deposit is discovered.
Those lands not included in a known geological structure

are leased noncompetitively on a first-come-first-served
basis or on a lottery basis in the case of simultaneous
filing.

## Location and Patent

Onshore minerals other than those listed above are
subject to location and, following discovery of a valuable deposit, may be patented at the option of the locator. The patentee receives fee title to all subsurface
minerals and to the surface of the property.

## Sale

The "common variety minerals" such as sand and
gravel are transferred by competitive sale. Outer Continental Shelf minerals are subject to lease only and competitive bidding is authorized. With minor exceptions,
timber is sold through competitive bidding and the land
is retained by the government.

## Pricing

Pricing of publicly owned resources is established
either by competitive bidding or by statute or regulation. In the case of timber resources sold competitively
by the U.S. Forest Service, bidding is on the basis of a
price per thousand board feet removed from the forest.
This method corresponds to royalty bidding for mineral
resources. No other payment is required for Forest Service timber. The sale of timber resources by the Bureau
of Land Management is subject to a lump sum bid, corresponding to a bonus bid for mineral resources. Again,
no other payment is required. Mineral resources sold
under competitive bidding by the Bureau of Land Management, whether onshore or offshore, require a bonus bid
to determine the successful bidder. In addition the
lessee must pay a fixed rental prior to production and a
royalty (fixed for the Outer Continental Shelf, and a
sliding scale onshore) on all production. Leasable
minerals subject to noncompetitive transfer require

payment of an annual rental until production begins (or the lease is surrendered) and a sliding scale royalty thereafter.

In the case of locatable (nonleasable) minerals, no charge of any kind is made for the resource.

The entire public domain, except for a few states and a few areas specifically withdrawn, is subject to the location and patent approach for the locatable minerals.

Of the leasable minerals, the record shows that the vast majority of acreage is leased by noncompetitive methods. In 1969, 36,969 acres were leased under competitive bidding for mineral development, and 13,378,265 acres were leased under noncompetitive methods. Thus, competitive bidding accounted for less than 0.3 percent of all acreage leased in 1969.[5]

The Public Land Law Review Commission examined the location-patent system and recommended a series of modifications. The present system involves administrative problems and equity problems.

## ADMINISTRATIVE PROBLEMS

Regarding administrative problems, the commission recommended that "locators be required to give written notice of their claims to the appropriate federal land agency within a reasonable time after location."[6] Under the present location-patent system, the federal agencies have no knowledge of mining activities on claims or the existence of such claims. Claims are filed in a multitude of county and state land offices. After filing a claim, the locator has a legal right to proceed with mining operations indefinitely on lands in the public domain prior to his application to the federal government for a fee title.

Lacking information on the existence and the operation of mining claims on the public domain, the government is not in a position to regulate mining activities in order to maintain environmental quality

in the area. Thus environmental quality control is non-
existent on mining claims. In order to correct this
omission, the commission recommended that "upon receipt
of the required notice of location a permit should be
issued to the locator, subject to administrative discretion exercised within strict limits of congressional
guidelines, for the protection of surface values. While
an administrator should have no discretion to withhold a
permit, he should have the authority to vary these
restrictions to meet local conditions." Further, the
commission recommended that "Where mineral activities
cause a disturbance of public land, Congress should
require that the land be restored or rehabilitated after
a determination of feasibility based on a careful balancing of the economic costs, the extent of the environmental impacts, and the availability of adequate technology for the type of restoration, rehabilitation, or
reclamation proposed."[7]

## Costs and Benefits of Rehabilitation

The report points out that "rehabilitation does not
necessarily mean restoration." The wording of this
recommendation reflects careful thought. The *cost* of
rehabilitation must be compared to the *benefit* of
rehabilitation. Where the cost exceeds the benefit,
rehabilitation should not be undertaken or a different
form should be considered where the cost is lower, relative to the benefit. The recommendation acknowledges
that rehabilitation should not be viewed as an absolute
requirement which must be undertaken at any cost.

## A Mass of Claims

The filing procedure without any central clearing
system has also produced a chaotic mass of claims against
the public domain such that the government is limited in
its ability to use or sell land from the public domain.
The commission urged that Congress "establish a fair
notice procedure (a) to clear the public lands of long-
dormant mining claims, and (b) to provide the holders of

existing mining claims an option to perfect their claims under the revised location provisions we recommend."[8]  A procedure of this kind is necessary to clarify the estimated 5.5 million existing claims accumulated over nearl 100 years.

## EQUITY PROBLEMS

Regarding problems of equity among citizen interest groups, the commission recommended the addition of "reasonable rentals" and added that "patent fees should be increased and equitable royalties should be paid to the United States on all minerals produced and marketed whether before or after patent."[9]  Under the present location-patent procedures, valuable minerals from the public domain belonging to all citizens are given away free of charge.  In the event that the locator wishes to obtain a fee title to the land (both surface and subsurface), he is obligated to pay only the nominal $2.50 or $5 per acre patent fee, as established by the Mining Law of 1872.  The Department of the Interior has estimated that in 1965 the value of production from locatable mineral production in the 12 western states was $2.1 billion.[10]  The net income from this production is less tha the $2.1 billion value of production, but is still a ver large sum of public wealth to be given away virtually free of charge.

## Separation of Subsurface and Surface Legal Rights

The commission also recommends a separation of subsurface and surface legal rights as follows:  "We propos that a mineral patent should carry only a right to use the surface necessary for the extraction and processing of the minerals to which patent has been granted," and further that "mineral operators, however, should have th option of acquiring title or a lease to the needed land areas when they are willing to pay the market value of the surface rights."

Finally: "If the mineral patentee does not acquire title to the surface, the right to the mineral interest should terminate *automatically* at the end of a reasonable period after cessation of production."[11] [Emphasis supplied] The commission does not specify how the market value is to be determined. An auction cannot be held since only one bidder would be permitted. Presumably an appraisal would be made, and this would be followed by negotiation wherein the interested party would attempt to (probably successfully) obtain a lower price. Since there is only one possible buyer, an agency would be under the usual pressure to exact a "fair price" which is a low price.

## Rentals and Royalties

The commission's recommendation that reasonable rentals be charged is somewhat misleading since it also recommends that "actual expenditures for exploration and development work should be credited against the rentals." If past history is a reasonable guide, every locator would be able to establish that improvement work has been undertaken having a value equal to or greater than the required rental and rental income would continue to be approximately zero. The objective the commission has in mind is to provide an economic incentive for the locator to develop his claim.

Under the present location-patent system no royalty charges are levied. The commission stated that "royalty should be collected on production both before and after patent."[12] Again, there is no specification of how the royalty is to be determined except that "as a general standard we recommend fair-market value, unless Congress expressly establishes another guideline for payment." The value of any mineral type will vary with its quality, quantity and accessibility. Therefore, it is difficult to imagine how Congress might *legislate* a price to be paid, other than a nominal price bearing no relationship to "fair market value." Again, the competitive auction approach is not suitable since the locator has a preference position which precludes other bidders.

The most likely solution is the appraisal procedure
similar to that used by the Forest Service in its sustained yield unit timber sales. The problem is that end
less conflict takes place between the selling agency and
the buyer since the latter has a strong economic interes
in obtaining a lower price regardless of what the appraised price might be.

## Minerals of the Future

With regard to the future development of minerals
from the Outer Continental Shelf, the commission notes
that the present law has worked very well in the case of
oil, gas and sulfur leasing. Other mineral development
from the OCS has lagged however. The commission felt it
would be premature to recommend a long-range policy
governing the development of these other minerals. Instead, it suggests that "Congress authorized the Secretary of the Interior to undertake experimental bidding
and leasing arrangements, assuring mining companies of
leases for a definite period, perhaps 10 years."[13]

The commission specifically rejected a recommendation advanced by the mining industry that the location-
patent approach established in the Mining Law of 1872 fo
the onshore public domain be extended to the OCS. The
commission stated that "although we recommend elsewhere
in this report continuance of a modified location and
patent system applicable to public lands generally, we
do not believe it feasible to extend this system to the
Outer Continental Shelf."[14]

As part of an interim experimental system the commission endorsed a recommendation of the Marine Science
Commission that "the flexibility given to the Secretary
of the Interior should include waiver of competitive bid
ding subject, however, to the principle we enunciated in
other parts of this report to the effect that, where com
petition is known to exist, competitive bidding procedures should be utilized."[15] This position seems appropriate in the interim period. If there is only one

interested lessee for a particular marine mineral lease, then competitive bidding is of no value in oral bidding and of slight value in sealed bidding. A lease that can be negotiated may be better than no lease at all in the early stage of OCS development.

The commission wisely did not recommend measures to require that the claims and patented lands be operated immediately or surrendered for operation by others. A requirement of this kind would possibly have introduced a problem of resource misallocation over time. Instead, the owner of mineral resources should be free to recover his minerals when market conditions are to his advantage. This economic freedom is likely to produce the best possible pattern of resource use over time and the highest degree of resource conservation.

The location-patent procedure was established first in common law, then codified in the Mining Law of 1872. In addition to its monumental administrative problems, it is a give-away approach that may have been appropriate a century ago when development was the primary concern and equity problems were secondary. It now seems clear that an overhaul of this law is in order and the recommendations of the commission seem more appropriate for the 1970s and the immediate future.

## THE LOTTERY METHOD v. THE FREE MARKET

Shifting our attention from the locatable to the leasable minerals, the commission has recommended an expansion of competitive bidding for mineral leases and a consequent reduction or elimination of the first-come-first-served and the lottery methods of noncompetitively allocating mineral leases. Specifically, the commission recommended that "Competitive sale of exploration permits or leases should be held whenever competitive interest can reasonably be expected."[16] In more detail, the commission noted that "competitive leasing would be appropriate (1) in the general area of producing wells, (2) for land covered by relinquished or forfeited leases or permits or (3) where past activity and general knowledge suggest reasonably good prospects for success."[17] This recommendation would vastly broaden the present "known geological structure" test and is intended to eliminate the need for the simultaneous filing system. Under simultaneous filing, each applicant pays a $10 non-returnable filing fee. Lottery tickets are then drawn at random from a vessel. The number of applicants have been in excess of 2000 for particularly attractive leases. Each applicant is limited to one filing. However, lease brokers are known to collect a large number of names that file on behalf of the broker.

The fundamental flaw of the lottery system is that chance rather than efficiency determines the winner and there is a haphazard relationship between the total amount of the filing fees and the value of the lease. A free market system provides a time-tested method of allocating the scarce resources among those desiring such resources, namely competitive markets. Use of competitive bidding, in the long run, insures that the most imaginative and the most efficient producers obtain the resources they desire and the least efficient are appropriately bypassed. The commission recommendation is consistent with this free market approach.

Shifting from first-come-first-served and the lottery system to an all competitive bidding system for oil and gas leases involves an equity issue again. The U.S. Department of the Interior estimated that such a shift would sacrifice filing fee income amounting to about $2.5 million per year but would increase bonus income "anywhere from $10 million to $100 million" per year. This study was based on 1967 conditions.[18]

## ALTERNATIVE BIDDING OBJECTIVES

If competitive bidding is chosen as the appropriate means of price determination and buyer selection, choices must be made concerning the alternative objects of bidding. The following are the principal alternatives: cash bonus (lump sum or cruise) bidding, royalty (scale) bidding and a combination of these.

In competitive bidding for timber resources, the commission recommended that "for both economic reasons and in the interests of conservation, the method of selling timber on the lump sum, or cruise, basis be adopted generally by the Federal land management agencies...."[19] For mineral leases, the commission noted that bonus bidding has been used by the federal government, but that in most cases the authority exists to use royalty bidding. The commission recommended on page 134 of the report that "The administrator should have the discretion to employ a combination of bonus, royalty, and rentals, or outright sale of the minerals in place as may be appropriate in particular situations. The tools available to him should permit the fullest exercise of sound business judgment." The commission's recommendation with respect to timber seems particularly wise. Problems of entry barriers into mineral leasing, as well as the great uncertainty characterizing hidden minerals seem to call for flexibility in mineral leasing, providing the recommendation does not mean that the administrator permits a combination of bonus, royalty and rental bidding on any one lease sale. The problem involved in combination bidding will be discussed later.

## ROYALTY BIDDING

Under royalty bidding procedures the contestants are asked to make their offers in terms of a specified price per physical unit of the resource or some specified percent of the value of the resource at a given point in the production process. Royalty bidding is normally subject to a minimum acceptable royalty and the amounts bid may be equal to or greater than the specified minimum. All other terms of sale are predetermined and fixed. Under pure royalty bidding there is no bonus payment. Royalty bidding requires a metering system to count the number of units of the product that have been removed.

The royalty bidding approach is in common use by the U.S. Forest Service in its timber auctions. The Forest Service must maintain checkout points on roads leading from national forest timber sale areas. This involves

112

social costs in the form of man-hours for those employed
as checkers as well as the cost of facilities and time
lost in transportation. Royalty bidding is less common
in oil resource auctions. The system has, however, been
used by the State of California in both its onshore and
submerged lands, oil and gas auctions.

An Economic Problem

The principal economic problem arising out of
royalty bidding is that the system requires that the
buyer pay for the resource utilized on a unit of production basis even though the cost to society may not be
a function of number of units utilized from any given
lease. Alternatively stated, the system treats a lump
sum cost to society as a marginal (incremental) cost and
accordingly leads to underutilization and resource misallocation.

The problem may be illustrated by royalty bidding
for national forest timber in the Douglas fir region of
the Pacific Northwest. As an initial step in the bidding
process, timber is identified on a particular area of
ground. The value of products into which the timber may
be converted is estimated. All costs of production are
estimated, including a normal profit for the operator,
and the sum is then subtracted from estimated revenues,
yielding a net value called the appraised value. This
becomes the refusal price.

Interested buyers are then asked to bid by oral
auction procedures usually and normally starting at
the appraised price. Bidding is by species and the high
bidder agrees to pay a specified dollar amount bid per
thousand board feet removed. If the amount bid by
species truly reflects the competitive equilibrium
price, then the amount bid corresponds to the *average*
value per thousand board feet of standing timber. But
timber is not a uniform commodity. The large logs, free
of knots and defects, command a substantial premium over
the small and the defective logs. Approximately half of
the volume of timber involved will in fact be of lower

unit value than the amount bid per unit.  A maximizing operator unrestrained by Forest Service regulations would choose to harvest only the timber having a unit value greater than its marginal cost, and to transport to his mill or market only those logs having a value greater than the marginal logging cost.

## The Utilization Problem

The Figure illustrates the utilization problem. Marginal costs (the additional or incremental cost for each additional unit of output) are shown both with and without a royalty charge.  In the absence of a royalty charge, a maximizing producer would utilize his timber up to point Y.  Where a royalty charge is imposed on each unit of output as illustrated, utilization would be halted at point X.

The prevailing and apparently optimum method of logging timber in the Douglas fir region is by clearcutting, that is, completely removing all standing timber on a specified area of ground so that the bare ground provides a seed bed for the next crop.  Small diameter logs and defective logs are either removed in the logging process or are destroyed.

Thus, the cost to society is the same whether submarginal logs are removed or not.  The operator must treat a royalty charge as a marginal cost in the critical decision-making area between points X and Y even though royalty is not a real cost to society.  Timber resource misallocation occurs if production stops at point X rather than Y.  The net cost to society is indicated by the triangle ABC.  The value of the net cost is a function of the value of the royalty and the slope of the cost and revenue curves at the margin.  Where bidding is based on royalty and the royalty is consequently high, the misallocation result will be great.

There is one exception to the single royalty rate applied by the Forest Service.  In the case of cull logs, the rate charged is a special appraised rate that is

FIGURE

MODEL OF MARGINAL OUTPUT

Dollars per unit of output

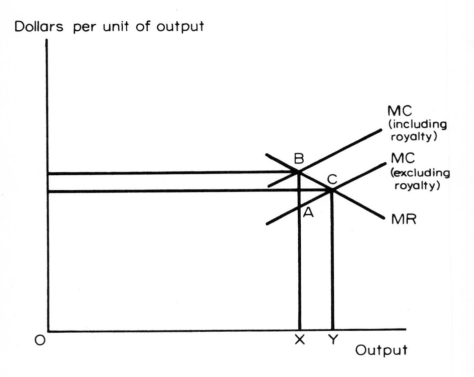

independent of the price bid.  The minimum rate in the
Douglas fir region is currently 50 cents per thousand
board feet and the highest rates seldom exceed $2 depend-
ing on local market conditions.  This nominal rate aver-
ages between 2 percent and 10 percent of noncull stumpage
prices.  Thus, for this single class of logs, low values
are accommodated.

Under prevailing Forest Service regulations timber
buyers are not permitted to seek their profit maximizing
output OX, but are forced to comply with the physical

utilization requirements prescribed by the Forest Service. These requirements presumably result in an output somewhere to the right of point X and possibly beyond point Y. Thus, regulations are substituted for economic incentives and require timber buyers to violate their own self-interest. This establishes a position of conflict between the buyer and the seller.

## The Case of Oil

With respect to petroleum, the same problem arises out of royalty charges. When a new oil field is developed, individual wells will normally yield a high output per day in the early stages of their life and subsequently decline as underground pressure is dissipated. In the oil field case marginal revenue is probably a horizontal line, rather than downward sloping as in the timber case, since oil is relatively homogeneous throughout the life of an oil field. A point is ultimately reached where oil recovery in barrels per day becomes so low that marginal revenues no longer exceed marginal costs.

Oil leases administered by the Bureau of Land Management require a minimum 12½ percent royalty on dry land wells and a 16 2/3 percent fixed royalty on Outer Continental Shelf leases. The 16 2/3 percent royalty charge, where the wellhead value of the crude oil is about $2 per barrel, requires a royalty payment of 33 cents per barrel, thus having a significant impact on the marginal cost structure.

As in the timber case, production will be halted at an output corresponding to point X in the Figure, unless producers are required by regulation to produce beyond their profit maximizing point. Again, the result is a misallocation of resources. The royalty charge takes the form of a marginal cost to the producer, but it is not a real cost to society. This argument assumes that petroleum which is not recovered at the point where lifting operations cease has approximately zero economic value to society.

The consequences of imposing a nonreal marginal cost in the form of a royalty requirement on oil production may be even more serious than in the timber case. The oil industry has developed a secondary recovery process by which water or some other agent is injected into an oil field in order to maintain or rebuild underground pressure and to facilitate the flow of oil. Production per month normally shows a decline in monthly output as pressure is lost. When secondary recovery operations are instituted, output per month is rebuilt and then declines along a new trend line. As output per month declines, cost per unit of production increases. Secondary recovery operations are introduced at considerable cost.

A profit maximizing operator must determine whether the added value realized as a result of secondary recovery measures will yield a sufficient discounted rate of return to justify the added expenditures. Where royalty charges are involved, it is possible that otherwise profitable secondary recovery operations may be foregone. Where this is the case, the net loss to society may be quite large.

## Sliding Scales

A sliding scale of oil royalty rates has been proposed as a means of minimizing the misallocation problem and also of capturing for the landlord a higher share of the profits from highly productive leases. A sliding scale would result in lower royalty rates as output per day declines in the later productive life of an oil field. The State of California permits the State Lands Commission to select either of two forms of a sliding royalty scale. It may specify a sliding scale having a minimum rate of 16 2/3 percent and require bonus bidding or bidding on a factor by which the royalty scale is to be multiplied.[20]

Where sliding scale royalty rates are in effect, supervision by the landlord is required to insure that the operator's self-interest does not result in either restrained daily production or overinvestment in drilling in order to qualify for lower royalty rates. Accordingly, all leases "contain a reservation to the Commission of the right to determine the spacing of wells and the rate of drilling and rate of production of such wells as to prevent the waste of oil and gas and promote the maximum economic recovery of oil and gas from, and the conservation of, reservoir energy...."[21]

The author of a consulting report prepared for the California State Lands Commission nevertheless pointed out that "the State would find it extremely difficult to impose controls that would force an operator to operate wells at the maximum rate at which there could be...[production] without waste, when it is obviously to the advantage of the lessee to produce wells under a sliding scale royalty at the lower rate of production per well per day." [22] Thus, sliding royalty rates establish a conflict between landlord and lessee that, unless effectively (and expensively) policed, will result in overinvestment in wells per lease, and underutilization of each well.

The sliding scale system suggests a means of avoiding the misallocation problem that arises at the margin illustrated by point X in the Figure. If the royalty rate could be automatically "triggered" to a zero rate at point X, then production would proceed to point Y. Further, if the system was introduced into all new contracts before they were offered for competitive bidding, and if competition  is reasonably effective, then the discounted value of the future anticipated royalty-free production would be reflected in higher bonus (or other variable) bids.

Alternatively, a formula royalty schedule could leave the operator with a profit incentive to continue operations while the landlord still collects most of the value represented by the area ABC. There is no obvious present solution to the problem of how point X can be unequivocally identified and specified in a contract. As pointed out above, average monthly production per well is subject to operator control.

Further, this arrangement is in conflict with some state prorationing systems--California does not have a prorationing system--which require a producer to restrict his output to some maximum permissible level in order to maintain a desired (high) price of domestic crude oil.[23] This approach has sufficient merit to justify further research.

## A Fixed Bonus

Another variation of a royalty bidding arrangement, as yet untried, would require a fixed bonus payment by the successful royalty bidder. Since the fixed bonus would increase the operator's cost, he would bid a lower royalty in order to earn his required discounted rate of return. In computing the royalty bid, a required fixed bonus payment is a trade-off against a royalty bid. The advantage of this variation of the royalty bidding system is that resource misallocation would be reduced as a consequence of a lower royalty payment.

The required bonus payment is a fixed cost for the purpose of determining when to cease recovery operations or to engage in secondary recovery. The disadvantage of the system is that given the great uncertainty of present value in the case of oil leases, the leasing agency could not establish a bonus requirement that would insure a relatively low royalty bid. If royalty bids substantially exceeded 16 2/3 percent on the Outer Continental Shelf, the resource misallocation problem would be substantial. If this variation produced royalty bids less than 16 2/3 percent on the OCS, then the resource misallocation problem would be moderated relative to the present system.

## Bonus v. Royalty Bidding

In spite of the resource misallocation that results from royalty payment requirements, royalty bidding is used in national forest timber sales and royalty payments are required almost universally in oil and gas leases, even though bidding for federal leases is not on the royalty. Personal interviews conducted by the author with oil company officials revealed a strong preference for bonus rather than royalty bidding but with a specified minimum royalty payment.

In the 1958 hearings conducted by the State Lands Commission for the State of California where alternative bidding procedures were considered, a majority of firm spokesmen expressed a preference for bonus bidding, but four firms testified in favor of royalty bidding: Richfield Oil Corporation, The Ohio Company, Hancock Oil Company and Signal Oil and Gas Company.

A spokesman for Richfield charged that "the cash bonus basis limits the field to the bidders of the moneyed few. Many companies and producers operating in California have the resources and the ability to develop these lands and they are completely responsible in every respect, but very few of them can bid cash in the amounts which the State ought to realize from these lands."[24] A Hancock spokesman testified similarly: "Obviously...if bonus bidding is embraced...the potential bidder with the largest bank account is of necessity going to be in the better position."[25] This testimony clearly indicates one of the advantages of royalty bidding: it minimizes the capital requirement for entry. Where barriers to entry are high, competitors are few, particularly in the case of the Outer Continental Shelf oil resource auction markets. Reducing barriers to entry must be considered a significant advantage of royalty bidding over bonus bidding. A second advantage of royalty bidding from the buyer's point of view is that payments are made for the resource only if an oil field in fact is discovered and production occurs. Under bonus bidding, in contrast, the bonus is due and payable whether production occurs or not.


BONUS BIDDING

By this technique an interested buyer submits a lump sum bid that would entitle him to exploit all of the

resources offered on or under a previously described area
of land. Any other fees are fixed and are not subject
to simultaneous bidding. After a bonus payment has been
made, it becomes a fixed cost with respect to the operator's decision-making problems, that is, the bonus payment is not a function of output. The buyer in effect
owns all of the resources offered. If the buyer is able
to devise better operating procedures that enable him to
economically utilize more of the resource, such resources
are available to him free of marginal charges, where no
royalty payments are required.

The Bureau of Land Management in its timber sales
program employs bonus bidding without royalty payments of
any kind. Thus, the commission recommendation urges the
Forest Service to shift to BLM method of bidding. Since
there is no charge based upon units of output, there is
no need to maintain and pay for a checkout point where
production is measured and recorded. Bureau of Land
Management oil leases, where there is a "known geological
structure," and all OCS mineral sales are offered on a
bonus bid basis. However, fixed royalty payments are
also required. On BLM dry land oil exploration leases,
the minimum royalty requirement is 12½ percent of the
wellhead value whereas on its Outer Continental Shelf
leases, the fixed royalty amounts to 16 2/3 percent.
Since a royalty charge is levied in addition to the lump
sum bonus, a check-out system must be maintained where
all oil production is recorded.

## The Uncertainty Problem

Like royalty bidding and charging, bonus bidding
also has its problems. First is the uncertainty problem
With respect to oil and gas leases, the lessees may conduct geophysical research short of actually drilling a
test well. These procedures are both expensive and of
questionable value. At best, they indicate an oil-
bearing structure. They indicate very little about the
quantity of oil present, let alone its quality. One oil
company landman testified "we bid in the dark, really."[2]

In petroleum resource auctions, the seller does not know what he is selling, and the buyer, who may have purchased some geological and geophysical research, has only a slight advantage over the seller. The bonus bidding procedure nevertheless requires a competitive bidder to estimate the probable flow of future net value of a given lease, discount it to the present and offer a present cash bonus. Where such great uncertainty prevails, only the large, well-financed firms or combinations of small firms can afford to accept the high risks of bonus bidding for resources of uncertain presence and value and commit present and irrevocable cash reflecting a reasonable present evaluation.

For oil shale resources, uncertainty is modest relative to crude petroleum. The presence of the shale resource is known absolutely. Much is known about its quality since core holes have been drilled. Any parcel offered for lease may be extensively core drilled by the seller and information made available to prospective bidders. There is considerable uncertainty, however, concerning the technology and consequent costs of oil from shale, as well as such public policy issues as import policy, taxation (depletion allowance) and substitute energy sources. There is no shale oil industry at present. In the early years of any such industry we should expect the learning curve to operate and produce sharply declining costs of production over time. There being less uncertainty in shale resource development than in liquid petroleum, bonus bidding would be relatively more appropriate.

In timber resource exploitation, the degree of uncertainty is even lower. There is some doubt about the quality of the resource hidden under the bark of trees. Also the methods used to cruise standing timber to determine the quantity involve a sampling error. Further, the timber buyer normally also buys a road construction requirement which may involve him in unforeseen difficulties. Again, however, the degree of uncertainty is low relative to that of shale and very low relative to crude petroleum. Therefore bonus bidding is relatively more appropriate for timber sales. But in any case the presence of unknown factors results in both windfalls and losses. In the case of crude petroleum the occasional windfall brings with it extremely large profits. These in turn must be more than enough to offset a large number of smaller losses.

## Barrier to Entry

The second problem of bonus bidding is that a significant barrier to entry may be added. In the 1964 Gulf of Mexico sale of oil and gas leases, the average lessee paid $2.6 million for his lease.[27] Where very heavy exploratory costs are added to the bonus charge, the cost of entry with its attending uncertainty may be very large. However even without the bonus charge the risks of submerged lands oil exploration and production are relatively high. This is an appropriate field for relatively large and well-financed firms. Others may, and commonly do, buy a participation in this high-risk activity through a multitude of joint ventures. For example, in Gulf of Mexico leases offered by the U.S. Department of the Interior from 1954 through 1964, 624 joint bids were submitted compared to 1577 single bids for tracts having two or more bids received. Thus 28 percent of all such bids were joint bids.[28]

The barrier to entry introduced by bonus bidding may be even more important in oil shale resource development. The potential entrants will be few in number, at least in the early years of an oil shale industry. The number of participants will be limited by two factors. First, there are only about 20 firms at most with a sufficient technological background to be considered serious contenders for oil shale leases. Second, the basic capital requirement for mining, crushing, retorting and upgrading facilities is estimated from $100 to $150 million.[29] Production facilities currently being constructed by The Oil Shale Corporation are estimated to cost $130 million.[30] Future bonus bidding may add substantially to this cost of entry.[31] Thus, a bonus bidding arrangement would increase the barriers to entry into the oil shale market.

Bonus bidding for timber sales, on the other hand, poses no great barrier to entry problem. The average timber sale requires relatively low bonus payments. For example, in the timber sales held during the second quarter of 1967, the average bonus bid per sale was $112,000.[32]

## Rate of Discount

A third problem arising from bonus bidding, one might argue, is that the discount rate employed by oil companies to convert expected future net income into present value may be inappropriately high as a representation of the public time preference rate. Presumably the discount rate used by oil companies will be based on their marginal internal rate of return. In effect, the bonus bidding system requires that the public landlord accept the private time preference rate. If there is an acceptable argument for holding that the public time preference rate should be lower, then the bonus system involving present payments for future values becomes less attractive relative to an alternative system that involves future payment.

The disadvantages of bonus bidding listed above must be weighed against the single advantage, that bonus bidding avoids the resource misallocation problem associated with royalty bidding where the latter imposes a nonreal marginal cost on marginal units of output.

In order to solve the barrier to entry problem, a schedule of delayed payments might be established to liquidate the bonus obligation. This procedure would permit some revenue from production to be utilized for the bonus payment. It is appropriate only on low-uncertainty situations such as the Long Beach East Wilmington oil field. In high-uncertainty situations, such as Outer Continental Shelf oil explorations, some irresponsible firms would probably choose bankruptcy where only dry wells are found, and would gladly pay the scheduled amount where productive wells occur. In the bidding process, and with this procedure in mind, they could outbid the more responsible firms. As a result, the seller would inevitably be placed in a risk-bearer position for which he receives little compensation.

## COMBINATION BIDDING

Instead of a single variable being the subject of bidding, interested buyers may be permitted to bid on two or more variables. Thus, one bidder may offer one-eighth royalty paired with $100,000 bonus. Another may offer a higher royalty, but a lower bonus, perhaps one-sixth and $75,000. Combination bidding of this type is permitted on mineral lands supervised by the State Mineral Board in Louisiana. Louisiana statutes state that "The Mineral Board has authority to accept the bid most advantageous to the State, and may lease upon whatever terms it considers proper. However, the minimum royalties to be stipulated in any lease shall be one-eighth of all oil and gas produced and saved."[33] In addition, regulations of the State Mineral Board prescribe that "The annual rental shall be at least (not less) one-half of the cash bonus offered."[34] Under Louisiana regulations, rent may also be a bid variable.

The dominant problem of multiple-variable bidding is that an objective judgment of the high bidder on at least one variable is needed and at least an equal bidder on every other variable. Where this situation does not prevail, the supervising agency is required to subjectively select the winning bid. This is a prescription for corruption. Even where the supervisory agency is as pure as the driven snow the members will still be vulnerable to the charge from the losing bidders that the agency was bribed by the winner.

The only conceivable advantage of multiple-variable bidding over single-variable bidding is that a board with superior insight into the probability of a given lease's being productive may select a combination that will maximize returns to the state. For example, if the agency

expects a given lease to be productive, it should accept
a combination of bids that maximize the royalty offered.
In contrast, if dry holes are expected, the agency presumably would choose the combination that maximized the
bonus offered.

## MISCELLANEOUS RESTRICTIONS ON THE PRICE MECHANISM

The commission is organized as a political body and
some of its recommendations clearly reflect the heavy
political pressure that a particular economic interest
group can bring to bear on a political body. Taking a
stand in opposition to continuation or expansion of the
sustained yield unit principle, the commission wisely,
in my opinion, stated: "We do not believe that a quota
system is a necessary tool for Federal (timber) policy
and, furthermore, we believe that it is inconsistent with
our free enterprise system."[35] However, the commission
also took equally strong stands favoring continuation
of the recently enacted ban on exports of public land
logs,[36] the longstanding primary processing requirement
for timber harvested from the national forests in
Alaska[37] and the similarly longstanding system of prorationing of oil production.

## PRORATIONING

In the case of prorationing, the commission rejected
the present practice whereby Louisiana and Texas prorationing regulations are mandatory for federal leases
in the Gulf of Mexico offshore from these two states.
Instead, the commission recommended that "the Federal
Government promulgate and administer its own rules for
controlling the rate of production from Outer Continental
Shelf oil and gas fields."[38] The report cited the need
for a "flexible system of allowables to meet the variety
of conditions which may be experienced." While the
report is not clear whether it is speaking of maximum
efficient rate (MER) prorationing or market demand prorationing, or both, I assume it is the latter.

MER prorationing is a necessity where more than one ownership draws on a single oil reservoir.  On the other hand, market demand prorationing is a simple conspiracy in restraint of trade legalized by Congress through passage of the Interstate Oil Compact Act and enforced by the Connally "Hot Oil Act."  Market demand prorationing limits the right of a producer to produce oil from his wells to some stated percentage of the predetermined maximum efficient rate of production.  By limiting output, price will be higher than under free market conditions.  The market demand prorationing system, in turn, is supported by the system of oil import quotas and could not survive without limitations on imports.

## THE LOG BAN

The ban on log exports from public lands prevents buyers of public timber from seeking out the best markets for their logs.  By precluding the best allocation of logs, the value of public timber is reduced and the public owners of this timber receive a lower value in public bidding than they would otherwise receive.  One side effect of the log export prohibition is to reserve this high-priced market for the private timber holding companies on the West Coast.  Private firms are not similarly restricted.  Another side effect is that an important incentive pressing for greater milling efficiency on the West Coast has been eliminated.

The primary processing requirement governing timber sold from national forests in Alaska prohibits the export of unprocessed timber from federal sources unless specifically authorized by the Forest Service.  In essence, the requirement prohibits log export, chip export and cant export where the cant is greater than a minimum prescribed size.  The intent of the requirement is to promote the development of lumber, veneer and pulp milling in Alaska.  One effect is that timber is misallocated from its most efficient processing locations.  Another effect is that some timber resources (both logs and chips) are wasted because their processing in Alaska is currently not profitable. A third effect is that public owners of timber resources in Alaska receive a lower value for their timber resources because the most profitable markets are constrained.

Each of the above restrictions of the free price system is "inconsistent with our free enterprise system." It is regretted that inconsistency with free enterprise principles which led to the commission's rejection of the sustained yield unit authorization did not also lead to the rejection of these three interferences with the same free enterprise principles.

# NOTES

[1] Texas and Florida control submerged lands "three leagues" into the Gulf of Mexico.

[2] U.S. Bureau of Mines, *Mineral Facts and Problems*, Bulletin no. 630 (Washington, D.C.: 1965), p. 638.

[3] U.S. Department of the Interior, "The Oil Shale Policy Problem, A Synopsis," background paper prepared for the opening meeting of the Department of the Interior Oil Shale Advisory Board, July 7, 1964, p. 20. (mim)

[4] Walter J. Mead, *Competition and Oligopsony in the Douglas Fir Lumber Industry* (Berkeley: University of California Press, 1966), p. 93.

[5] U.S. Bureau of Land Management, *Public Land Statistics, 1969* (Washington, D.C.), pp. 112-113.

[6] U.S. Public Land Law Review Commission, *One Third of the Nation's Land* (Washington, D.C.: 1970), p. 126.

[7] Ibid., p. 127.

[8] Ibid., p. 130.

[9] Ibid., p. 126.

[10] U.S. Department of the Interior, *Task Group Study on the Pricing and Disposal of Federally Owned Mineral Resources*, June 1, 1966, p. 2. (mim) An open-file report available at the Interior Library.

[11] Public Land Law Review Commission, p. 128. See note 6 above.

[12] Loc. cit.

[13] Ibid., p. 194.

[14] Loc. cit.

[15] Ibid., p. 195.

[16] Ibid., p. 132.

128

[17] Ibid., pp. 132-133.

[18] U.S. Department of the Interior, *An Analysis of the Impact of An All Competitive Leasing System on Onshore Oil and Gas Leasing Revenues*, by John W. Sprague and Bernadette Julian of the Bureau of Land Management, Division of Energy and Minerals. See footnote, p. 20. (1968) (mim)

[19] *One Third of the Nation's Land*, see note 6 above, p. 98.

[20] State of California, *Public Resources Code*, Section 6827.

[21] Ibid., Section 6830.

[22] Herman H. Kaveler, "Recommended Tidelands Oil and Gas Leasing Policy," submitted to the State Lands Commission, State of California, February 3, 1958, p. 11. (Consultant's report, mim)

[23] While this paper is concerned with resource misallocation due to the pricing system employed, the reader should be reminded of the more serious problems of misallocation that result from prorationing and other interferences with the market mechanism that abound in the petroleum industry. See M.A. Adelman, "Efficiency of Resource Use in Crude Petroleum," *Southern Economic Journal*, 31: 101-121 (1964).

[24] California, State Lands Commission, *Public Hearings on Oil and Gas Leasing Policies and Procedures*, Vol. II, p. 24 (February 27, 1958).

[25] Ibid., p. 10.

[26] Statement of Paul Ottoson, Signal Oil Company, in *Public Hearings...* p. 10. See note 24 above.

[27] U.S. Department of the Interior, Bureau of Land Management, *Oil and Gas Lease Sale Reports*, 1954-1964 (New Orleans). (mim)

[28] Ibid.

[29]These estimates are based on interviews conducted with oil shale development personnel employed by major oil companies.

[30]Statement by Morton M. Winston, Executive Vice-President of The Shale Corporation, Sept. 15, 1967, *Hearings before the U.S. Senate Committee on Interior and Insular Affairs on the Federal Oil Shale Program*, 90th Cong., 1st sess., p. 421.

[31]A production facility capable of producing 50,000 barrels of oil from a retort per day would require a shale lease large enough to yield about 500 million barrels of oil over a 25-year amortization period. A bid amounting to 20 cents per barrel of oil would require a bonus of $100 million which, in the pattern of bonus bidding for oil resources, must be paid in advance of production.

[32]U.S. Forest Service, *National Forest Advertised Timber Sales*, Region 6, April 1-June 30, 1967 (Portland, Oregon). (mim)

[33]*Louisiana Revised Statutes* (LSA-R.S.), Title 30, Sec. 127.

[34]"Rules and Regulations for the Leasing of Oil, Gas and Minerals on State Owned and State Agency Tracts," p. 3.

[35]Public Land Law Review Commission, p. 100. See note 6 above.

[36]Loc. cit.

[37]Ibid., p. 99.

[38]Ibid., p. 189.

# PANEL DISCUSSION ON POLICIES FOR THE USE OF THE PUBLIC LANDS

Moderator:   John A. Zivnuska, *Dean*
*School of Forestry and Conservation*
*University of California, Berkeley*

Panelists:   Brock Evans
*Sierra Club, Seattle*

Frank J. Hortig, *Executive Officer*
*Division of Lands*
*State of California*

George H. Ketchum, *Manager of Lands*
*Western Oil and Gas Association*

Carl Stoltenberg, *Dean*
*School of Forestry*
*Oregon State University, Corvallis*

*Zivnuska:*   Before we have a floor discussion, each of our four panelists will speak to the general topic of resources being made available to the public through the processors. Our first panelist is Mr. Brock Evans, the Pacific Northwest representative of the Sierra Club.

## Sierra Club

*Evans:*   I am very glad to be here to speak on this important subject. I feel constrained first of all to state that I was a little surprised and disappointed this morning at some of the strong criticism made by other speakers of the environmental groups that have expressed concern about the thrust of the report. I was disappointed to see the use of the straw man technique of ascribing positions to our organization that we do not, in fact, hold, and then knocking them down to prove we are wrong.

131

We heard that environmental groups see zero population growth as the *total* solution to the problem. Well since this isn't going to happen, they say, the concern was then expressed that this "position" of ours somehow may result in millions of people being out of work and a denial of the aspirations of the poor. Again, these are positions that we have never taken. I think we all know that there is a lot of room for valid discussion on this subject, but we should be frank about what interests we represent and not misrepresent the interests of others.

## ASSUMPTIONS: POPULATION GROWTH AND MAXIMUM OUTPUT

Coming to the policies and conclusions of the commission's report, the argument there seems to be that since the population won't stop growing and millions more are going to demand more and more goods and services, the basic policy emphasis on maximum economic output is justified. If the attitude is being taken that the gross national product must expand and, therefore, we must continue to extract more materials from the public lands, then we feel the commission should have vastly expanded its basic policy recommendations.

It should have looked at oil import quotas and ways of maximizing production in this country. It should have looked at log exports from private lands that are sending timber overseas, increasing demands on public lands here. It should have looked at the 100-plus million acres of private forest lands not reforested in this country. All should have been the subject of the policy recommendations.

It should have looked at the waste of power and what it consumes in excess energy in this country, in what we consider to be extravagant patterns. There should have been policy recommendations to deal with these fundamental factors as well.

Unfortunately, as we look at the report, we don't get very much of this. The policy recommendations seem basically to promote maximum feasible extraction from the public lands. In view of the strong emphasis we have heard so far on the necessity of keeping the work force going and having a rise in the gross national product, these are some things we do feel that the report was very inadequate in, because it looked only to the public lands for a solution.

## Commercial Interests

Our objections to the report are well known, and I will not go into them all since we are dealing just with policies here. But the heart of our objections is that the basic policy recommendations appear to give maximum possible advantage to western commercial interests in this country. We feel that the environment will suffer despite a lot of words about it and despite some genuinely good recommendations--and I want to make it plain here that I and others think that there are some very good and important recommendations, too.

One way to test this out is to just take a look, for example, at what would happen if the most basic policy recommendations in timber and mining and the environment were enacted tomorrow. What sort of system would we have?

In mining, we would have some improvement. Exploratory permits would have some rehabilitation requirements. We would have a protective system of sorts. We certainly would have more bargaining power relative to the government. But there is a basic flaw, as we see it.

No one still has the right to say "no." No federal administrator can say, "There shall not be mining, regardless of the value of the other resources in the land." If areas do have what are considered such "unique public values" that it would not be in the national interest to permit such operations, then there is a chance that they might be set aside. But it's not said exactly how. Presumably, it would be done through a long classification process of elimination at the political level.

And again in timber policy if a commission-recommended law were to be passed tomorrow, we would have immediately an allocation of dominant use to at least 45 million acres of federal timberland for cutting purposes. We would have a special fund for intensifying management. We would have greatly increased liquidation of timber, acceleration of construction of timber access roads into wilderness areas, all subsidized through this fund.

In environmental policy, we would have a few things like talking about making environmental quality a purpose of land management. We'd have a classification system of tolerable impacts and some guidelines, and we would also have an inventory of areas that might qualify for additions to special natural systems, as well as wilderness and parks. We would also, of course, have a repeal of the Antiquities Act, which is a present important means of protecting areas like these.

In brief, if these laws were enacted tomorrow, more land would be opened up. There would be no authority to say no. The national monuments would be reviewed and other wilderness areas would be reviewed again as well. In timber, we would have an accelerated cut and more roads to be built through, say, a special fund.

## INVENTORY, WITHDRAWAL, CLASSIFICATION

Well, those of us who see other values in the public lands, would get an inventory and a temporary withdrawal and then a long congressional political classification process. If certain areas were sufficiently unique--and this is the word you see again and again--then maybe they would be set aside after years and years. In other words, as we see it, if you will bear with special funds and special priorities, after inventory and temporary withdrawal, maybe, if they are unique enough, certain areas might get set aside.

It's obvious to us that the commission at least could have recommended an immediate policy on this subject. It could have made a recommendation for a law to protect de facto wilderness until the review. It could have given administrative power to say no to the mining interests. We don't share the view that was mentioned on the subject of mining: some of us wanted a mineral leasing system, but we didn't get it, so let's compromise and take what we can get. I have great difficulty compromising beautiful natural resources; these are the places where there will be mining, if there aren't substantial and real changes in the mining laws.

Regarding the policy of dominant use, which is another fundamental policy expressed in the report, the statement has often been made that this is okay for wilderness areas and parks. Why not for other uses, too? The fundamental distinction seems obvious to me; that is, that the parks and wilderness areas have to go through a long political reclassification process in the interim. The other uses don't have to go through the political process the way that wilderness and parks do.

## WASTING RESOURCES

Finally, I was going to remark on Mr. Mead's paper, which, I think, has a lot of worth to it. About royalties, there appears to be a feeling here that if we have a bonus system, then this will better conserve either timber or oil resources. We think that we should go further than that and use economic incentives. We think it's a waste of usable resources to have timber left on the ground, or the minerals that we take out not fully utilized. Or if a well is drilled, it is wasteful for some to be left in there. We would like to see some regulations and laws passed to require that all resource be used and to have the industries then retool and take account of these things, too.

Well, there's too much more to say here. What I can basically say is that we felt the report could have been broader in scope. It should have considered all aspects of the uses that our society is making of its private and public lands, since all of these have an impact on what happens to public land. We wish it could have included a lot more.

## AN OIL INDUSTRY VIEW

*Zivnuska:* Thank you, Brock, for a very full seven minutes--really packed. As our next panelist, we have George Ketchum who is Manager of Lands of the Western Oil and Gas Association. Mr. Ketchum.

*Ketchum:* As the oil industry's representative here today, I am pleased to report the favorable reaction on the part of our industry to a large majority of the commission's report.

This report, as it concerns our industry, strikes a fair balance in recognizing the nation's continued need for more energy resources and concern for the quality of our environment. As you may know, from the founding of the oil industry in 1859 to the present, the American people have consumed an aggregate total of about 100 billion barrels of oil. Yet in the next 30 years this nation's demand, on a conservative basis, for oil is expected to represent a cumulative total of over 230 billion barrels. In other words, the nation is expected to consume 2 1/3 times more oil in the next 30 years than it has in the past 111. Our job in the oil industry is to find and produce it, compatible with environment and ecology needs which we as citizens share with all the rest of the people.

## Potential Sources

Increasingly, our industry looks to the public lands, onshore and particularly to the Outer Continental Shelf, as potential sources for new supplies of oil and natural gas. As this nation's onshore producing capacity dwindles, our national reliance on the offshore increases. From zero percent in 1946 the nation now obtains in excess of 28 percent of its oil from state and federal submerged lands adjacent to our coasts. This share is expected to increase substantially in the future.

We are pleased to note that the commission in its report recommends that the federal government generally should rely on the private sector for mineral exploration, development and production by maintaining a continuing invitation to explore for and develop minerals on the public lands.

## A New Leasing System

Turning to specifics, private enterprise needs a reliable leasing system, which we now have in the Mineral Leasing Act and the Outer Continental Shelf Lands Act. It needs a regular schedule of OCS lease sales, which we do not have, and the right to explore as far seaward on the Outer Continental Shelf as our technology is capable of taking us.

The commission has recommended that the Outer Continental Shelf Lands Act should be amended to give the Secretary of the Interior authority for utilizing flexible methods of competitive sale, and that the present exclusive reliance on bonus bidding, plus a fixed royalty, should not necessarily be followed.

We believe a combination of bonus, royalty or rental bidding would be generally undesirable. A system having more than one variable would be impractical in most instances because of the difficulty in assigning competitive values to various combination bids so as to identify the optimum bid.

## OBJECTIONS TO ROYALTY BIDDING

There would appear to be several objections to royalty bidding. One is that poorly qualified bidders tend to be attracted who will bid high royalties in order to win leases. This can result in early abandonment of wells because of the heavy royalty charge as an operating cost. As a result, such leases would tend to be bought and sold as speculation rather than for bona fide exploration and development.

Another consequence of royalty bidding might be loss of cash bonus revenue to the government, with no off-setting royalty advantage. For example, a winning bid might be a high royalty and a nominal cash bonus. In the event of a dry hole, the government would receive no royalty and would not have received a large cash bonus that might otherwise have been paid. The government would not have benefited as it did, for example, in connection with a parcel sold on the Outer Continental Shelf off Southern California in 1968. The successful bidder paid in excess of $45 million for this parcel, drilled two dry holes and quitclaimed the lease in 1969. The government's net gain was the $45 million cash bonus. Had the bid been made on a royalty basis, the government would have received little or nothing. We believe what is illustrated here is that such risks should be taken by the private sector and not by the government.

## Regularizing Sales

The commission has recommended regularization of the timing and size of Outer Continental Shelf lease sales. We agree. Recently lease sales have been held on a hit-or-miss basis, but new factors in the form of sweeping environmental quality legislation require that in the future much more lead time be given industry, government and other interested groups in preparing for an OCS sale. Therefore, we strongly support the commission's recommendation and urge that a five-year schedule of lease sales covering the time span through 1975 be released by the federal government as soon as possible.

## Balancing Hazards and Rewards

Here on the West Coast there is interest in the Gulf of Alaska and offshore from Southern California, the latter including areas as distant as 170 miles from the mainland. There have been, and probably will be, operational accidents on the Outer Continental Shelf, but efforts--brains, plus imagination and large amounts of money--are now allocated to minimize them. We fully support the commission's concern about the environment and we are dedicated to its preservation. On the other hand, it is clear the federal government must as a matter of policy recognize this nation's dependence on petroleum energy and join with environmentalists and the oil industry in reaching a balanced solution to facilitate the large investment and additional work that must be expended to explore and develop our OCS.

We have noted Professor Mead's statement on market demand factors and would simply like to say that court cases have held that market demand prorationing is not a conspiracy in restraint of trade, but is a valid conservation law within the authority of each state.

## NO SPECIAL FAVORS

The oil and gas industries' position with respect to many of the problems treated by the commission report was well summarized by O.N. Miller, who is chairman of the board of directors of the American Petroleum Institute, in his address at the annual meeting of that organization in New York City last month. Mr. Miller said:

We ask no special favors from the public or government. We do ask that they recognize that development of greater petroleum production and preservation of our country's independence from foreign energy sources do cost a price that must be paid. This price is eminently fair to everyone, and it is established in the open market by vigorous competition which keeps the price as low as possible.

A vocal minority is hindering industry from meeting the public's energy needs. This minority seemingly wants to preserve the environment at all costs.

Crucial examples of the effects of this attitude are the disappointing delay in development of Alaska's north slope reserve, postponement of offshore lease sales and proposals to prohibit offshore development entirely.

With respect to offshore oil particularly, the public must understand the importance of these reserves.

It should not be, however, and is not necessary to choose between clean water, clean air and the preservation of wildlife areas on the one hand, and the progress of the economy on the other. It is necessary to exercise balanced judgment and common sense in setting up the rules and the timetables by which Americans preserve their environment.

That concludes Mr. Miller's statement.

In summary, I would like to say that the oil and gas industry looks forward to working with the Congress as it begins to implement the suggestions contained within the commission's very excellent report.

*Zivnuska:* Thank you very much. As our next speaker, I would like to introduce Dean Carl Stoltenberg, who is Dean of the School of Forestry at Oregon State University.

## THREE COMMISSION VIEWS OF PUBLIC LAND

*Stoltenberg:* Thank you.

I should like to comment on three views of the commission related to the use of public lands: (1) the commission's propensity to classify and manage public forest and range lands for dominant use, stressing a single, high-priority benefit; (2) payment of full value for the use of public lands; and (3) the problem of developing policies that reflect the relative importance of local community costs and benefits in evaluating total benefits of various use alternatives.

## NECESSARY TRADE-OFFS v. DOMINANT USE

Quite appropriately, I believe, the commission has selected maximization of net public benefits as the goal of public land policy, and simultaneously has also recognized the exploding demand for all of the many benefits that can be derived from these lands. Accordingly, the commission recommends permitting on each land area the maximum number of uses that are compatible. However, the commission does not appear to recognize the necessity of trade-offs in optimizing net public benefits, even though the term "net" would imply acknowledging such costs.

The commission evidently felt more comfortable with planning for "dominant" uses for most areas, permitting other uses only when they do not in any way conflict with that dominant use. Now, in preparing planning maps, I agree that it is convenient to place use titles on various areas which refer to one use as the highest priority, guiding or dominant use for that area on the map. However, both conceptually and practically this is neither a necessary nor a sound step in seeking to manage that land so as to maximize net public benefits from public forest use.

Considering all possible use combinations and then selecting that combination which provides the highest net public benefit requires knowledge of the relative benefits to be derived from each use and each use combination, but neither a priority ranking nor recognition of a dominant use. In fact, simple priority rankings prevent effective use of systems analysis in determining the optimum combination of uses, and they retard the process of promptly reflecting changing public value systems in more appropriate land management and use practices.

Priority rankings, dominant-use classifications and single-use designations simplify the decision process by simply eliminating user groups. Thus they may be appealing to legislators, and they evidently were to the commission, but because of the interrelatedness of the processes by which the many benefits are produced, restricting uses to a single or dominant use is an extravagant and unnecessarily wasteful way to use most public forest lands.

## FULL-VALUE FEES

My second point is to agree with the commission's wise recommendation for a consistent policy of full-value fees for all uses. Effectively implemented, this policy would help identify the relative values of various uses, and thus managerial systems analysis could identify that combination of uses for any area that

would maximize net public benefits. Full-value fees
should provide dynamic guidance on changing user preferences, help evaluate current and changing priorities for
resource development investments, and assist in resolving land use conflicts.

## How "Consumption" Occurs

I also agree with the commission's recommendation
to exempt nonconsumptive uses from full-value fees,
but only if opportunity costs are acknowledged and time
use, as well as physical use, is recognized as consumption. Consumption can occur in many ways. In effect,
consumption occurs when an area, commodity or an environment becomes unavailable for use by some consumers
because of its use by others. Thus, a wilderness classification that prohibits intensive recreation use or
the growing and harvesting of timber and wildlife makes
such wilderness reservation a consumptive use. Similarly, capacity use of a recreation area constitutes
full consumption of that area for that period of time,
and thus constitutes a use that is every bit as consumptive as if these resources were removed geographically:
that is, "consumed" for that time period. All such consumption should be reflected by the full-value fee
policy, unless consciously and specifically subsidized
under congressional authorization.

## Establishing Legislative Guidelines

My third concern lies with the difficulty of establishing legislative guidelines for maximizing net public
benefits, guidelines that will deal fairly with both
dimensions of user interest, scope and depth. Scope or
nature of benefits of interest to individual users is
rather well reflected in Congress through the political
process, but depth of interest is not, in my opinion.
Depth of concern with public land policies is not distributed in the same pattern as voting power. In
general, those people geographically nearest the public

lands have a greater personal stake in policies affecting public land use. But they do not have any greater
voice in management and use decisions.

Federal legislative power is concentrated in states
with relatively few public lands, whereas benefits and
costs associated with public land use decisions tend to
be concentrated in the public land states. If the commission's goal of maximizing net public benefits is to
be realized, Congress must provide criteria for evaluat
ing public land decisions which appropriately reflect
the exceptionally strong impact of these decisions on
local people, local communities and local firms. This
is recommended by the commission, but is indeed a very
difficult task to accomplish.

*Zivnuska:* Thank you.

Our final speaker is a representative of state
government, Frank J. Hortig, who is the Executive
Officer of the Division of Lands of the State of California.


## EIGHT, NOT THREE, POLICY ELEMENTS

*Hortig:* Dean Stoltenberg has just outlined three major
policy elements that become problems in any administrative policy practice with respect to the public domain.
Under the general heading of multiple use today, references were made in various degrees to such uses as oil
and gas, to which both Dr. Mead and Mr. Ketchum referred, and to other minerals, timber, recreation and
wilderness reserves, which of course were of primary
concern in the presentation by Mr. Evans. It has not
been mentioned that there are such vital uses as power
sites, reservoir sites, the opportunity for exploration
and development of geothermal resources--that is natural
steam from the ground--particularly in California and
Alaska. And of course, water, which has been referred
to previously. On a fast count, there are about eight

major policy elements to be melded into some coherent
administrative practice and policy.

I ask you to visualize an eight-armed seesaw, that
is, one with eight seats and an assortment of eight
people standing around, ranging from youngsters to full
adults. It would be infinitely more simple to get those
people assigned to that seesaw in the first instance and
then have the thing balance, than to have to try to
balance this multiple-use seesaw so that it will include
the type of advances, the type of programs, the type of
economic benefits, the type of esthetic and recreational
benefits that will satisfy or come close to satisfying
the majority of the citizens, whether it be in the State
of California or nationally.

One of my fellow panelists said, "Well, everything
that's left now, you can have." I commend the other
panelists for their comprehensive coverage in such a
short period of time of the elements to which they
directed their attention. But, I did suggest that there
are eight major elements that should be considered, not
only the two or three that we have heard about this
afternoon. This is predicated upon the fact that Dr.
Mead, in his statement which set the tone for this
panel, had to concentrate on two primary elements for
illustration--timber and oil and gas--as examples of
resource allocation. But in the process of so doing--
and also in Mr. Ketchum's presentation--I did note that
there were some elements that probably were deserving
of possible clarification. I think that there are solutions to some of the problems that have been raised here
this afternoon, or at least routes toward solutions, and
particularly, in all modesty, since some of these solutions, in whole or in part, are applied in the public
land administration policies of the State of California.
All of these have, in turn, during the consideration by
the Public Land Law Review Commission been communicated
by the State of California to that commission for their
consideration through our governor's representative to
the Public Land Law Review Commission, our Secretary
for Resources, Norman Livermore.

## PREQUALIFYING BIDDERS

As an example of what I mean, Dr. Mead was properly concerned with the possiblity of unqualified bidders bidding on a royalty bid lease on whatever commodity was being offered. Because this did not require any large cash outlay in the normal sense at the time of bidding, an utterly unqualified bidder could bid wildly and then peddle the lease subsequent to award. This problem was resolved both by statute and by rules and regulations of the State Land Commission in California by prequalifying bidders to ascertain that they do have the technical know-how and can acquire the capital, if they do not have it at the moment, to proceed with the development of the lease, so that a lease can not be transferred to anyone in the category of a lease broker under normal lease awards. Also, it was suggested that royalty bidding on timber leases was just like royalty bidding on an oil and gas lease.

Generally speaking, when oil and gas lease areas are offered, the oil and gas content is not known very clearly. It is a hope, whereas with a timber lease bid, a previous cruise of the timber as to quality, size, condition and known market conditions at the time, of course puts the buyer in a much better position to know what he is buying.

I should like to point out also, finally, that the market demand proration which Dr. Mead spoke about, and which he indicated was being revised with respect to OCS lands off Louisiana and Texas, has never been an administrative element and has never been permitted in the State of California with respect to production of oil and gas. Also, I noted Dr. Mead referred to "maximum efficient rate," MER, in distinction to the market demand proration. There is a second version among some elements of the industry to make that maximum efficient rate read "maximum economic rate," and then of course the market demand proration is injected right back into that same terminology.

## DISCUSSION WITH THE AUDIENCE

*Zivnuska:* Thanks to the fine cooperation of our panelists, we do have our full 45 minutes for discussion
with you in the audience. If you can't direct your
question to a member of the panel, I will try to allocate it to one of our resource people here.

With those rules of the game, let's proceed. Please
volunteer your questions.

### MULTIPLE USE AND DOMINANT USE

*Hill:* My name is Clair Hill. In the recommendation
that refers to multiple use and dominant use, the sub-
section reads: "To provide the positive statutory
direction and strengthening for multiple-use management
which we now find to be seriously lacking, recommending
that Congress provide for dominant uses only."

Having served some years on the Secretary of Agriculture's Committee on Multiple Use, I would like a
little further explanation of the problems with multiple
use. It seems to me that dominant use as defined here
means single use as against multiple use.

*Zivnuska:* The only member of the panel who referred to
this tended to agree with you. Would anyone like to
volunteer an answer? How about a member of the commission? Milton Pearl?

## Resolving Conflicts

*Pearl:* Okay. The problem we are talking about is one I
touched on this morning. The statutes at the present
time provide no guidelines for resolution of conflicts,
and the commission's recommendations for dominant use
or primary use are related only to the times when conflicts arise.

As I said this morning, inevitably a conflict will arise. Multiple use will continue and should continue wherever possible. But, for example, when the time comes that you want to picnic in the same area that you want to cut timber, there are no guidelines at the present time, either statutory or in the development plans, that tell you which use has to give way. If, however, you could go through a public interest test with everyone involved and decide that certain areas should be set aside for recreation, then you would know that timber would have to give way if and when there is a conflict.

On the other hand, the reverse would be true if the area was declared available for timber production.

*Zivnuska:* I think Dean Stoltenberg wants to say a word on this, too.

*Stoltenberg:* I don't believe the proposal to identify an area for a single dominant use resolves the conflict problem. It just means that you have said, "From here on out this is what we are going to do." I don't think this helps at all in providing criteria to choose which use should be dominant or in what combination.

I think it's very comforting to have a dominant use, and the commission evidently found it so. The things that it liked were those areas that had been set aside for one use. It's very comforting, but I don't think that is evidence that it maximizes public benefits, and I don't think the commission has provided any indication that it would maximize public benefits either.

*Zivnuska:* Thank you. Do you have another question?

## REDUCING CONSUMPTION

*Barry:* I am Frank Barry from the University of Oregon. One of the policies that the commission didn't consider and one that I think the panel ought to comment on is

pointed up by a figure to the effect that we were going
to consume in the United States--correct me if I am
wrong--230 billion barrels of oil in the next 30 years.

Well, I have been doing a little arithmetic on the
back of my pad here and that comes out to 21 million
barrels a day. Now the policy point that really challenges me is this: Haven't we got to do something
about the consuming side of our natural resources problem to solve the problem of the public lands? If this
is the kind of population growth and the kind of consumption we are going to have, then I have to tell Mr.
Brock Evans, with whom I sympathize completely, "Don't
worry about wilderness; there won't be any. Don't
worry about parks; there won't be any."

If we have this many people and we do nothing at
all to reduce the per capita consumption in the United
States, we will continue to use half or more of our
timber to make paper cups and continue to use all of
our oil to sit in traffic while we wait, trying to get
to the city, burning up the oil from Alaska.

*Zivnuska:* I will first get Mr. Ketchum and then Mr.
Evans to comment on the point that was raised.


## Youth and Energy Consumption

*Ketchum:* Well, I don't know that I can disagree with
Mr. Barry's comments. I only know that it isn't the
function of the oil business to establish limitations
on population. The recent report of the Chase Manhattan
Bank brings out the interesting point that there is a
wave that will last through the 1980s of young people
who are in the maximum period of consumption. A young
couple consumes far more than a man and wife of the age
of myself and my wife. This is a factor we already
have and I don't know the solution to it. In the oil
industry, we are doing everything we can to promote a
legislative environment that will help solve this and
at the same time not destroy our physical environment.

*Evans:* I sympathize with Mr. Barry completely. I think we all need to work together to seek restraints on our consumption patterns. My experience has been, too, that the oil industry hasn't done this yet.

Canadian oil already has existing fields producing 50 percent of capacity, but would like more of the American market. Middle Eastern oil is available to us at $1.30 a barrel less than we pay for oil produced in this country. There are a variety of other ways of producing oil from existing places, if we are talking about the problems of Alaska.

## Horsepower Tax

How about a horsepower tax? We haven't thought of that yet. Supposing, you had a $10 horsepower tax on every horsepower over 60, that would cut down oil and gas consumption a great deal, too.

There are lots of other ways. For example, I think we should ban the internal combustion engine. I think we will have to do that eventually, and I would like to know the oil industry's position on that.

Regarding young people, maybe we know different kinds of young people. Many that I know are abandoning the wasteful consumption patterns that their elders have followed, and I think this is also a trend that we have to take into account. I don't think we can just automatically draw a straight line from junction X and assume it's going to be this way on and on. As Mr. Barry so well pointed out, we have got to stop somewhere.

### THE MARKET MECHANISM

*Zivnuska:* Do you have another question?

*Moshofsky:* My name is Bill Moshofsky. To partly respond to Mr. Barry's concern, I wonder whether the market itself will tend to correct some of these problems. As oil gets more scarce, won't people look to other sources? I wonder if Dr. Mead might have a comment on the effect of the market in dealing with these shortages?

*Mead:* I think anyone in economics would go down that particular road. The reasoning is as follows: We have a resource here, namely, oil. One problem is to allocate it among different uses--for example, chemical use and automobile use. Well, we have a market mechanism to do that. We also have a market mechanism to settle the problem of allocation over time, if we in fact are going to run out of oil shortly. The price is going to go up very sharply and that will do some of the allocating for us. The market mechanism can handle this.

I would like to take this chance to respond partly to Brock Evans. We have another mechanism that we have never used: the right to tax something that imposes burdens on society if used. The use of oil imposes burdens on society because it pollutes the air, yet the cost that society bears is not borne by motorists. You ask yourself: Should I drive to work? And your answer is that the cost of gasoline is 31 cents a gallon or something. But society is paying perhaps another 10 cents a gallon.

In other words, if we are really concerned about pollution of the air, there is an external social cost to society, and we have not exploited the possibility of imposing a tax to reflect this cost.

I also want to comment on a point brought out by Frank Barry and referred to by Mr. Ketchum. The estimate of 230 billion barrels is a fantastic figure. I suspect it's right, but that gets us into the issue of oil import quotas that Brock Evans spoke of. Do we realize what we are doing? We are prohibiting the

import of oil from abroad, and now Mr. Ketchum tells us
we are going to consume 230 billion barrels of it in the
next 30 years. The fact that we have oil import quotas
is justified on a national defense basis, so we will not
become dependent upon Middle Eastern oil. But we are
going to run out. The fact of oil import quotas is
going to make us absolutely dependent much sooner.

*Zivnuska:* Thank you. I hope we can cover some areas in
addition to oil, important though it is. The gentleman
over there?

*A member of the audience:* You talked about the consumption of oil, and the figure of 230 billions of barrels
is quite outstanding. I wonder about its disposal.
What do we do? Dump it in the ocean like the Navy is
doing now? I mean, it's all right to consume something,
but what about the waste end of it? If we are talking
about ecology, saving the land and saving the environment, what do we do with the used product or the used
end product?

## CONCESSIONAIRES AND THE LOCAL COMMUNITY

My other question relates to the use of public lands
for concessions. What happens to small communities when
the government sets up concessions and the towns furnish
housing for the concessionaire and accommodations for
the tourist, and the sewer system and all these functions that a small community has to provide for the seasonal tourist? Also in this regard, it seems as though
the federal government wants the fat tourist dollar, and
is willing to give back a little tax. But what happens
to the small business people in these towns who are
going to be deprived of this concession dollar, while
the money is received by the government? The little bit
of tax to the county that the government gives back
doesn't subsidize the small business people who are in
business to provide the concessions for the tourist. In
a sense it sounds as though we are putting the county
on a welfare system.

*Zivnuska:* Thank you. I think that raises an important area that hasn't been raised before--the concessionaire approach. Would any member of the panel like to respond to the question about concessionaires in relation to the local community?

*Hortig:* I might make one comment. From my own knowledge, I know of no concession on public domain lands that isn't under a lease from the Bureau of Land Management. Therefore it is being operated at that location by that small businessman on land that he happens to lease from the federal government because he chose to or because there wasn't other land available to lease. Many of these small communities do not have room to expand.

*A member of the audience:* Well, the commission report is more or less projecting going into the concession business on Forest Service land, and this is what I am relating to.

*Edmiston:* My name is Buela Edmiston. Many of us would like to see our public lands kept for their environmental and esthetic quality and leave the goods and the services--the concessions, if you will--to private enterprise on private land adjacent. We feel that the public lands should not be so used. We feel it is not the province of the government to go into concessions. We do not feel it's a way of improving environmental quality and we do believe that it would certainly make the local people feel a whole lot better about public lands to be able to provide the goods and the services themselves as private enterprise.


## A STATEMENT OF CONCERN

*Zivnuska:* Thank you. I promised the gentleman back there the floor next.

*Schoewe:* My name is Lee Schoewe. I'm President of the California Association of the Four-Wheel Drive Clubs,

and I am also acting on behalf of the California Wildlife Federation Lands Committee. I'm here today to
present a statement to the panelists, a statement of
conservation-oriented organizations as the result of
a meeting in Sacramento on November 28, 1970 on the
Public Land Law Review Commission report.

We had over 18 organizations; among them were Cali-
fornia Outdoor Recreation League, National Wildlife
Federation, National Audubon Society, the Sierra Club--
Mother Lode Chapter, The Wildlife Society, the Western
Rockhounds' Association and others that I will not list
at this time.

The statement is as follows:

> We believe that the federal public
> lands in the United States belong to
> all the people and must be managed
> and used in the best long-term inter-
> est of the people. The Public Land
> Law Review Commission Report recently
> submitted to the President and Congress
> has pointed out clearly that the mul-
> titude of archaic land laws governing
> the management and use of public lands
> must be updated.
>
> We strongly urge immediate national
> legislative action to fully protect
> the public interests in the public
> lands which will insure the long-term
> productivity of the natural resources
> of the public lands, including the
> soil, water, air, vegetation and wild-
> life. Such legislation should contain
> the following provisions:
>
> 1. There should be no further major
> disposals of public land and the pres-
> ent ratio of public to private land in
> this country should remain stable in
> the future.

2. That public lands be managed first
and foremost in a manner that will
not endanger the quality of our
environment.

3. That public lands be managed and
made available for a wide variety of
uses to meet the diverse needs of the
people, and that these uses must be
determined on the basis of sound public land use planning. Planning for
the management and the use of public
lands should not be subject to the
domination of dollar-oriented values.
Rather, it must be primarily based
on the integrity of the natural resource values in the broad spectrum
of social values.

We will strongly support such legislation when it is introduced.

Thank you.


## BEYOND 30 YEARS

*Peart:* My name is Ray Peart. Maybe I am a little con-
fused, but it seems to me that the commission could
have looked further than 30 years ahead. I have the
feeling that it sort of measured our remaining tin,
copper, oil and timber and said, "Can we stretch it
out for 30 years?"

I think we have evidence that some of these resources will be gone, and yet the need for wilderness
in the future beyond 30 years is going to be a lot
greater. With our increasingly complex society, we may
value a chance for solitude very greatly in the future.
It doesn't make sense to just plan for 30 years on this.

*Zivnuska:* This was the topic discussed by other panels
this morning. Do you have a question relating to the
land use policies as an aspect of this problem?

*Evans:* This does relate somewhat, and it goes back to the oil and mineral problems in general. We can use all the oil or minerals or copper and whatever we have right now, and when it's all gone, it's all gone. But we would like to see a little bit of wilderness left before that happens.

Let's not wait until we run out, but let's draw the line and have other resources and other values, too, such as wilderness and many other kinds of environments on the public lands.

## TIMBER AND ACCESS ROADS

*Blayganny:* I would like to offer a brief comment about another resource that keeps replacing itself: timber. My name is Howard Blayganny. I represent a firm that is one of the largest national forest timber operators in California, and we are critically dependent upon public timber.

Our industry attaches great importance to timber access road construction, which the commission, under its Recommendation 33, believes should be accelerated for the many good reasons given in the report. I would hope and trust that your panel fully concurs with this recommendation.

*Zivnuska:* I am sure that there are differences of opinion on the panel.

*Evans:* I absolutely do not concur. I would like much more detail of what's involved here.

Accelerated roading is one of the things that destroys natural and scenic environments on our public lands. We see road construction as one of the primary detractions from other values and other environments. So I couldn't concur, but I would like to look at it on a case-by-case and place-by-place basis.

*Stoltenberg:* I think it's a very general recommendation. Depending on the kinds of usage that you are attempting

to develop, you either do or do not favor increased
access roads. Obviously Brock Evans favors the kinds
of uses that do not require access by vehicle. Until
you study what combination of uses is optimum, the decision on increased access roads is a very difficult one.

I think it's a general statement. I think you can
get greater use available to more people of the public
if you had greater access to the public lands, so I
would favor the general approach of this recommendation.

*Zivnuska:* The recommendation of the commission report,
of course, was particular to timber access roads.

## Trees, Charges and Reseeding

*Teller:* I am Otto Teller, director of Trout Unlimited.
I would like to ask a question: Has any member of the
Public Land Law Review Commission ever made an onsite
inspection of the timber resources of this country--the
Oregon Cascades, the Washington Cascades, Montana, Idaho
or Colorado?

The reason I ask this question is that I asked a
Forest Service supervisor what was the average age of
the original timber that was on these various public
lands, and he said 150 to 300 years was the age of the
trees. That was the spread.

I further asked how long the Forest Service has had
a planting program. I know of one forest where people
have logged 200,000 acres in five years and they report
that the reseeding is a total failure at the present
time because the cutting was done on grades of 45 percent and over. The large percentage of the planting is
washed down into the rivers due to the fact that the
roads that were built for the logging trucks to get up
were never reseeded. So what is left in many areas of
the Cascades? Fly over it, walk through it--all you
can see is devastation to a point that is shocking to
anybody who looks at it.

It's simply because the Forest Service has spent all of its money. The budget is funded on income from timber sales and there isn't any money left for planting, and when they do attempt it, it's done in a slipshod manner on very small percentages.

So, projecting housing requirements to 1980 or the year 2000, we only have 15 years of an adequate supply of timber left in this country.

One more thing I would like to mention: Some omnipotent man in the Forest Service said that any tree that is less than 11 inches in diameter, breast height, is not to be harvested. It's not counted against the allowable cut. It means you can knock a tree down with big machinery or you can take it to the mill and make chips out of it, but the man who is cutting the logs isn't to be charged for that.

## A Renewable Resource

*Craig:* I am George Craig, and I represent people who buy timber from the national forest.

I fear that this last statement is typical of some that may be generated by observation of a problem area that causes an emotional reaction and damnation of an essential practice.

I think that one of the reasons there's been interest in the dominant-use approach is that there are areas where substantial volumes of timber can be produced regularly on a crop basis, and the concern has been similar to that expressed about the high-quality agricultural lands in the Santa Clara Valley that are paved with asphalt instead of being put to the highest and best use for society.

There are substantial parts of the national forest that were originally established to be protected and developed to meet the needs of the citizens for wood and water.  And until we do get some direction for some of these high-quality lands, until we do make the proper investments and protect these areas and restock them, we are not using this growth potential and we are, in effect, in the same position as the petroleum industry which does not have this opportunity of a renewable resource.

Whether we like it or not, we are going to have tremendous needs for construction materials.  You have indicated here today that the petroleum industry does not offer good prospects, and we can also go to other resources which are so-called substitutes and find that they all have shortcomings in the energy that they require for producing and in the disruption of the land in other ways.  Here we have a beautiful tree which is renewable and which can be handled in a way as a crop that is esthetically pleasing.  We should all accustom ourselves to the idea that wood does come from trees and that wood is essential for our economy.

## Roading and Primary Use

*Mead:*  Just one comment on this matter of roading.  I think that it's easily possible to examine situations where roading in a forest has produced erosion and where reseeding, either by natural or artificial means, has not succeeded.  However, in an area where the primary use--I use the word "primary" rather than "dominant"--is timber production, you cannot get an area under management without roads.

We have, as was pointed out by the last questioner, areas in the natural forest where the timber is vastly overmature.  It's sick.  It's disease infested, and if you don't get roads in there you can't get the timber out.  It's our timber.  You can leave it there and let it die.  The timber is there and we need a lot of housing construction for various purposes in this country.  That has to come from timber, and the roads are necessary to get an area under efficient management.

*Zivnuska:* Thank you.

I would like to thank the panel and the members of the audience. I hope we can follow these points up over coffee. But before we do that, I would like to turn the meeting back to Chairman Lee.

## A CHANGE IN SCHEDULE: TIME FOR INDIANS

*Lee:* Thank you, Dean Zivnuska. Let me explain a readjustment in our schedule. During the last few days, as I have come to know the subject of this conference, it has been brought home to me--and perhaps to you--that there are views that have not been fully represented in the planning or in the agenda of the conference.

I refer specifically to the views and feelings of Native Americans--our Indians--concerning their rights not only to the reservation lands, but to the public lands generally. I am pleased to say that it has become possible, with your cooperation, to respond constructively and creatively to remedy this deficiency. Three Indians will participate in our next panel on Alaska, presenting remarks as a part of that panel discussion.

I would like to ask John Borbridge to comment on this change in our agenda and some of the reasons for it.

*Borbridge:* Thank you, Dr. Lee.

As mentioned, there are some voices that haven't been heard and some of the people who want to be heard have agreed tentatively that they will go on in the evening. Now, you and I know that we can approach this in two ways. One is to go ahead and please the Indians, give them the last part of the day and perhaps half of us can walk out right in the middle of their presentation, secure that we have done our duty and have been fair to everyone. Very frankly, we are almost afraid to even try that.

I think it all depends on you. I call this simply laying it on the line. If you feel that these viewpoints are important, if you feel that a simple matter of justice warrants your staying here and being present and if you feel that you want to uphold our judgment that you are willing to do this, then I think we can go ahead and proceed.

We are asking that you at least give us our opportunity. There are many of you, very frankly, who have never heard the things that we have to say.

I will conclude with this, Dr. Lee: That even as pertains to the Alaskan situation, it's all very fine that you are talking about policy and regulations and laws. Let's start to talk about the ownership of those 340 million acres that we Indians claim, and if that subject just isn't important enough to keep the audience, then I think much of this conference is a facade. But if it is important, you will stay, and I am asking you to stay. And, very frankly, we would appreciate it.

*Lee:* I have absolutely no doubt as to the participation of this group.

# PART FOUR

# Alaska

# THE RIGHTS OF NATIVES

John Borbridge, Jr.

*President*
*Tlingit-Haida Central Council*
*Juneau, Alaska*

I would like to say at the outset that the human
factor has been sadly minimized in today's discussion of
the use of the public lands. This is a factor I intend
to emphasize, particularly as it pertains to the ownership of approximately 340 to 350 million acres of land
in Alaska.

In doing so, I am fortunate to be accompanied by
other Indian members from the Bay Area, who also will be
stressing the fact that we can't possibly begin to talk
about planning for the optimum use of lands without
alluding to the concerns and experiences of the Indian
people. It is not enough at this point to say that by
definition the commission is excluding from consideration
a detailed discussion of the Indian reservations and
Indian lands.

## ABORIGINAL LAND RIGHTS

I am a Tlingit Indian. I am one of approximately 55
to 60,000 Natives of Alaska who collectively comprise
three aboriginal ethnic groups--Indians, Eskimos and
Aleuts. It is most appropriate that the viewpoint of
the Alaskan Native should be presented at a conference
focusing on recommendations pertaining to the public
lands of the United States, since we are presently seeking a congressional resolution as to the precise extent
and nature of our aboriginal land rights. And remember,
this is not a one-way proposition. A claims settlement

bill will not only benefit the Natives by defining the extent of that land which they shall be allowed to retain, but it will be of inestimable benefit both to the State of Alaska and to the nation to do justice.

That the Alaska Indians, Eskimos and Aleuts should be party to what promises to be the largest real estate transaction in the twentieth century in no way establishes a precedent for the role of American Indians as the true owners of vast areas of land, a part of our history that somehow has been generally ignored. We fin in tracing the development of national policy that: "Th historic fact is that practically all of the real estate acquired by the United States in 1776 was purchased not from Napoleon or any other emperor or czar, but from its original Indian owners."[1]

## Treaty and Negotiation

The total of these numerous acquisitions enabled ou fledgling nation to acquire more than 2 million square miles in what was then probably the largest real estate transaction in the history of the world. I defy you to find these facts in most of your textbooks and authoritative studies. Curiously, history has tended to minimize the fact that the bulk of the public lands were pur chased by treaty and other negotiations with the Indian owners. It is only right that we should be here to spea to you today on this subject.

The Alaskan Natives were never conquered by force of arms. As a matter of fact, my Tlingit ancestors destroyed two Russian settlements and forts at Sitka and Yakutat respectively. The Russians generally did not hunt or fish in Tlingit or Haida territory. They usuall traded with my ancestors for such necessities. We asser ed dominion over our land.

Further, in a unanimous decision in October 1959, the Court of Claims held that the use and occupancy titl of the Tlingit and Haida Indians was not extinguished by the treaty.[2]

This disposes of the question as to whether or not we Alaska Natives lost any land rights in that sale.

Native use and occupation of the lands of Alaska, which had persisted for centuries before the area was "discovered" by Bering, was hardly disturbed at all during the Russian era, or for two decades after the Treaty of 1867. The first organic act for the District of Alaska, enacted in 1884, provided:

> That the Indians or other persons in said District shall not be disturbed in the possession of any lands *actually in their use or occupation, or now claimed by them*, but the terms under which such persons may acquire title to such lands is reserved for further legislation by Congress. [Emphasis added]

## Waiting for Legislation

Today we are awaiting that legislation. This provision expresses what has been the policy of the United States respecting the rights of aboriginal peoples within its political boundaries since before the adoption of the Constitution.

Today Alaska, the last great frontier and wilderness region of our nation, is the sole remaining part of the United States that includes extensive areas *still used and claimed by the indigenous inhabitants, based on rights of aboriginal occupancy*. The aboriginal titles of most Native groups in the United States were extinguished during the eighteenth and nineteenth centuries. In the main, they were extinguished under bilateral treaties between the United States and the Native groups.

These treaties were intended to effectuate the policy that Natives should be paid the full and fair value for lands they cede to the nation. These treaties did not always achieve their aim. Later, when it became apparent that the Natives in many cases had not been fairly dealt with, the Congress provided forums where they could establish and collect the difference between what they had been paid and the fair value of the lands they had ceded. But, where the nation failed initially to deal justly with Native peoples, the remedies later provided proved to be something less than satisfactory. Over half a century of litigation has resulted. It is still in progress and, what is worse, the mistrust sown by these inequities continues to poison relations between Natives and the government.

By and large, the aboriginal rights of the Natives of Alaska have not been extinguished. On the contrary, they have been carefully preserved by Congress in every important statute relating to Alaska, including the Statehood Act, and exist today little diminished from what they were in 1867. The Federal Field Committee, which recently studied the matter for the Congress and submitted a comprehensive report, concluded that Alaskan Natives have a substantial claim upon all the lands of Alaska by virtue of their aboriginal occupancy.[3]

### ALASKA'S LAND CHOICE

By its Statehood Act, Alaska was given the right to select and have patented to it approximately 103 million acres of the 375 million acres of land contained within its boundaries. In other words, it was given the right to pick and choose for grant to itself in excess of a quarter of the area of the state. Additionally, it was provided that the state should receive 90 percent of the mineral revenues realized by the United States from the remaining public lands within its borders.

When the State of Alaska began to select lands under the Statehood Act, the Native groups that hold aboriginal title to such lands protested the selections. After reviewing the situation, former Secretary of the Interior Stewart Udall concluded that Congress had not intended to

extinguish Native titles by the Statehood Act. The law
is clear that only Congress can extinguish such titles
by action clearly calculated to do so, and that, until
Congress has acted, anyone, including a state, that takes
paper title to lands subject to an unextinguished aboriginal title receives a naked fee--that is, a technical
estate completely subject to the continuing rights of
the Natives to the use, occupancy, returns and profits
of the lands.

Accordingly, Secretary Udall ordered a halt in the
processing of state selections to afford Congress an
opportunity to determine how the Native rights should be
dealt with. As you are aware, the "land freeze" due to
expire December 31, 1970, was extended to June 30, 1971.
This will give the Congress and the Natives a very tight
time schedule for the enactment of legislation in 1971.

But apart from the view that sound public land use
policy supports Native utilization of the public domain,
the fact that the Native claims have a firm legal ground
was further evidenced in *Alaska v. Udall* and *Alaska v.
Native Village of Nenana*, decided on December 16, 1969
by the United States Court of Appeals for the Ninth Cir-
cuit here in San Francisco. The court held that if it
can be shown that public lands in Alaska are used and
occupied by the Natives, then they are not "vacant,
unappropriated and unreserved" and hence, they are not
available for state selection. This imposed, in effect,
a judicial land freeze on public lands in the State of
Alaska.

But before Secretary Udall imposed what is commonly
referred to as "the freeze" on state selections, Alaska
had obtained paper title to approximately 5 million acres
of land and had obtained tentative approval of selections
covering another 8.5 million acres. The state received
approximately $900 million as bonuses for oil and gas
leases which it sold on some 450,000 acres of the tentatively approved lands in September 1969.

Meanwhile, the Natives of Alaska were organized on a statewide basis as the Alaska Federation of Natives. After considering the alternative of seeking the authorization of a judicial solution, they decided to press Congress for a direct legislative settlement of their historic rights. This in itself was innovative since previously such determinations had been referred to the courts for adjudication. So we determined to ask Congress to legislate what land should be retained in Native ownership and the amount of compensation we should be paid for the rest.

## THE NATIVE PROPOSAL

Essentially, the Native proposal calls for the confirmation of Native title to about 60 million acres of land; for Native retention of a 2 percent royalty on the production of resources from all lands in Alaska presently in federal ownership; and for the payment to the Natives of $500 million. It also provides for the establishment of state and regional Native corporations to administer the funds and property received pursuant to the settlement.

Presently the Natives are the beneficial owners of virtually the whole state. We are prepared to agree that our title to all but 60 million acres may be extinguished. In other words, our proposal contemplates our surrendering title to 300 million acres of land. And yet this matter is still discussed as though it were a widespread social welfare program for the Natives. Perhaps when the bill is finally passed, there should be two representatives present: one for the Alaska Natives because the matter concerns the welfare of all people; and one representing the United States. Both would participate in a ceremony in which the Natives would have their title formally confirmed and the remainder of the Native-claimed lands would be conferred upon the United States. Under the law and the policy of the United States, we are entitled to full market value for the 300 million acres we contemplate surrendering.

## Royalty Interest

We support the retention by the Natives of a royalty interest in the resources of the land as an element of the compensation we ought to receive. Retaining such an interest will give the Natives a continuing stake in, and identification with, the land and tie the compensation awarded to the developing value of the land itself. Nothing would be more cruel and ironic than to have the Native owners of the land observe the riches flowing from the resources of their land, knowing that both the land and its resources were forever lost to them.

Regarding the 60 million acres that the Alaska Federation of Natives bill proposes should be confirmed to the Natives, it should be pointed out that as the Natives presently possess full beneficial rights in the land involved, adoption of this part of our proposal would not result in our receiving anything that is not already ours, except a firming up of tenure. This would amount to 16 percent of the land for 20 percent of the people. How easily we seem able to reduce justice to a simple formula! This grant will not deter the development of Alaska. It will enable Alaska Natives to share in that development. Land equaling more than three Californias will remain in public ownership. Thus, we would have the opportunity to shape our destinies from a land base--the base we love.

Regarding the compensatory elements of the Native proposal--the $500 million and the 2 percent royalty--I have already pointed out that these would be given in exchange for over 300 million acres of land. No one knows what the present fair market value of the 300 million acres is, but certainly it is many times over $500 million, and a 2 percent royalty interest in the resources.

## A Common Interest

As I have said earlier, until Congress provides for the extinguishment of Native titles in Alaska, the state cannot obtain beneficial title to the lands it was given the right to select under the Statehood Act. Because the state is the party principally interested at this time in having Native title extinguished, because it will be a principal beneficiary of a settlement of the Native rights and because it has been treated with extraordinary generosity by the nation, I submit that every consideration of justice and equity dictates that the state should agree to the 2 percent royalty provision. I am highly pleased to note that a flexible and cooperative attitude has been indicated by Governor-elect William Egan on this very vital question.

I will say to the conservationists, the sportsmen, the miners, the lumbermen, the oil men and to all who have stakes in the development of Alaska, that if they will look with enlightenment to their own interests, they will conclude that they have a great deal more in common than in conflict with the interests of the Natives. The Natives are not going to lock up-- either physically or economically--the lands that are confirmed to them. It will be to their interest to make their lands productive, to promote their multiple use and development for purposes of recreation, environmental protection and resources production.

Specifically, leases, contracts and other valid existing rights involving lands confirmed to the Natives will not be disturbed. Anyone who fears that the Natives may be careless of the demands and practices of conservation exhibits a profound want of knowledge of history and of the essential character of the Native people. The traditions, life patterns and economic interests of the Alaska Natives insure that Native utilization of lands from the public domain will be in strict conformity with protection of the environment. I am pleased to note that my people, who have been in Alaska for untold centuries as practicing conservationists, are pleased to have you at this somewhat late date join us in our concerns.

## NATIVE DEVELOPMENT CORPORATIONS

The administration of the land claims settlement offers the opportunity for an innovative, highly imaginative, people-oriented approach--if we dare to cast aside the shackles of past failures by the Bureau of Indian Affairs. The idea of Native development corporations is as exciting as it is innovative. Substantial, well-financed development capabilities, not mere token play businesses, can give the Natives whatever opportunity there is for their independence in the new technological environment that is coming. The dual purpose of profit and service to its public can be achieved by a statewide Native development corporation and Native controlled and directed regional development companies sensitive to vast local variations in need and opportunity. Both entities can go to work to develop Alaskan resources, including the greatest resource of all, our people.

I therefore agree with the Public Land Law Review Commission's recommendation that, "we strongly recommend the early enactment of legislation to resolve the problem of Native claims and end the current impasse." I also contend that you cannot be for justice in a specific circumstance without making an effort to analyze the substance of the case.

Because of a lack of Indian involvement in the discussions and the recommendations, I oppose, on behalf of the Alaska Natives, the commission's efforts to terminate the Indian Allotment Act.

A just claims settlement would enable the Native people of Alaska to attack existing disparities in levels of education, health, housing and employment. This could mark the beginning of a truly large-scale effort to equip our people to attack their problems. We won't need anyone else to do this for us; we will do it ourselves.

PREROGATIVES OF CHOICE

In short, the settlement the Natives are seeking
is compatible with the interests of all who are genuinely
concerned about the future of Alaska. The Alaska Natives
seek justice, not charity. We seek the dignity of being
able to exercise a prerogative of choice--within the context of our needs, our goals and our desires. We recognize that many of our people will choose to continue life
in the villages because it is for them a fulfillment and
a satisfaction. We will assist them in uplifting the
qualities of life. Others of our people desirous of
projecting themselves into the free enterprise system
will have the means to do so. Surely there is room for
both! Americanization does not demand that we must all
be alike. Our native culture and heritage can contribute
a great deal to our society and, frankly, we need those
contributions.

Comedian Pat Paulsen was asked what his Indian
policy would be if he were successful in his campaign for
the presidency. He replied, "Attack; we haven't taken
all of their land." At the time that he said it, it was
a joke.

## Varieties of Pollution

We Alaska Natives share your concern about the
existing and potential pollution of our bays and rivers,
the land and atmosphere. But we are also vitally concerned today about the possible pollution of the heart,
the mind and the human spirit. We are concerned that
you may develop a rationale to justify the expropriation
directly or indirectly, of our lands on the basis of a
"higher use or purpose." This would be in direct dero-
gation of our historic, legal and moral rights and to
our mutual loss.

We are concerned because there is an attempt to
quantify, in economic terms, what in actuality is for
us a way of life, utilized by our ancestors since time

immemorial. You cannot quantify or completely analyze our ties to our land or our desire to maintain its original beauty. We are concerned because our ties to the land are spiritual as well as social and economic, and we depend on it in great part to support current subsistence hunting and fishing use at a time when other nomenclature is applied when others use the land in a similar manner. What is *recreation* to you may be a *way of life* to us. Our heritage does not cause us to view land as a commodity to be automatically subjected to analysis, pricing and subsequent disposal. This would be virtually tantamount to selling a part of ourselves, and this we will not do.

## The Last Opportunity

What, then, is the justification for assuming that the development of an economic analysis and data based on non-Native use habits and criteria will be a sufficient basis for measuring the competency of Natives to administer their affairs when a claims settlement bill is passed? How can you answer this question without understanding us as a people? You should not impose your values on us as a prelude to your effort to do justice to us.

The nation is now presented with what will probably be its last opportunity to deal justly with a Native people who possess unextinguished aboriginal title to a vast land. It would be difficult to exaggerate the importance of the outcome to the Natives, the state and the nation. But as certainly as history repeats itself, the practice of inequity or parsimony at this time would cause disruptions in the future; the cost of repairing them would certainly far exceed the cost of doing justice now.

Support for the Native land claims should be forthcoming because we come before the Congress by right, and because it is not only the claims issue that is on trial, but also the willingness of the institutions to do justice. We have steadfastly sought justice within the institutions of our society for more than 100 years. They must now respond.

I invite you to participate in this opportunity to face with honesty this issue, knowing that doing justice will not be easily accomplished, but that the returns will be equally beneficial to the Native and the non-Native, to our state and the nation.

# NOTES

[1] Felix J. Cohen, "Original Indian Title," 32 *Minnesota Law Review* 1: 28-59 (1947), p. 35.

[2] See The Tlingit and Haida Indians of Alaska v. the United States, 147 *United States Court of Claims Reports* (Ct. Cl.), 315-439 (1959).

[3] [U.S.] Federal Field Committee for Development Planning in Alaska, *Alaska Natives and the Land* (Washington, D.C.: 1968).

# ALASKA AND THE PUBLIC LAND LAW
## REVIEW COMMISSION RECOMMENDATIONS

George W. Rogers

*Professor of Economics*
*University of Alaska*

The specific assignment given to each panel speaker was to "deal with the key recommendations of the commission's report that relate to the topic in question." In my case the topic in question is Alaska. The commission has made a number of recommendations relating specifically to Alaska, and others of general application that have special application or meaning in Alaska. In terms of the specific recommendations, it could be said that the State of Alaska fared extremely well at the hands of the commission. Some of the deadwood in existing laws and regulations were cleared away, basic policies of fed eral and state governments on the public land issues were brought closer together, the critically important matters of determination of Native land claims and state land selections were given top priority and institutiona᾿ arrangements were established for the continued coordination of Alaskan and federal public land policies and programs.

## OMISSION OF COMMUNITY AND HUMAN ASPECTS

On a laundry list basis we got from the commission virtually anything any reasonable Alaskan could hope for. It is not out of any sense of ingratitude, therefore, that I will address myself to what has been left out of the report in its treatment of Alaska as a whole based upon an understanding of the meaning of the creation of a new state from the public lands. Looking beyond Alaska, I would expand these observations to conclude

that what the commission has left out has been the community and human aspects of public land management. This
implies a major shortcoming, but it was inevitable given
the analytical system and assumptions they subscribed to
for arriving at decisions. Although the commission may
have believed it was entitled to overlook these factors,
a critique cannot.

I could have saved myself and this audience considerable trouble by simply identifying, describing and
evaluating the clearly Alaska-related recommendations of
the report. These might be identified as being the "key
recommendations" intended by the assignment, but beyond
giving footnote references I will pass them over here to
be taken up in the discussion following as appropriate.[1]
Rather than making a selection of key recommendations, I
will relate what appears to be the basic pattern which
underlies all of the 137 recommendations of the report
to the idea of Alaska as a new and still developing
state.

## Alaska--The Federally Owned State

According to the report of the Public Land Law
Review Commission before us, public lands under the
jurisdiction of federal agencies in 1968 comprised 95.3
percent of Alaska's total land area, in effect making it
a federally owned state.[2] Also in 1968, 46 percent of
the United States' public lands were in Alaska, which
makes our state of special importance to this conference
or any other consideration of the recommendations of the
Public Land Law Review Commission. (It should be noted
that 64 percent of the United States' continental shelf
area is off our shores, the implications of this fact
having been overlooked or ignored in the commission's
report on the management of the Outer Continental Shelf.)
As the State of Alaska makes its selections under the
land grant provisions of the Alaska Statehood Act these
percentages will decline, but even if we succeed in completing the process by the 1984 deadline the federal
government will still own 67 percent of the state's

land area, and 38 percent of all public lands of the
nation will be located within Alaska.  If this represents
a significant reduction in the relative areas involved,
it does not, however, alter the generalization drawn
from the 1968 statistics that on the one hand Alaska
is important in any consideration of the nation's public
lands, and on the other hand public lands play a key role
in any consideration of Alaska.

## Lands Excluded from State Selection

Furthermore, 24 to 26 percent of the federally
managed public lands in Alaska have been reserved or
withdrawn from entry by past executive and congressional
actions.  With the exception of limited areas within the
national forest reserves to allow for community expansion, these lands are excluded from selection by the
state and represent an important restriction on what can
be accomplished by the state in reducing the continued
dominance of federal land management on future developments.  The two largest urban centers in Alaska, Anchorage and Fairbanks, in which reside approximately 57 percent of the state's total current population, and the
next ranking centers in southeast Alaska, containing an
additional 14 percent of the population, are almost
totally dependent upon activities related to or taking
place on the large federal reserves adjacent to or surrounding them.

The future of these communities, therefore, will
continue to reflect how the federal government manages
public lands under its jurisdiction no matter how much
land is selected by the state.  For the most part, state
selections have been made opportunistically on strictly
real estate grounds or in order to bring the emerging
petroleum provinces under state ownership.  This will
provide enlargement of "living room" and sources of
funds to finance state and local government programs,
but the primary employment of most Alaskans will still
depend heavily upon how the federally retained lands
are used.

## Conflicts and Claims

The commission clearly recognized this. In discussing the need to set up a joint federal-state natural resources and regional planning commission for Alaska under Recommendation 15, it notes that although

> a significant part of that land
> base will belong to the state in
> the future....the state's desires
> and needs underscore[s] the Federal
> responsibility to plan for the
> retention and management or dispo-
> sition of the lands that it will
> have after the selection process
> is completed, in a manner not to
> thwart the state's effort to chart
> its own destiny.[3]

In addition to the importance of these continuing Alaska-federal public lands relationships, Alaska is currently caught in the crosscurrents not only of conflict and interaction between federal and state land policy and the shift of ownership reflected in the accelerating selection of public lands by the State of Alaska, but also in a number of other pressures. These include: the claims of the descendants of the aboriginal inhabitants of Alaska to title to most of the land (and the attendant land freeze of Public Land Order 4582, U.S. Department of the Interior, January 17, 1969); the private development and transportation land and right-of-way requirements following the discovery of a major petroleum province on our arctic slope and the sale of timber from large tracts of our southeastern forest lands; and the concern of many Alaskan and outside conservation groups over the threat of environmental degradation implied in major land use contemplated. All of these are of vital concern to us as Alaskans and probably of interest to non-Alaskans in the audience, but given the manner in which my topic is to be developed time would not permit even a cursory treatment. Furthermore, we have on our panel able representatives of the

principal "contending groups" (the state legislature,
the petroleum industry, the Alaska Natives, and conservation interests) and they will be presenting their special views of current public land issues in Alaska, which
I could here only anticipate or duplicate.[4] Here I will
deal with what lies behind or beyond current Alaska land
issues.

## MANY ALASKAS

My past attempts to understand and explain Alaska
have much in common with the commission's attempts to
present the "general public." There is not one Alaska,
but a compound of many "Alaskas." There are several
quite distinct and different regional Alaskas. There
also have been several distinct socioeconomic Alaskas
defined by quite different objectives and patterns of
development (Native Alaska, colonial Alaska, military
Alaska), each having dominated a discrete historical
period and all continuing to exert some influence in
the whole that is contemporary Alaska.[5] Each of these
regional and historical Alaskas would relate differently
to the commission's report, but for this discussion we
will focus on the essential meaning of Alaska as a state
in process of development. For more than 25 years I
have been a resident of Alaska and have been deeply
and continuously involved in the process, so I cannot
be objective. What is perhaps even worse is that over
time my very subjective views also have fluctuated widely
because the involvement has been a long one.

## The State of Alaska as an Anachronism

The idea of Alaska as a state has appeared at times
as a hopeless anachronism in an age of increasing urbanization and specialization. This mood comes over me
following certain happenings--exposure to a chamber of
commerce or tourist industry refurbishing of the "Last
Frontier" image, hearing a speech or reading a report
urging construction of a railroad into the arctic as a

means of "opening the country" or hearing plans to resettle unemployed urban workers on Alaska's "vast and empty lands." All of this is an attempt to replay the nineteenth century "winning of the West" in a northern frontier setting. When Alaska became a state just past the mid-twentieth century mark, this was the final act in a process designed in the eighteenth and nineteenth centuries and here set in motion late in the nineteenth century when Alaska was created as a district of the United States. Statements justifying or explaining the creation of a new state out of the raw materials of the public lands have a stirring ring to them, but they also sound like an echo from another time, a long-gone heroic age. The statement by a congressman two years after Alaska was organized as a territory, the last step in the process before becoming a state, is typical: "When the United States acquires extensive domain over extensive tracts of territory, the duty devolves upon it not so much to exploit the natural resources for the benefit of the people of the States as to build there a civilization, to induce immigration and settlement...that homes may spring up and that that territory may contribute to the general strength and happiness of the whole Union."[6]

## The Wrong Century

But aren't we in the wrong century to carry out such a program? According to a 1937 report by the National Resources Committee on the value of Alaska to the nation:

> In the past, the empty spaces of the
> earth were peopled gradually over a
> long period of time. Immigrants were
> at first predominantly subsistence
> farmers. They expected to hew down
> forests, to work from dawn to dark,
> to do without any luxuries, to live
> in isolation, to do without schools,
> police protection and doctors--they
> were ready to live at a very low
> level of subsistence provided they

> could look forward to ownership of a
> piece of land that in the second or
> third generation might yield a com-
> petence and a reasonable degree of
> comfort.
>
> Migrants of this type are becoming
> fewer and fewer in the world, and
> it is doubtful if the United States
> has even its proportionate share....
> The modern 'pioneer' thinks in terms
> of government and what it will do
> for him. If settlement is not made
> easy for him, the present-day pioneer
> will seek more sheltered spaces or
> call upon his government to discharge
> its social responsibility toward him.[7]

Based upon this line of reasoning, the 1937 report recommended against federal investment in programs to "force-
feed" settlement and, indirectly, against the creation
of a state.


## A Modern Approach

Looked at realistically, it appears that the development of whatever economic value Alaska held for the
nation could best be done without the encumbrance of
settlement and the political development represented by
statehood. This was substantially the pattern that had
been followed from the period of Russian ownership to
the date Alaska actually became a state. Hundreds of
millions of dollars of products were drawn from Alaska's
resources by seasonal or temporarily imported labor,
with virtually no change in the levels of population
from the turn of the century until the construction and
manning of the military establishment in World War II
and after.

Elsewhere in the polar lands a similar pattern was
being followed. After an initial drive to settle its

North in the 1920s and 1930s, the Soviet Union substantially abandoned this approach to northern development
in the 1940s and 1950s. The approach to development in
the forest and tundra zones of the northern regions,
according to studies of official policy available was
by the "selective method of developing lands by separate
oases and areas" and with

> periodic importation (for definite
> terms) of labor force from other,
> more southerly regions of the country.
> The principal aim of creating a com-
> plex is the working of especially
> valuable mineral resources, forests,
> and the wealth of fish and other sea
> animals. Modern technology and eco-
> nomics permit the development of this
> northern wealth through especially high
> mechanization of the processes and the
> shifting of the process to such forms
> of energy as water and oil power, which
> make it possible to reduce sharply the
> expenditure of live labor.[8]

This approach has a sound twentieth century ring to
it and, if intelligently implemented, would maximize the
net economic contribution of these regions to the gross
national product of their national owners, the United
States, the U.S.S.R., Denmark and Canada. In terms of
the stereotype of frontier development going through a
set series of stages or being based upon agricultural
settlement of the land, the idea of Alaska attempting
to recreate the process is not only an anachronism but,
given the limited agricultural lands, the climate and
other factors, either a grossly expensive undertaking
or an impossibility.

## THE STATE OF ALASKA AS A POSSIBLE
## MODEL OF THE FUTURE

Having gone to this limit, anyone who is a resident
of Alaska or who has visited it will immediately recognize that the potential of Alaska's public lands offers
more than merely being a supply depot to be drawn upon
for certain economic goods when the price is right
according to the calculations of the analytical system
devised to maximize these values. Richard A. Cooley
sums this up for most of us in his classic work on
Alaska's public lands, a basic work which surprisingly
I found neither mentioned nor reflected in the commission's report.

> In years past, Alaska was thought
> of primarily as a place to go to
> work, to acquire money and to leave.
> The population was highly transient.
> In the last decade, however, more
> and more people are coming to Alaska
> with an altogether different purpose
> in mind. They have become dissatis-
> fied with their hurly-burly, complex
> and often meaningless existence that
> offers comfort, entertainment and
> security but little real satisfac-
> tion. They are well enough off
> financially, but happiness seems
> to be absent from their lives, and
> they come to Alaska seeking a new
> environment that will fulfill this
> need.... What happens in Alaska
> could prove to be a kind of refor-
> mation; a discarding of the old
> mythology and a creative adventure
> in shaping new approaches to land
> and resource policy adjusted both
> to nature and to man's needs and
> values in the modern world.[9]

Not all that is happening in Alaska fits into this ideal presentation of what could be realized. As a resident, I would say that the majority of those who have come in during the last decade are still motivated by the old drive of acquiring money quickly and leaving as soon as possible. Many of the mistakes made to the south also are being repeated in the development of our communities and industries. But there is a shift in public opinion and a growing concern about what happens to the land and the environment, and a comparison of the characteristics of the last three decennial census reports reveals a growing balance and stability in the total population which was absent from previous reports. Even if Alaska is hardly more than a state in name only, the fact that it is so considered has put a definite pattern on what has happened over the last decade tending to direct development toward realization of the ideal of creating a real human community.

At other times, therefore, the idea of Alaska as a state appeared to me not as an anachronism, but as a model of the future. This mood comes over me most strongly following a trip Outside, such as the present one. Many of us who are long-term Alaskan residents have been able to sense and see, on periodic trips Outside, the progressive destruction of the physical conditions essential for life more clearly than those who have acquired a protective immunity by reason of living with daily increments of environmental degeneration and social decay.

In our efforts to prevent these things happening here, we are finding allies in new Alaskans who represent a growing body of contemporary refugees seeking a new life in a frontier not yet totally lost. But more than escape for a fortunate few is involved.

## Problems of Scale

At the heart of the multiple crises facing our society are the excessive concentrations of population

until they go beyond the scale which the natural environ
ment can carry without destruction and beyond the scale
in which the individual can survive as a human being.
Over the last 25 years I have made regular visits to
several of the great metropolitan centers of the United
States and Canada and have seen them grow steadily bigge
and at the same time more chaotic, shoddy and dehuman-
ized. They now face either being dismantled and recon-
structed in an attempt to make them fit places for human
habitation or being burned down by their inmates. Over
the past decade combinations of both alternatives have
been taking place.

The commission report recognizes the need for model
for something better and has recommended that steps be
taken to make some public land available for a prototype
"new city" on an experimental basis to provide information and guides for a building of a better future.[10]
The discussion in the report is limited to narrow real
estate considerations and would appear to view the problem as primarily one of passively responding to population and industrial growth. It ignores the fact that
even without any population increase, there is right
now a need for new cities, as well as for a redistribution of population. It also points out that such experi
ments are complex and costly and, therefore, would be
limited. In attempting to develop a new state in Alaska
we are using the public lands in a similar but broader,
more complex and costly experiment in trying to create
a model for an entire new society.

## Providing Employment

The public lands must do more than provide space
on which to build towns and cities in this experiment.
They must be used in such a manner as to provide local
employment to support the population of these communities. It was the recognition of these goals which
caused the U.S. Forest Service management programs in
Alaska to include not only the principles of multiple
use and perpetual yield, but also the requirement that

"logs, cord wood, bolts, and other similar products not be transported for primary manufacture outside the State of Alaska."

The working circles which form the basis of the timber management programs are based upon both inventories of forest resources and plans for establishment of new industrial enterprises at each of the major existing population centers within the forest reserve. There is an economic cost involved in that the return to the U.S. Treasury on the stumpage is not maximized by the primary processing requirement (the purchaser will reduce his bid by a factor representing the cost to him of constructing and operating a plant in Alaska), but the primary object of this policy is to realize other values from the commercial use of the forest resources.

The experiment involves other departures from policies that an adherence to limited systems of economic development would dictate. Additional economic costs must be assumed by developers to protect the physical environment and the other necessities and amenities for the "good life." Certain lands and resources must be withheld from use and harvesting for commercial values, in the interest of preserving higher environmental values for the enjoyment and benefit of nonresident visitors as well as residents of the developing state.

None of these departures from traditional development and land management goals would pass muster with the analytical systems of traditional liberal (or Marxist) economics, but the discipline itself is in a period of change reflecting the underlying ferment in contemporary society. As in all such periods of ferment, it is not certain whether the process is one of chaos or creation, although the latter at one time came from the former. What is needed is a laboratory for the testing of new approaches and hypotheses, as well as demonstrations of new models. Alaska, in carrying out its experiment, can serve as such a laboratory for the nation and could make a contribution toward the "general strength and happiness of the whole Union" which goes far beyond what the congressman quoted in the previous section could ever have envisaged in his less developed and less threatened time.

## THE STATE OF ALASKA AND THE NATIVE PEOPLE

It is no chance occurrence that the emergence of Alaska's Native people (Indian, Eskimo and Aleut) as a potent political force coincided with the opening decade of Alaska's experiment with statehood. This movement deserves more than the quick look afforded it here, because a full understanding of its meaning leads to an understanding of the ultimate meaning of Alaska as a state--a political means of attempting to reestablish in our society a real relationship between people and place. More is involved than simply getting an answer to the question of who owns Alaska's lands, although this is the only avenue that conveniently presents itself.

The approximately 55,000 people of aboriginal ancestry living in Alaska today are descendants of an estimated 62,000 population in this region at the time of the first Euro-American contacts in the mid-eighteenth century. They lived under several distinct social, economic and cultural systems, reflecting the adaptations made to the limitations imposed and the opportunities offered by the physical environment and the harvestable natural resources in each area.

## Human Habitat or Supply Depot

These sensitive and durable human adaptations to the various natural environments of Alaska were disrupted, and in many areas completely destroyed, by invasions of outside economic forces which looked upon Alaska not as a home but as a short-term supply depot from which to ruthlessly extract, while they lasted, a specialized list of raw materials of high value in the distant markets. The true cost of these outside economic developments was not paid by the outside exploiters (or "spoilers" in the old Alaskan idiom), but by the Native people who only participated in a marginal way in the related activities and benefits. Survival was achieved by maintaining a greatly degraded semisubsistence way of life (resulting in a decline in numbers to 26,500 by 1920), more recently combined with "benefits" from the welfare state branch of the dominant non-Native society (resulting in a rise to 43,000 by 1960).

The non-Native society was neither heartless nor unaware of their inability to assist the Native people in coping with their tragic situation. Attempts were made to provide escape routes. From the beginning some form of educational program was provided with the objective of assimilation of the Native people into the new dominant landless culture and wage-labor economic system.

Where the traditional aboriginal pursuits had some affinity for the new commercial enterprises, as in salmon fishing and canning, there appeared to be some progress toward these goals, but subsequent developments (i.e., the crash of the salmon resource in the late 1940s and 1950s and the failure of Indian fishermen to move into new jobs created in forest products) have proved even these cases to be illusory.

A comparison of vital statistics and census data has revealed that in each decade several thousand Alaska Natives "disappear." Allowing for statistical errors, this is an indication that a significant number who migrate from the villages or even from Alaska do cease to be "Natives." But the majority have stubbornly rejected the route of assimilation as a means of escape from the poverty in which they are caught.

Other alternatives were suggested by the statehood movement of the 1940s and 1950s. The basic objective was to obtain more local control over or ownership of Alaska's natural resources and to substitute resident

for nonresident interests as the guide in their utilization and management. Self-determination and other
political values were also involved, but these were means
toward the economic and social development aims of the
majority of Alaskans who supported the movement. This
was the broad political context in which what started
as simply a protective reaction of Alaska's Natives
became something more basic and universal. As they
found their ancestral lands threatened in the post-World
War II period by a formidable array of federal giants--
the Atomic Energy Commission with its plans to convert
the Alaska arctic into a nuclear testing ground and the
Corps of Engineers' giant Rampart power development--
and then the invasion of the international petroleum
industry, regional Native groups set up organizations
to protect their interest in their land and their way
of life. These were transformed into the statewide
Native land claims movement and the development of a
unified political force in the Alaska Federation of
Natives. Thus the entire movement is more than a
parallel to the statehood movement which preceded it
and goes much deeper.

## The Meaning of Land

Land is more than a convenient economic symbol or
a commodity for the Alaska Native. He finds his whole
identity as a human being tied up with it, whether he
still lives in the village of his people or is making
his way in the white man's world at Anchorage or elsewhere. It has become an effective political tool or
weapon in dealing with the white community. Depending
upon the terms of the settlement arrived at, it will
provide in itself or through revenues derived from its
use by petroleum and other industries a set of meaningful alternatives for the Native to choose from in selecting his future.

No longer will he face the alternative of continued
poverty on a subsistence village life with a depleted

resource base or one of making a full assimilation into a foreign culture. As in the case of the broader experiment of creating a state, this will also require programs for its realization that will be justified on values other than purely economic.

## THE COMMISSION'S PUBLIC BENEFIT:
## A CASE OF MISPLACED CONCRETENESS

Developing a state has basic implications for ownership and use of public lands. Land is seen as a place to live as well as the source of making a living, as a home as well as a supply depot. The benefits to be promoted appear to be primarily regional and local, but as I have indicated they could have significant national benefits implied in the whole legal process of advancement to this status. The commission's concept of maximizing public benefits and recommendations must be related to Alaska as a state in the making, given the dominance of federal public lands in Alaska and the dominance of Alaska in the total public lands of the nation.

The Organic Act under which the commission was created and has functioned sets forth specific duties to be performed and the general charge to report to the President and the Congress on the legal and administrative actions needed to assure that the "public lands of the United States shall be (a) retained and managed or (b) disposed of, all in a manner to provide the maximum benefit for the general public." A study of the efforts of the commission as reflected in the discussions of the 137 recommendations, the preface, the program for the future, and Chapter Two and Chapter Three of the resulting report is of critical importance in relating the recommendations to the topic of this panel. The heart of the report is the determination of the meaning of the "general public" and the "maximum benefit" that will guide continuing decisions as to disposal of public lands and management of those retained. In approaching these two objectives, the report follows two different and sometimes conflicting routes.

Public benefit is an evolutionary and highly subjective and relative concept. It cannot be determined
by reference to absolutes. This is properly the objective to be served by the *political* process of a democratic society. In turn, this is properly the subject
of Professor Caldwell's panel. My remarks will be
limited to noting that this is the arena in which divergent opinions and interests come into contact and conflict and in an ideally functioning democracy resolve
themselves into a consensus approximating what the
general public, as it might define itself at any given
time and place, believes to be its maximum benefit.

The commission has recognized this and gives recommendations that could make existing political institutions and machinery more effective in discharging this
essential task in relation to public land issues. The
first basic premise of the commission's program for the
future, for example, is that "Congress, elected by and
responsive to the will of the people, makes policy; the
executive branch administers the policy." Some of its
recommendations would enlarge the role of state and
local governments, provide for public discussion and
participation in all major decisions and create regional
commissions for land use planning.

## The Commission's "System" Personality

The commission (or its members and staff), however,
is only human, and as such has an underlying split personality which would support a more certain, objective
and "scientific" means of achieving these aims. This
surfaces in response to the charge to produce a report
at a set date and the bit of Platonism to be found in
all of us. It also probably reflects the professionalism
of the staff and those who prepared the special reports
that are referred to, but that I have not seen. Throughout, there is a strong urge to discover or create some
order in the subject, to make the definition of public
good objective and the measurement of the maximizing
effects of existing or proposed policy as scientific
as possible.

From the outset we are told that there are to be "controlling standards, guidelines and criteria," although it is noted that "judgment would be required." We are told in the preface that in considering its task, the commission used a check list of "justifiable interests" that led it to its subsequent recommendations and conclusions, which met "the test of providing the maximum benefit for the general public." We are also informed in the preface that "the Commission considered all the resources and uses of the public lands to be *commodities*," [emphasis added] which would lead us to anticipate an analytical system drawing from the academic discipline of economics rather than politics. In fact, there is strong evidence that economic factors alone are to be the primary measure of public benefit. This approach reaches its most complete statement in the discussion of Recommendation 2.

Maximum public benefit in planning for public land use will be obtained, according to the recommendation, when the Congress specifies the factors to be considered in making the decision and an "analytical system" determines the application of these factors to the specific decision by the executive agency involved. Having made this recommendation, however, the commission immediately deprives Congress of its role by going on to list the several general categories of factors that "can serve all of the agencies equally." In order to assure consistency of results and effort among the several agencies "this process should be standardized with common units of measurement and a system for the comprehensive analysis of the factors considered." After considering benefit-cost analysis, the executive branch, PPBS (Planning, Programming and Budgeting Systems) and the techniques used by the Department of Commerce in its national income measurements, the commission concludes that a regional input-output analysis is "the only approach that provides a reliable basis for making comparisons of economic impacts for different land uses." Although the commission intends "the factors and procedures suggested above to be the primary basis for land use decisions generally...*for those limited situations where choices among*

*conflicting uses cannot clearly be made after applicatio*
*of this system,* Congress should attempt to provide guide
lines that could be used to resolve such conflicts."
[Emphasis added][11]  In other words, even those factors
and goals which at present do not fit the "common units
of measurement" are not to escape what will eventually
be an all-embracing machine system or possibly an alli-
ance of systems covering economic, social and other
factors and goals.

## The Commission's "Nonsystem" Personality

The other half of the commission's personality,
however, asserts itself repeatedly throughout the report
and even in this crucial section.  When the system personality of the commission asserts in Recommendation 30,
for example, that "dominant timber production units
should be managed primarily on the basis of economic
factors so as to maximize net returns to the Federal
Treasury," its nonsystem personality counters.  It
asserts in Recommendation 34 that the "Federal Governmen
has an obligation to those who depend on public lands fo
their livelihood" and that they "should be given consideration in the management and disposal of public land
timber" even to the extent of continuing such uneconomic
practices as the ban on export of logs from public lands
and setting "the size limit for this industry in terms
of qualifying for Small Business Administration assistance."[12]

This seesawing is continuous from the beginning to
the end of the report, but it is in no sense a real
debate between opposite views.  The most the nonsystem
side of the commission does is seek recognition that son
minor exceptions must be made as we go along.  Ultimatel
the analytical system should determine the correct decision in each public land issue.  Full realization of thi
only awaits further refinements of the system to embrace
those "limited situations" that at present do not fit ir
and the generation of appropriate data.

## THE COMMISSION'S ANALYTICAL SYSTEM:
## THE WRONG TOOL KIT

It could be argued that I am in error in seeing the commission as split into system and nonsystem personalities. The true split may be between accepting only economic factors and analysis as determinants of all decisions or allowing exceptions only until companion systems can be devised to take care of all general categories of factors. Limiting our observations only to the forms of economic analysis considered by the commission and thus implied in its assumptions and approach, however, we find a further narrowing of scope and vision. With the exception of the chapter dealing with the environment and passing references to it elsewhere in the report, I had the impression of reading a report of the 1940s or 1950s when the national crises focused on the natural resource base and progress was still defined in terms of economic output of goods and services. Now economists are recognizing such additional values as the "quality of life" and the environment as something embracing the resource base and transcending it in terms of economic welfare.

The commission gave no evidence of being aware of these changes, or possibly the evidence was that they chose to ignore them. In the consideration of goals and systems of analysis, they showed no awareness that we are finally freeing our choices of futures for our society from the tyranny of economic growth and traditional analysis. The sacred gross national product is being treated with diminishing awe by a new generation of economists. As defined by Edward J. Mishan,

> This index, as economists know, is an
> artless though effective device which
> can be counted on to register some
> economic gain for almost any country from
> from one year to the next. For the
> principle employed is simply that of
> totting up the values of all man-made
> goods while assiduously ignoring all
> the man-made bads that are produced

simultaneously. These bads (or
'spillovers' as they are commonly
called) include development blight,
the erosion of the countryside, the
accumulation of oil and sewage on
our coasts, contamination of lakes
and rivers, air pollution, traffic
congestion, and shrieking aircraft.[13]

## Amenity Rights and Property Rights

Professor Mishan has proposed a number of approaches
to including these "bads" or social costs in the economist's calculus, among them the recognition of "amenity
rights" on the same basis as the traditional economists
have recognized property rights. Regional economists
have for some years included "amenity resources" (i.e.,
natural resources that do not enter directly into the
production process, but condition the manner in which
economic decisions are made) in a region's natural resources endowment.

Professor Mishan is not alone in pointing out that
the contempt that the so-called hard-boiled economists
heap upon the "soft" or "sentimental" economists is based
upon a "misplaced concreteness which, despite occasional
disclaimers in our more civilized moments, tends to associate utility, or value, with market prices. But if all
that is priced has value, the reverse is certainly not
true."[14] Among economists interested in welfare, he is
not alone in putting a "price" on those things that
escape the market mechanism. Inspired by the teachings
of Galbraith, Ayres, Myrdal and others, for example,
there have emerged the first steps toward an institu-
tionalization of the search for new approaches in the
recent establishment of the Association for Evolutionary
Economics.

Addressing himself primarily to young economists
in underdeveloped countries in the 1950s, Gunnar Myrdal
urged them to

have the courage to throw away large
structures of meaningless, irrelevant
and sometimes blatantly inadequate
doctrines and theoretical approaches
and to start their thinking afresh
from a study of their own needs and
problems. This would take them far
beyond the realm of both outmoded
Western liberal economics and Marxism.[15]

His advice of over a decade ago to this group of economists has application to the young economists of the
so-called developed nations and we have had an upsurge
of unorthodoxy within the profession in response to
recognition of the failures of traditional approaches
to meet the critical needs of our times. Unfortunately,
none of this is reflected in the report.

## The Public Benefit Revealed--Over and Over Again

It is not my intention to belabor this point beyond
noting that the evaluation of any system of analysis
should not be in terms of its elegance and appearance
of precision, but in the identification of what the
system takes as given (i.e., not problematical). Ideas
and factors that would disrupt or cannot conveniently be
assimilated into the system are consciously or uncon-
sciously discarded and what is left in does not necessarily reflect what is strategically important in the
real world or the objectives and aspirations of real
people.

The regional input-output systems favorably considered by the commission as a means of establishing
benefit maximization, or any of the other systems considered, can only treat those factors which are subject
to common units of measurement and included within the
framework of the system. In short, they are capable of
treating in only a limited way a narrow range of economic
values, factors and goals. Virtually everything I have
discussed as representing the values, factors and goals

inherent in the experiment of creating a state from the
public lands of Alaska and the more basic Native law
issue, therefore, would be off limits in any analytical
system of the sort considered. The commission's view
that all resources and uses of the public lands are to
be considered as commodities, for example, is incompatible with the land ethic of the Native Alaskan which
treats it as home. This relation of the underlying
pattern of the recommendations to Alaska raises the
question of their relevance in the determination of any
other version of the public benefit.

I repeat that the public benefit is an evolutionary,
highly subjective and relative concept. It is not an
absolute and it cannot be discovered and measured and
weighed and described by application of a set of absolute principles, standards, criteria and analytical
systems. Granting all of the truly great accomplish-
ments of the commission in performing this tremendously
important and difficult task, one basic flaw is the
search for concreteness and stability where it could
or should never be found, in a concept of the public
benefit.

## The Rules of the Road

In preparing for this conference, I found in my
files a form letter from the director of the commission
dated 13 October 1966 inviting me to provide suggestions
for "identifying and structuring criteria" for determination of the maximum benefit for the general public which
would "put decisionmaking within the Commission on a
plane above reliance on divergent opinions arrived at
without reference to a common base." At the time this
letter was received I was reading a journal article by
my friend and former colleague Harvey Perloff on "New
Directions in Social Planning." The original source
and reference is lost, but I had written the following
quote on the bottom of the letter, "Voluntary and democratic processes have been built into social planning
operations; broad citizen involvement has been sought;

a pluralistic approach to the definition and solution
of social problems has been accepted." This was the only
reliable formula I could offer to the commission for the
determination of the public benefit and the only approach
toward maximization.

The comments of Director Pearl this morning were of
considerable interest and concern to me in this regard.
To paraphrase, he concluded that policy *must* be established in advance in accordance with a "public interest
test" so we would "know the rules of the road" in arriving at the correct decisions. If we are to follow this
approach, there will be no voluntary and democratic process or broad citizen involvement. With a hygienically
predetermined test, there will be no pluralistic approach
to the definition of the benefits to be maximized, the
determination of policies of maximization and the solution of problems. Goals and objectives will all be determined by the system.

# NOTES

[1] [U.S.] Public Land Law Review Commission, *One Third of the Nation's Land* (Washington, D.C.: 1970) (hereinafter referred to as PLLRC). Recommendation 8, pp. 54-56; Recommendation 15, pp. 64-65; Recommendation 34, pp. 99-101; Recommendation 49, pp. 132-133; Recommendation 68, pp. 177-178; Recommendation 70, pp. 180-182; Recommendation 78, pp. 198-199; Recommendation 107, p. 249; and an unnumbered but strong recommendation for "...the early enactment of legislation to resolve the problem of Native claims and end the current impasse," pp. 248-249.

[2] PLLRC, p. 327.

[3] PLLRC, p. 65.

[4] I am having duplicated for distribution with my paper a current treatment of these matters by my colleague, Professor Arlon R. Tussing, "Issues of Land Use Determination in Alaska," September 11, 1970. One of the best treatments of Alaska land administration and the implications of statehood is contained in Richard A. Cooley, *Alaska, A Challenge in Conservation* (Madison: University of Wisconsin Press, 1966). A comprehensive background analysis of the Native claims issues is contained in [U.S.] Federal Field Committee for Development Planning in Alaska, *Alaska Natives and the Land* (Washington, D.C. 1968) and U.S. Senate, Committee on Interior and Insular Affairs, *Alaska Native Settlement Act of 1970: Report* (91st Cong., 2d sess., Report 91-925) (Washington, D.C.: 1970). G.W. Rogers, ed., *Change in Alaska: People, Petroleum and Politics* (Seattle: University of Washingto Press, 1970) presents an anthology of essays treating th petroleum and environment issues.

[5] G.W. Rogers, *The Future of Alaska, The Economic Consequences of Statehood* (Baltimore: The Johns Hopkins Press, 1962), pp. 60-104.

[6] Representative Halvor Steenerson, Minnesota, February 5, 1915. Quoted in Ernest Gruening, *The State of Alaska* (New York: Random House, 1968), p. 191.

[7] [U.S.] National Resources Committee, *Alaska--Its Resources and Development* (Washington, D.C.: 1938), pp. 22-23.

[8] N.N. Kolosovsky, "The Territorial-Production Combination in Soviet Economic Geography," *Osnovy Ekonomicheskogo Rayonirovaniya* (Moscow: 1958). Quoted in Rogers, op. cit., p. 286. For a full historical treatment see T. Armstrong, *Russian Settlement in the North* (Cambridge, England: Cambridge University Press, 1965); also T. Armstrong, "Soviet Northern Development, with Some Alaskan Parallels and Contrasts," *ISEGR [Institute of Social, Economic and Government Research] Occasional Papers,* No. 2, October 1970 (College, Alaska: University of Alaska).

[9] *Alaska, A Challenge in Conservation* (Madison: The University of Wisconsin Press, 1966), pp. 129-130.

[10] PLLRC, p. 227.

[11] PLLRC, p. 47.

[12] PLLRC, pp. 96, 99-100.

[13] "The Spillover Enemy, The Coming Struggle for Amenity Rights," *Encounter*, 33(6): 3-13 (December 1969), p. 4.

[14] Ibid., p. 11.

[15] Gunnar Myrdal, *Rich Lands and Poor* (New York: Harper & Bros., 1957), p. 104.

# PANEL DISCUSSION ON ALASKA

Moderator:          A. Starker Leopold
                    *Professor of Forestry and Zoology*
                    *University of California, Berkeley*

Panelists:          Representative Eugene Guess
                    *Alaska Legislature*

                    Joseph H. FitzGerald
                    *Atlantic Richfield Oil Co.*
                    *Anchorage, Alaska*

                    Robert B. Weeden
                    *Alaska Conservation Society*

Panel of
Indian Spokesmen*:  Michael Rogers, *Chairman*
                    *Paiute-Shoshone Indians*
                    *Owens Valley*

                    Roque Duenas
                    *United Indians, Seattle*

                    Bela Cortief
                    *Bay Area Native Council*

                    Mrs. Mitchell
                    *Quinault Tribe, Washington*


*Leopold:* We will follow the format of previous panels
by having a relatively brief analysis of either Dr.
Rogers' speech or the commission report itself by our
several panelists. First, I would like to present to
you Representative Eugene Guess of the legislature in
Alaska, a resident of Anchorage.

---
*See p. 215.

## THE ALASKA GOVERNMENT'S VIEW

*Guess:* I view my role here as representing the government of the State of Alaska and its feelings toward the report as it affects the state and its responsibilities. Nevertheless, it would only be realistic to say that my thoughts are tempered by the fact that I feel an elected politician cannot and should not be afforded the luxury of operating in a vacuum.

In the context of land management and disposition, the State of Alaska is a political entity and has specific responsibilities to carry out on behalf of all of its people, subject to the just settlement of the Native land claims. The state first must complete its selections from the public domain, including Forest Service lands which are badly needed because of rapid urbanization in the state, and this should be done pursuant to the method established by the compact at the time of the admission of Alaska as a state. Otherwise, the state should decide within a specified time frame that it does not wish to utilize the full selection during this period of time, so as not to disturb the relationship set forth by the compact.

## Contending Groups

Now, secondly, the state must solve within the framework of its government the conflicting interests surrounding land utilization. Several of the papers submitted to the panelists referred to these conflicting interests as contending groups; that is, conservation groups, Native groups, oil and gas and mining groups. And the State of Alaska was placed in the same group on somewhat an equal basis.

I noted with some interest that neither the 20 or 30 percent of the Alaskans who subsist below the poverty line nor the some 17 percent of the Alaskan work force that is unemployed was considered in these various papers as contending groups. Nevertheless, as I see it, the alignment in this particular manner calls for initially only three groups: the federal government and the state government composing two with their initial obligations established by the statehood act, and, third, the Native groups whose rights established, both legally and morally, transcend the relationship between the federal and the state governments.

The other various contending groups, as I see it, fall within the present or subsequent responsibilities of federal and state governments. In carrying out its obligations to solve both the vocal and nonvocal conflicting interests in land utilization, the state also must see that there are sufficient producing economic units allowed to maintain governmental services, and that solutions are found for "people problems" of unemployment, poverty, health and those problems created by the rapid urbanization now taking place in Alaska.

Because of the conflicting interests of the contender groups as dual citizens and because the federal government, after its selection, will control some two-thirds of the land within the State of Alaska, the state has the further obligation to coordinate its present and future programs with the federal government. I think this will succeed and succeed, however, only on the basis of mutuality and respect of the desires and obligations and problems of each of these entities.

## A Mutual Effort

In view of this mutual standing between the state and federal governments, the state should move immediately with the federal government to solve or bring about a just settlement of the Native land claims, thereby clearing the relationship between the federal and state governments, or, if you will, eliminating the contending groups with the highest priority. Then we should move jointly to establish machinery through a joint commission, as suggested in the report.

It is necessary for this to be accomplished if we are to feed the necessary data into the federal and state political process to carry out its varied but mutual obligations to the other groups involved.

Thank you.

*Leopold:* Our next panelist is Mr. Joseph FitzGerald, who represents the Atlantic Richfield Oil Company in their operations in Alaska. Mr. FitzGerald is a resident of Anchorage and comes to us to express the view of industry as it is involved in public land problems.

## AN INDUSTRY VIEW

*FitzGerald:* I would like to say immediately I agree with George Rogers' analysis that the valuation of the various uses of land as we envision them is truly a political decision and not an economic one. The economic arguments enter in order to provide facts to buttress the analysis, but basically the problem in Alaska is a political one. I want to emphasize this because the actions that will be taken are political and must be faced in that manner. These will include getting a declaration of parks, recreational areas and other things that many of us have believed to be necessary for a long time.

Now, I want to make only a few brief points, because I think that there is no possibility of analyzing the problems in depth here in the space of a few minutes. Most importantly, I want to say that the recommendations of the Public Land Law Review Commission are probably on the whole acceptable as a basis for the future management of Alaska. There are modifications that must be approached, but it is a reasonable rationalization of the land system. It brings the federal law into conformity with that of the state, and we have a good state system of laws. I think that we could move forward under these recommendations in many ways.

## The Real Issues

Having said that, I must point out immediately that
the real land problems of Alaska are not encompassed in
this proposed legislation. We have four major land
issues that have been building up largely since statehood 11 years ago. They must be resolved, and resolved
now, by legislation or administrative action, or a combination of the two. These issues are the land claims,
the pipeline permit, a state selection of lands and the
outline of a conservation program. This last problem
will involve the setting aside by the state and federal
governments of land, not only for parks under the federal law, but also for all kinds of uses of land for
recreation and conservation purposes.

Let me give you some background on these issues.
I think it's very easy to assume that the land problems
of Alaska are similar to the land problems found in the
western United States; they are not. In Alaska approximately 914,000 acres out of 375 million acres are in
private ownership. That is approximately one-fourth of
one percent of the land. But the cities in Alaska with
a population of a thousand or over occupy 20,000 acres
of land. Now, we assume that the various governmental
uses which give any real intensive use to land constitute possibly up to 3 million acres.

## Ninety-Nine Percent Wilderness

You realize that we are talking about an area where
99 percent of the land today is wilderness, and it is
wilderness under very special circumstances. Alaska
is composed of two basic areas: the Middle North and
the Arctic. The Canadian Middle North, which is north
of where 95 percent of the Canadians live in Canada,
is a vast area inhabited by some people, but basically
wilderness. North of that lies the Arctic, as it does
in Alaska, and the Arctic is a harsh and hostile land,
a land to which man may go to extract resources or to
do something on a minimum penetration basis, but it's

not a place where we are going to build cities or have extensive development as we know it here.

The possibility for the Middle North development of Alaska comes in the rail-belt area--Seward, Anchorage, Fairbanks and the Kenai Peninsula. This is where such development is taking place, in a small core area buttressed by a development of communities along the coastal fringe, where there is basically a maritime civilization.

Inland from the coast there are mountains and wilderness. One of our challenges in dealing with the land is what to do with the wilderness from the standpoint of 100 years or 500 years or 50 years from now. We must project into the future how we wish this land to be used and to be protected for the future.

## Alaska's Economic Base

It is also, I think, important to realize that land is peculiarly the base of the economy of Alaska. We don't have an industrial base. We don't have an agricultural base, other than forestry. We have fisheries, but essentially we are dealing with the products of the land.

At the time of statehood, the large users of the land were the military and other governmental agencies, so we had no tax base of any extent. The focus was therefore on the development of resources: timber, oil and gas, fisheries, and then recreational uses. This fact remains today. Whether Alaska stands on its own two feet or moves ahead progressively, whether it conserves its land through its own efforts or whether it can do any of these things, is dependent upon its ability to derive revenue from its own resources. When you deal with the problem of Alaska, that is one of the two key issues that you must bear in mind. I don't want to prolong this, but I feel that you must realize that these four land issues must be resolved as quickly as possible.

You have heard John Borbridge's speech on the Native land claims issue. He speaks sincerely. He speaks eloquently. I think you get the sense of urgency that exists. It is equally true that the timetable on the construction of the pipeline and the extraction of resources of the North is just as crucial to the Natives, to the State of Alaska and to conservationists. It is true this is where the money must come from. It is also true that we must do the other things. We must allow the state to select the land, because it cannot be a state if the people are going to live on a vast reservation.

The role of a state in the United States is to manage directly the affairs of the people who live within its boundaries. That takes a land base.

## The Highest Priority

Finally--and I want to end with this, because I think it's the most important of all--we can, of course, immediately send to Congress a list of the land areas that ought to be withdrawn as national parks. This work is largely done and well buttressed by analysis. It should go. But if we are going to have a joint federal-state planning commission, then I think the highest order of priority should go to analyzing in depth all the things that the state and the federal governments could and should do.

And it is going to take innovative thinking. There are many things that we now realize should be done quite differently in Alaska than we are doing them down here. For example, we must solve the problem of giving people access to the mountains and glorious scenery of Alaska, while at the same time preventing deep penetration of the wilderness, which cannot take a great deal of use. There are ways of doing this, and speaking as an Alaskan, we think that we can do this. We think we should do it immediately. Once we have solved these immediate problems, we can move on

to rationalizing the laws under the public land laws
of the United States. But we can only come to that
after we have taken major intermediate steps.

Thank you.

*Leopold:* The fourth member of our panel is Dr. Robert
Weeden, a fellow professional biologist and professional
conservationist, who has lived for some years in Alaska
and has been connected with the government and the university and with conservation organizations, including,
most recently, the Alaska Conservation Society. Bob
Weeden.


## A CONSERVATIONIST VIEW

*Weeden:* I would like to add one thing to my own intro-
duction. I am a member of the Saxon Tribe and some of
my ancestors are now pursuing aboriginal rights in
London.

I wanted to relate to you a really glorious irony
that has developed during this process of restoring
the identity of the Natives. One of the few reservations we do have in Alaska is across from Anchorage.
It's called Tyonek, and oil was discovered close to
there. The companies wished to drill within the area
and paid quite a considerable sum for the rights to do
so. The Natives then invested, very sensibly, and one
of the things they invested in was office buildings in
Anchorage. They later leased one of these office buildings to the Bureau of Indian Affairs.

## Personal and Brief

Public land laws are among the most important of
the institutions that have made Alaska what it is and
are likely to direct its future. I simply can't discuss
the ways these laws are influencing how Alaskans use
their natural resources or how and where people have

settled in Alaska, or the appearance and social usefulness of the landscape as a whole.  Instead, I have
elected to be fairly personal in my approach to this.

   I have been trying to find something that is at
once brief and different from what has been done before
I am afraid that, in trying to be personal and brief,
I am going to sound dogmatic.  I will have to run that
risk, because I am trying to distill some fairly complex and dynamic thoughts on these problems in a very
few words.  These statements I will make don't necessarily represent the full range of my thoughts and
feelings about land strategy any more than, for example
the 10 biggest trees characterize a forest.

   Everyone knows that Alaska has very few people in
it.  Everybody knows that Alaska has vast reaches of
uninhabited country.  As Supervisor McSheehy must have
said sometime, it's country where the hand of man has
never set foot.

   Alaska has varied natural resources that can contribute to its own and the nation's welfare.  And every
one knows, too, that Alaska is in the mainstream of
technological society and is there to stay.  These are
just some of the major elements in the substrata of
facts in the reality that we call Alaska, and they don'
imply anything at all about the social purposes that
could flow from them or be derived from them.

## For and Against

   I oppose any policy that aims to increase population.  It's going to come anyway; we don't need to
encourage it.  I oppose any policy that aims to settle
uninhabited country.  Elbow room is already too rare to
tolerate an anachronistic nineteenth century approach
to the remaining space.  I oppose the view that all
resources must sooner or later be converted into commodities and profits.  Economic exploitation, however
sanitized environmentally, cannot be allowed free acces
to the whole of Alaska's landscape.

What am I for? I am for the expression in all public policies of the importance of environments of high
quality, beauty, diversity and natural productivity. I
am for the preservation of extensive areas of natural
landscapes, not as an unwanted residual, but as an
essential part of the human estate.

I am for the development of economic resources on
a scale sufficient to provide a livelihood for Alaskans
and particularly to provide an opportunity for an economic livelihood for those who now have none; and also
to provide a share in the balancing of exports with our
fantastic imports which are needed because of our geographic position and small population.

I am for the widening of land planning horizons to
include all levels of government, all human and technical knowledge that's pertinent, to include reference
to a substantially longer time frame than is normal,
and to include an integrative perspective of social
purposes.

Last, I am for public policies arrived at through
maximum public participation, carried out by a strong,
responsible and visible government.

## Areas of Disappointment

I will have time only for a very short look at the
commission's report, and I think some of you can anticipate the directions of my thoughts in this regard.
First, my biggest disappointment is that the commission
did not state and hew to the most important fact of all,
and that is that the nation should retain responsibility
for the management of all but a tiny fraction of vast
public lands. (I have to make two exceptions: the lands
that the Natives derive from their claims, and the land
that will be transferred to states, mainly to Alaska, in
satisfaction of their statehood land grants. And, incidentally, to put it in perspective, if you haven't made
this connection yourself, the land grants to Alaska will

amount to the transfer of one acre out of seven that
now exists in the public domain.)

In expressing this disappointment, I might say that
although I recognize the commission spoke against a
wholesale disposal of the federal public lands, I
detected that the commission envisioned a fairly brisk
retail trade. I ask the commission to think again of
the millions--tens of millions--of Americans who can
never own land, and to remember that we now have only
one-third of the nation's lands left.

My second criticism is merely an echo, I think, of
what has been said before by many people, and that is
that the commission apparently embraced inappropriate
or only partly appropriate systems for deciding who
should use the public lands in specific cases. These
systems express the failure of American culture to
recognize basic human values apart from economic survival.

## The Positive Side

On the positive side, the commission certainly
understood the new role of comprehensive planning in
public land management, especially as it applied to
Alaska. I think their recommendations relating to
Alaska land planning are excellent. I hope that an
Alaska Land Commission of some sort can be established
soon. Representative Guess and others have outlined
why it is absolutely necessary.

In summary, then, the work of the Public Land Law
Review Commission reflects the deep interest of the
commission and the whole nation in the struggle of
Alaskans to find themselves. Still it's plain that the
commission worked with only a few, although very important, pieces of the puzzle that is our state. We
couldn't expect anything else. The mark wasn't missed;
it simply was not aimed at. The commission worked by
analysis, and I think that a state can only be built by

synthesis. It's up to Alaskans to take what pieces of
the report they can use and fashion new ways of life for
themselves out of respect for, and an understanding of,
both man and nature together.

## PANEL OF INDIAN SPOKESMEN

*Leopold:* Now we may proceed to the unstructured part
of our modified program. First of all I would like to
introduce some of the other Native representatives who
have come to our conference and who by virtue of this
slight reorganization we are able to have on the program with us.

First, Mr. Michael Rogers on the left, who is
chairman of the Paiute-Shoshone Indians in the Owens
Valley. I have not had an opportunity yet to speak to
Mr. Rogers or to the other members to ask how much
time each wants.

*Rogers:* It will only take about three minutes.

*Leopold:* Great. I wonder if we could ask each of you
to give a short résumé, based perhaps on the more extensive coverage that John Borbridge gave us about the
general problem, and then we can open our discussion
to cover Alaska in general and native land problems
in particular. The questions can go in either direction. Is that suitable?

All right. First, Mr. Michael Rogers.

*Rogers:* First of all, I'd like to speak about the commission's report and give my own opinion.

After taking the dollar sign out of it, I have
found one sentence that I can really relate to, and
that's on page 88. It says: "Everything is connected
to everything else."

I would like to compare this with the Indian religion or philosophy that says: "We are no less or no more than any living thing." We are all connected through life itself; this is the only sentence that really struck me in the whole report.

I feel that the commission concentrated more or less on the dollar value to the government without taking a deep look at the concerns of the average American.

## WITH AND WITHOUT A CONSCIENCE

The Indian truly lives in two worlds. One is the dollar world which has no conscience, and the other is his own world of humanity which has a conscience. And it's in trying to make this transition that we sort of get fouled up. We just don't know when you are not supposed to have a conscience, because we have always been taught that life is important, regardless of what the dollar has to say.

We are truly concerned with the Indian people-- Indians in Alaska, here in the continental United States and in Peru--with all Indian people. Our religion was based on the land, but the coming of the non-Indians caught our attention and made us look up toward the heavens. Pretty soon we wound up almost without any land, and therefore we now keep one eye on the heaven and one eye on the land, and this is the way it is going to work.

## The Life of the Future

We are concerned. We are concerned because our forefathers left us a vast resource for future generations, and we are interested in protecting it at all costs. We are not interested in leaving a dumping ground. We are concerned about the life of the future and hoping that it can come about more reasonably to resolve the problems that face us.

I don't know how our Indian people were able to
live in this nation for some 25,000 years without the
dollar, but they surely managed.  And thanks to the
coming of the dollar 300 or 400 years ago, all we have
to do today is press a button to blow ourselves up.
It's a tragic transition in a sense, and sometimes we
really wonder where it's all leading.  When is the dollar going to begin to have a conscience?

There is a good aspect to a meeting like this,
although I wish it wasn't after the fact, as the commission related here.  It seems to me that what has
taken place today is that the commission has been perhaps listening to some people, but I wonder if they were
the right people.  Has the commission really been talking to the average Americans about their concerns in
their everyday lives?  If this is what the commission
really wants, I haven't found it here yet.

## In Search of Justice

In regard to Mr. Weeden and his land claim in
England, I hope that he receives more than we did
as California Indians in 1970:   43 cents an acre at
today's prices.  And we are supposed to call this justice.  It's hard for the Native American to seize upon
the fact that this nation can spend its youth and money
in foreign countries trying to bring about freedom and
justice, when it can't take care of this little problem
at home.

The injustices done to the American Indian cannot
be erased, but we sure can plan for tomorrow.  And the
compensation to the Indian for the injustices of yesterday can be made by the people of the United States and
the vast resources that they possess.  There are no
problems that we cannot resolve if we care to do so.
We feel this because of the evolution of the United
States which has been built upon the contributions,
the sacrifices and the cultures of all people, of all
colors.  There is no reason why we cannot work out

our problems and somehow come to an understanding to
live together and work together in peace.

*Leopold:* Thank you, Mr. Rogers.

Next I am pleased to present to you Mr. Roque
Duenas, who is a representative of the United Indians
of all tribes from Seattle.


## THE ISSUE OF SURPLUS LAND

*Duenas:* First of all, on the commission's recommendation
that the Allotment Act be repealed, I would like to go
on record as being against that, since it is one of the
only channels left by which Indians can reclaim some of
their land and put it to use. And Indians have the
right to it, because all of this surplus land is covered under one treaty or another in this country.

The other matter concerns Alcatraz and Fort Lawton,
which are both pieces of federal surplus land. Right
now, due to the government's different programs of
termination, education and relocation, a lot of our
people are situated in urban areas where they suffer
the highest unemployment, lowest annual wage, highest
infant mortality rate, you name it. All of the social
ills befall our people in these urban areas, as elsewhere. We would like the commission to recommend that
some consideration be given to requests by the urban
Indians for the surplus properties.


## The Coming Blowup

These are matters that I didn't come prepared to
talk on at all. First of all, a lot of things have
been said here today concerning, on the one hand, economics and social welfare and, on the other hand,
environment and environmental control. There seems
to be, as has been admitted, no stopping population
growth, whether you are for or against it. Yet

environmentalists request that there be no more substantial population movement into the wilderness areas or the unpopulated areas.

Consequently, it seems to me that everything is leading to one path, which unavoidably and likely will end in some kind of blowup where the problem will be resolved out of our hands. This has to do very much with the dollar signs that Mr. Rogers talked about as compared to the human factors discussed by Mr. Fitz-Gerald. It has to do with a legal world versus a natural world that is very evident to the Alaskans-- the Native Alaskans--living with nature, with their environment. You have to live that way. It progresses in a certain way and, if you misuse it, it's going to come to an end.

## Legalisms

These are the things that concern all of us, or should concern all of us. And yet when you talk about economics and the programs that have to be instituted for social welfare, all these are talked about in the legal world way. You can't change natural facts. That chair there is naturally a chair. You can legislate it to be a table, but it's still going to be a chair. And this is what has been happening to us all along, while all these programs have been instituted. I don't really know what to say.

I don't think much of anything I say is going to do much good. If nothing alters the course that we are following now, maybe we should help you speed it along to get it over with.

*Leopold:* Thank you, Mr. Duenas.

Now we have Bela Cortief who is a Sioux and a member of the Bay Area Native Council. Do you wish to speak, Mrs. Cortief?

INDIANS' CONCERN:   CONSERVATION AND ECOLOGY

*Cortief:*  There is a possibility that everything has
been said pertaining to the way the Indians feel about
their Native lands.  I represent an organization con-
sisting of 27 Indian organizations in the Bay Area.
Most of the Indians are on what you would call a relo-
cated basis.  Although we are trying to exist and trying
to adjust to the urban society, we still maintain our
culture and our heritage.

For instance, we work eight or nine hours as the
non-Indian expects us to do, but in the evenings we
have our singing, our dances, and we speak in our own
language.  So don't forget that we are still basically
Indian, even though we are here.

Now to get to the Indian land situation:  The Indian
has always thought that the land is a sacred duty: that
everything relates one to the other--the moon, the
stars, the sun that shines.  We pray for these things
to exist.  But listening to these oil men talk, it
sounds like if they run out of oil here, pretty soon
they will be going to the moon.

The Indian is basically concerned with conservation
and ecology.  We have been preaching this for many
years.  Now we hope that you will finally start to listen to what we have to say.

On my Indian reservation, for instance, we have
thousands of acres of land.  On it there are oil wells
capped which have never been opened, and yet our Indians
dwell in dire poverty there.  And there is also the
Homestake Mine in Lead, South Dakota, the highest gold-
producing mine in the western hemisphere.  Our Indians
live 65 miles south from there in dire poverty.  This
is what the Indian movement is about.  A little justice
along the way.

When you take the treaties, for instance--and the
treaty was the non-Indian's idea; we signed it as an

agreement and tried to live accordingly--those treaties
have been abused and not even mentioned here. Moreover,
this commission did not give many of the Indians notice
of this meeting. The only way we found out about it was
through a rumor or a word from a friend.

Now, what I would like to see on this commission is
an Indian representative to speak for the Indian, so
that you will know what we are about. We are basically
ignored.

The Indian is also concerned about land development.
But we have to maintain some of this benefit for ourselves.

There is a song I hear every night on TV and the
last line of it is: "We crown our good in brotherhood
from sea to shining sea." Let's do it.

*Leopold:* Mrs. Mitchell would like to speak.


SELLING INDIAN LAND

*Mitchell:* I was one of the Indians who got an invitation to the affair today. But I didn't have time to
go to my tribe and ask for the participation of my
tribe, so I am here as an individual. I'm from the
Quinault Tribe on the coast of the State of Washington.

As I said, I received an invitation and although
I'm busy 24 hours a day trying to save the lands of
my tribe, I came down to find out what the commission
was talking about, what it was doing and what effect
this would have on our lands. And I appreciate whoever
is responsible for me being here.

When I was sitting out there and you began talking
about Alaska, I felt that I would be very much out of
my element, although I have sat in national meetings
before and listened to the Alaska Natives, and I do
know a little bit about their situation. But I can

relate to you that I certainly hope that the same thing
doesn't happen to them that happened to us.

For years our lands were contracted out and sold to
large timber interests, and it appeared to me that we
weren't going to have a Quinault Reservation if someone
didn't do something about it. The sale of our timber
to private timber interests, I feel, was totally unjus-
tified. I think they could have sold the product without giving up our lands.

So, after I reviewed the situation and it appeared
that our lands were going faster than we could stand,
I decided to try and find out if an Indian could actually log the timber on the reservation and save the
land for the tribe and exist. It's been rough, real
rough, but we did stop the land sales.

## Resisting Materialism

One of our greatest difficulties is that our culture is so different from the rest of the country.
Our Indians are not materialistic, and when an outside
interest comes in, we are totally defenseless against
it. The people, my people, have resisted the dollar
value as being the uppermost thing in life. One of
our problems is, "How do we recover the lands lost?"

Just in the past session--and I haven't the exact
quotes--I understand a senator, in discussing the return of the Blue Lake lands to the Taos Pueblo Indians
in New Mexico, stated that he felt that this was not a
good idea because Indians did not know how to use the
land. The Taos Pueblo people, if you have ever actually
watched them in operation, live the right life, and they
want this land for religious purposes, not to exploit
it.

The Indian Claims Act was supposed to be designed
to give Indians compensation for the land that they
gave up to the rest of the country. But, as the

gentleman said, we got 40 cents an acre. I would like to see some legislation that would give us our lands back at 40 cents an acre. Until we control all of our land within the boundaries of our reservations, it's going to be a total wasteland.

## Zoning for the Reservation

Our tribe proposed zoning ordinances for the Quinault Reservation. At that time there was a question over state jurisdiction on Indian reservations in Washington. So as one of the provisions for passing our zoning ordinance, the Secretary of the Interior asked that the county pass the same zoning ordinance so that there wouldn't be a conflict between state and federal law on the reservation. As a result, the county declined to pass our zoning ordinance, because they said they don't have jurisdiction over our land, which is true. They don't have jurisdiction over Indian trust land within the boundary. As I understand your zoning regulations, you cannot spot zone; in other words, you can't just zone the lands that have been alienated within our boundaries. So since you can't zone our lands and we can't zone your lands, we have no zoning in this area. This is a situation I fear, because our people want to protect those lands for their natural qualities; this is a way of life to our people.

So we have many problems, and I could stand here and talk to you until tomorrow and we wouldn't even touch on them. But to express the same thing that the rest of the Indians have said, since we were the originators of the totem pole, it's rather difficult to accept being low man on that totem pole.

## DISCUSSION WITH THE AUDIENCE

*Leopold:* Time is slipping by and I would like to open this panel for questions from the floor or comments.

*A Member of the Audience:* Somebody touched upon the freeze on land in Alaska, and I would like to know what the implications of the lifting of the freeze would be and what lands it could affect.

## THE FREEZE: TO LIFT OR EXTEND?

*Borbridge:* The situation at the present time is this: The freeze, previously due to expire on December 31, 1970 has been extended to June 30, 1971, which means, in effect, that this is a timetable that has been set up for land claims action.

I might add that had there not been an extension of the freeze, the Alaska Natives were preparing to take the whole situation into the courts to protect their rights. The order itself pertains to the restrictions put on the future change in status of any of the public lands in Alaska. This means, in effect, that since we have slightly in excess of 5 million acres which have been patented to the state and slightly in excess of 8.5 million acres which have been tentatively approved, that pending either the resolution of the claims or the end of the newly extended freeze, there will be no further change in status. Thus no further selections will take place.

The state itself has presently selected, I believe, over 12 million acres, but again this has to go through the process of legal publication and other matters which would put it into the status of tentatively approved.

*Leopold:* Another question?

## Pipelines and Roads

*Barry:* I'm Frank Barry of the University of Oregon. I have a question for Mr. Guess: If the Alaska land freeze is lifted, in your opinion, will the State of

Alaska select the route of roads and pipeline right-of-way for the construction of the Alaska pipeline?

And then, for Mr. Borbridge, the same question but in respect to the Indians' attitude: If the Natives get a bill passed by Congress to their satisfaction, will they agree to the construction of the pipeline from Prudhoe Bay to Valdez, Alaska?

*Guess:* I would say that the past administration would have probably selected the pipeline route and the road route. The new administration was just sworn in about two hours ago, and I don't know what its policy is going to be. I would speculate, however, that before it took such a measure it would confer with the various Native organizations as well as the legislature. So I would not expect any rapid action in that area, Mr. Barry.

*Borbridge:* I think that describes much of what we consider to be the basic facts. The Natives have obviously been well aware that the question of the pipeline for the extraction of the natural resources has lent a pressure point which has been very helpful. Since we have waited over a hundred years, we frankly doubt that without the dramatic discovery of oil and the desire of the state to select lands, we would be receiving this much attention at the present time.

As to the pipeline route, the attitude of the Natives basically has been that we are quite anxious to see that safeguards, such as the criteria established by the Department of the Interior and demanded as a prerequisite to approval, are forthcoming. Likewise, we are concerned that we be sufficiently informed so that such important factors as the subsistence hunting and fishing--more precisely, the migration pattern of the caribou--can be guaranteed and safeguarded in some way. We have seen some attention given to these concerns through, for example, plans for elevated ramps or raising the pipeline in areas where there are large herds of caribou.

## An Equal Basis with Developers

Another thing that the Natives have been concerned about is the opportunity for the owners of the land to deal on a basis of equality with the developers of the land. In regard to the mechanics of oil extraction, we are not prepared to agree that there should be a token force of Natives, for example, working in the industry.

We feel further that this is an ideal opportunity, once the safeguard conditions have been mutually agreed to, for the Natives themselves to enter into some specific developmental or allied activities relating to the oil companies. In other words, we just don't foresee that there will be a pipeline running across our land without our being involved in every step of the way from the guaranteeing of safeguards to the environment to the construction of the pipeline.

*Guess:* I would like to add that if the land freeze were lifted tomorrow, I doubt seriously if the state could survive an immediate injunction in that particula: situation. There is a grave question as to whether the} would have rights, or whether their rights would supersede those rights reserved for Native Alaskans.

*Leopold:* Another question. Yes, sir.


### HOW MANY ACRES FOR NATIVES?

*Dixon:* My name is Dixon, and I am from Alaska. I would like to address this question to Joe FitzGerald. Befor you went to work for the Atlantic Richfield Oil Company you were head of the Federal Field Committee in Alaska, which under your direction published a report on Alaska Native lands that is one of the most comprehensive book ever published in that field. I believe it recommended that the Natives be given 4 to 5 million acres of land in fee title.

Could you explain the disparity between that and the 40 million acres that the Natives are asking and the 10 million acres that the Senate is offering in their bill?

*FitzGerald:* I can only speak for myself. Let's go back to when we wrote the book. At that point we didn't know what the attitude of Congress might be, but as far as we could see, there was a need for two things. There was a need for substantial sums of money and there was a need for land that would protect the homes, fishing sites and hunting sites of the natives and also provide hunting areas on their particular campsites.

We also recognized the great trade-off between money and land in this area; that Congress might, for example, go more towards land than money, or more towards money than land, so we specifically spelled it out in those terms in our proposals to Congress, which were separate from the large book.

## Land or Money

As far as I am concerned, the Senate is well within the parameters that we set for it. We tried to indicate to them the areas where flexibility existed in a way which would advance the cause without doing any damage. It may well be this Congress will increase the number of acres. I think that we all have different attitudes, and I think the Native people see land a little differently than I do. I see money as one of the more important things, because I feel so strongly that one of the failures of the BIA [Bureau of Indian Affairs] is that it has done things on behalf of Native peoples rather than aiding them to do things themselves. And the only way to break this cycle is to give them large sums of money under their own administration to develop their own institutions.

So my fixation was probably a little different than some other people's fixation, but I think that the land

claim today is in good shape. I think we are within
striking distance of getting a settlement. The state
itself has indicated its flexibility, and that's really
the moving point that we needed. I think the Native
people themselves wish to settle it. All the rest of
us in Alaska who are responsible citizens wish to settle
it. And I think when it is settled, it's not only going
to be good for the Native people, but all the rest of us
as well.

## The Generous Government

*Rogers:* Well, I can hardly agree with that. As the
man from Alaska pointed out before, they are not going
to go anywhere with the land, and you can bet those
resources and values will still be there when the rest
of the earth becomes a dumping ground. The Indians
have preserved the area and this is their reward in the
end. The government is so generous about making land
available for Indian people that out of 365 million
acres in Alaska, after having lived there for thousands
of years, under government control the Indian is only
entitled to 10 million acres. They couldn't give them
the 40 million they are willing to settle for, yet we
can go to foreign countries and tell them how to run
their country, which costs our country in blood and
youth and astronomical expense. Yet we don't even
think enough about the Native Americans to really do
justice.

The time has come, and we are crying out. We are
not interested in just us; we are interested in justice.

*Leopold:* Any more questions? Way in the back, sir.

### THE QUESTION OF RESERVATIONS

*Collins:* I think one short statement is in order. I'm
a lawyer. My name is Richard Collins. I have represented Indians for several years.

If one reads the Public Land Law Review Commission's report, it seems not to have any significant impact on Indian rights. But that is not true. It has some very important impacts, although they are hidden underneath the table.

*Leopold:* I thought the Indian reservations were specifically excluded from the charge by the commission.

*Collins:* That's true. They were specifically omitted from the jurisdiction of the commission, and the commission has only transgressed on that limitation once and in a relatively minor manner. There is one report published by one of the subsidiaries of the commission-- not a commission report itself, I will grant--which recommends that jurisdiction on Indian reservations be turned over to the states in certain areas. It recommends this specifically. This is a Navajo Reservation on the recommendation of the Bureau of Indian Affairs. It is a matter of vital concern to Indian people and they weren't consulted.

Now, admittedly, it's not a commission report, but I think that could be lost sight of. That report could be cited as a staff report, or whatever you want, of the Land Law Review Commission. In many people's minds, it's going to have the imprimatur of the official commission, even if it doesn't represent the views of the commission. That report was based on evidence given by the Bureau of Indian Affairs officials, not upon the views of the Indian people themselves. Were those recommendations to be followed, you would have a large number of very angry Indians, to say the least.

That's the only case where that limitation of dealing with the reservations themselves was directly violated. However, there are a number of other recommendations in the report that have important impact on Indians. One, of course, is the recommendation that the allotment laws be abolished. That has already been mentioned. Indian opposition to that has already been mentioned.

## Grazing, Hunting and Fishing

Another example is the recommendation concerning grazing leases. The present practice in the public lands is essentially a low-cost lease to grazing interests, lower than the market would bear if it were a free market. This has an important bearing on Indians in South Dakota and other states where a lot of their lands are leased out by the Bureau of Indian Affairs for grazing. They suffer from depressed prices because of the competition of subsidized public land alongside their reservations. They don't get market return for leases of their lands. In many cases, and especially in the Dakotas, this is the only source of income for some families, and when they are getting a dollar an acre a year for a lease, it doesn't go very far toward feeding the families.

## Federal v. State Jurisdiction for Off-Reservation Rights

Another example is the report's recommendation that certain areas of the public land, where there is now exclusively federal jurisdiction, be turned over to state jurisdiction. In some of those areas, there are tremendous rights of Indians to hunt and fish. These are not on the reservations. They are called "off-reservation rights" in the Northwest and in Alaska. These rights are extremely important to the Indian people who hold them, and the Indian people have learned the hard way that state fish and game authorities have a great deal less respect for their rights than federal authorities. So they have a strong interest in not having jurisdictions ceded to the states in some of those areas, but again, their interests are not represented or even discussed in the commission's reports and findings.

I think I have outlined the high points of how the issues that the commission is dealing with will affect the substantial rights of Native Americans.

*Leopold:* Thank you very much for that informative contribution to our discussion.

I think there can be no doubt in any of our minds that, irrespective of what the limitations might have been in the charge to the commission by the Congress, the problem of Native people's lands cannot really be separated from the specific areas that the commission covered.

Another question?

## MINING LEASES AND CLAIMS

*Parks:* Alan Parks is my name.

Since Alaska is trying to develop an economic base, and has yet to be involved in large mineral exploitation and also has a land freeze on, this would seem to me to be an ideal time to take advantage of some of the recommendations of leasing.

Has the state taken the lead and gone towards this direction, or are they going to sit back with the old claim situation?

*Leopold:* Let me clarify that question. Are you talking about mining leases?

*Parks:* Primarily mining leases and mining claims.

*Guess:* In the area of oil and gas we have a firmly competitive system, and in the mining area, the state government has not taken any action. The legislature, through the legislative counsel, has under study an analysis of the Alaska mining law with an eye to attempting to modernize it. Hopefully the study will be completed during the next session, which starts January 11. I would agree with you in your analysis.

*Rogers:*  I think it's important to add that the state system for minerals, other than oil and gas, does differ from the federal one in two ways.  The state, by our constitution, will not allow the rights to the land to pass in a patenting system or a fee simple title system to a private landholder.  Only the minerals themselves are leased to the developer.  I think that's a crucial difference.

### SERVING AND MAINTAINING THE PIPELINE

*Crutchfield:*  I would like to address a quick question to either Joe FitzGerald or Bob Weeden.

It seems to me there has been little attention to one of the greatest potential dangers to the Alaskan environment.  This involves the pipeline, not in the line itself or its direct effects but the fact that access must be provided for service and maintenance of the line.  And the effects of access to that particular part of Alaska through careless hunting, careless mineral exploration, all of the damn kinds of carelessness that we are capable of, can even in very, very limited ventures take very long periods of time to recognize.

Is it possible to provide the necessary access but also the necessary control over that access so that uncontrolled spilling out of people into the northern part of Alaska can be prevented?

## Access and Control

*Leopold:*  Rather than relay that question, let me give my impression of the issue.

I had a meeting with George Collins and others set up a month or two ago at White Horse.  We were talking there with the oil line people from both our own interests in the United States and those in the MacKenzie

Delta and with the Crow Indians and the other conservation groups and the government groups. These issues bother everybody. Obviously, if you are going to find a way to extract oil, there is going to be an access. There is no way around it. You have to have maintenance of pipeline and, even if it's done by helicopter, it's access of a sort. And moreover, you can't lay a pipeline by helicopter; they are going to have to build a road.

This imposes, then, upon the government, local and federal, a regulatory responsibility to see that this is not abused. Now, we do have a prototype of that. Roads can be built even in our dedicated wilderness. This is certainly very much in the minds of the people who are going to administer this country after the pipeline is installed. Such regulations will indeed be necessary at both the state and the federal levels. It is not going to be easy.

I am afraid that we have run out of time.

## A Last Word

*Borbridge:* Just a very brief comment, because I know you are going to have to leave.

One is for the record to express the opposition of the Alaska Federation of Natives to the termination of the Allotment Act.

Second, at the beginning of this panel, we said we were kind of laying it on the line and depending on you to hear us out. This you did, and I wish to thank the panel members, the moderator, and those who did give us an opportunity to express our views. This is what makes, in the end, a successful conference.

Thank you very much.

# PART FIVE

# Administration of the Public Lands

# ADMINISTRATION OF FEDERAL LANDS

## Charles H. Stoddard

*Resource Consultant, Duluth*

A great deal has been written about public administration and a lot more about various aspects of land management, yet satisfactory organizational structures and effective administration seem as elusive as ever.

## WHAT WE HAVE LEARNED

Ordinarily land administration and management essentially means managing people's use of the land--hopefully so that it sustains a steady yield of raw materials and services without depletion of the resource base. To do this, we employ an increasingly complex technology to manage the land and an equally complex social psychology to handle the people in the large organizations who control the public's use of the land's resources. It is important to remind ourselves that the people in so-called land managing agencies are not the direct users of the land; they do no logging, grazing of livestock, mineral extraction and too little recreating.

## A Safety Valve

The public lands of the United States are coming to serve as a safety valve for millions of urban people. They provide a form of diversity as well as escape to freedom from the monotony of city life and routine jobs and in addition are a source of many kinds of raw materials, valuable yields of water, homes for fish and wildlife and numerous other benefits. Whether they will continue to provide these useful yields depends in large measure upon

how well we, as a society, use the social sciences to
apply what we have learned from the natural sciences.

My paper today will make an effort to review something of what we have learned about public land administration up to this point in history, particularly as
revealed in, but not limited to, the studies of the
Public Land Law Review Commission.

Frederick Jackson Turner pronounced the year 1890
the end of the frontier as a force in American life.
But until now we have maintained a frontier "growth"
psychology. For the past 80 years the momentum of
onward and upward, of expansion, of opportunity, of
bigger, better and more production, of greater economic
efficiency, has continued to be our national goal. Even
as recently as 1961 President John F. Kennedy called his
administration "The New Frontier." Most economists are
still seeking the elusive pot of gold in an endless national economic growth--for bigger and better materialisr
and the great benefits derived from a multiplicity of
necessities and gadgetry, without consideration of the
social and environmental costs.

## Social Earthquakes

There is more than skimpy evidence to indicate
that the great social earthquakes that are taking place
in our civilization today are the result of a sudden--
almost too sudden--slowing down of our 300-year plunge
forward of economic conquest. We haven't learned to
live and be satisfied with what we have. Within only
the past few months some have come to realize that growtl
in itself is not a stable goal for a society, nor will
it end in the civilized relationship between men and
nations, nor between men and their natural environment
that we really seek. Furthermore, we have abruptly realized that three centuries of economic and technological
development have laid waste such great portions of our
fragile planet that our very biosphere is threatened.

Fortunately, in the midst of or the latter part of its studies, the Public Land Law Review Commission became aware that its responsibility was to the natural environment as well as to the political economy. It was a recognition of transition--albeit belated--and because the trend of environmental concern has swept the country so suddenly, the commission cannot be blamed for not supplying all the answers. One responsibility we have here today is to pick up where *One Third of the Nation's Land* stopped nearly six months ago and provide a much greater ecological input to the consideration of public land problems, policies and decisions.

Yesterday we discussed the whole question of reviewing economic projections, and this is certainly something that should be done and done quite soon, I think, if we are going to get a more realistic look at the future and the demands on the public lands.

PUBLIC LAND OBJECTIVES:   THE RESERVED LANDS

The first great period of concern over the environment took place in the late 1890s following the post-Civil War public land exploitation in the "Lake states" pineries. It gave impetus to rescuing western public lands from a similar fate. The damage wrought by logging and forest fires in northern states led to the forest reserve system for watershed protection and for the provision of future timber supplies. That future, incidentally, is right now if we examine the source of much of our timber production.

To preserve wildlife from further decimation by overkill due to poaching and inadequate game laws, national wildlife refuges were established in many areas. National parks were originally instituted to secure for public use our great scenic treasures--more recently to provide public recreation and scenery on lands less spectacular but close to urban centers.

## The Symbols

Thus a long history of well-defined political movements with quite specific social objectives has governed and influenced the administration and management of these reserved public lands under tenure systems secured by law. They are distinguished in the public mind by the conventional symbolism associated with permanently well-managed public lands--defined boundaries, entrance signs, blocked units in colors on maps, resource management plans, an adequate staff of managers headed by a district ranger or superintendent, congressional budget support and wide public recognition. The fact that we have these lands is a tribute to the foresight of our forebears who had the courage to stand up to the short-sighted land grabbers and exploiters of their day.

## Challenge to National Forests

It is unfortunate that of this triumvirate of reasonably well-administered lands the Public Land Law Review Commission chose to challenge the national forest system in several ways--almost to the point of jeopardizing 70 years of hard-won conservation gains. That it did so first by questioning the method of withdrawing national forest land from the public domain and then by recommending that commercial forest land be zoned into dominant use areas for timber production instead of multiple use is an unfortunate fact. The first failed to recognize the foresighted statesmanship of the Clevelands, Roosevelts and Pinchots and the benefits we today are reaping from their foresight. The second, which would build in a procedure for forced liquidation followed by monocultural forestry, appears to be simple retaliatory action against the wilderness area setasides. The Public Land Law Review Commission did not seem to be aware of the fact that multiple uses are really dictated by the natural combination of resources found in any area and not by legislative or administrative fiat. A system of multiple use can also be a method of balancing one pressure group against the other!

I shall not dwell on these challenges to the integrity of our reserved public lands because I do not believe the political mood of the American people will permit any threatening recommendations to go into effect. The goals and objectives for these reserved lands have stood and will continue to stand the test of time.

## THE RESIDUAL PUBLIC DOMAIN: THE NEED FOR STABILITY AND CONTINUITY

The public domain lands, however, are another matter. The much larger area of 450 million acres of undedicated public domain lands poses a very serious challenge for immediate solution. These lands have never had a clear charter either for long-term management or for disposal. They still don't. There is a first set of goals that we still need to establish. These lands have been suspended between retention laws, including some (but not enough) management authority and laws authorizing disposition, for scores of years. Management, due to the uncertainty of tenure (scrambled land pattern, in effect) and lack of policy continuity, has been inadequate and has led to resource deterioration and ineffective administration. The Public Land Law Review Commission recognized that the great era of disposal was over and wisely suggested that land use planning was needed to determine which lands would fit which disposal or retention classification, but then made the serious omission of not spelling out planning objectives. (Planning land use without stability of tenure or continuity of management is an exercise in futility.)

This was done in spite of the fact that nearly seven years of careful application of the temporary 1964 Classification and Multiple Use Act (C & M U Act) gave guidelines for classifying tracts fitting disposal or retention categories. Criticism of the C & M U Act is abundant in the commission's report, but the Public Land Law Review Commission would have made a better case if it had evaluated through careful analyses the useful

242

experience gained by the Bureau of Land Management's application of it. Rarely, if ever, has a study commission had the benefit of a "going" experiment--an experiment concurrent with a study providing an opportunity to observe and weigh the results and determine their usefulness in solving the problems before the commission. The fact that it did not do so lends its criticisms of BLM's application of the act much less weight.

## Three Land Categories

During this period BLM--following specific instructions of the Congress--developed careful planning criteria, made field investigations and held hundreds of local meetings to obtain viewpoints and involvement of those directly affected before any classifications were made. Here is one area where there has been participation by the people directly affected by the decisions of the big federal government, and it is hardly mentioned as an uncomfortable fact by the PLLRC. Out of this process three major categories of land emerged:

1. *Scattered*--fragmented tracts not suitable for federal management and administration. Some of these acres logically belong with adjacent private lands, some are needed for community expansion and some for locally administered parks and open space.

2. *Intermingled*--federal with state and private lands, amounting to around half the area with no distinct land pattern. Railroad checkerboard grant lands (as with O & C lands in western Oregon) are one example of this pattern. Some of the lands in the eastern Montana Valleys, where bottom lands were homesteaded and the pine ridges left in public domain, are another example.

3. *Larger, solid blocks*--more remote lands (much greater in total acreage than the others), with a variety of uses taking place, running the gamut from

grazing and forestry, watershed cover, wildlife habitat
and rock hounding to mining or oil shale exploitation.

## A History of Opposition to Disposal of Lands

It is significant to observe that at local public
meetings held by the BLM, there was almost unanimous
opposition to disposal of these larger tracts and many
of the smaller ones. No group of users wanted to·grant
the right of exclusive ownership or single use to other
users! Thus, the concept of multiple use has arisen,
not out of a carefully drawn system of mixed land management, but rather as a practical response to the experience of accommodating a variety of users who are
willing to share their use of the land but not surrender
it.

Having recognized this fact in opposing further
large-scale disposal, it is paradoxical that the commission, instead of supporting multiple use, proposes the
granting of exclusive dominant use to an especially
privileged few users. This is tantamount to providing
private rights in public lands in lieu of sale--the
very issue which has been fought long and hard by conservationists since before Bernard DeVoto when he wrote
his famous essays in *Harper's*, "The West Against Itself"
and "Sacred Cows and Public Lands." The experience
gained from the Cooperative Sustained Yield Act of 1944,
which provided for the same dominant-use principle and
has been totally rejected in practice, has been almost
totally ignored by the commission.

Since the application of the C & M U Act has provided a going experiment in land use classification and
planning and a rich experience to draw from, we must do
so and do it rapidly. The new Congress will be looking
for answers.

## POSSIBLE COURSES OF ACTION

In the five years of its existence, the commission authorized a wide variety of studies and held many hearings before it reported its findings to the President ar the Congress. But the commission did not define possib1 alternative goals or directions as guidelines for its policy recommendations. At first glance, the multitude of existing laws and land uses seems to suggest a confusing welter of possible policy directions from which the commission could have chosen. But this need not necessarily be true. As a practical matter, if we look at the lands before we look at the laws, there appear to be only four main possible courses of action open:

1. One alternative advocated by representatives of several user groups is complete disposal of all residual public lands.

2. Another one advanced by some conservationists is retention of all lands.

3. A third course of action would be to continue the existing rudderless, case-by-case drifting and confusion.

4. And a fourth opportunity presents itself in the procedures established by the Congress in 1964 under the Classification and Multiple Use and Public Sale acts: Use the C & M U Act as a land use planning process to determine which blocks should be retained and managed by the U.S. and which should be transferred out of federal ownership for well-defined and properly considered higher usage.

A reasonably clear choice of one of these possible alternatives must be made by the Congress for the 450 million acres in the 12 western states and in Alaska, if the public domain dilemma is to be resolved. But the first goal must be one of settling the uncertainty of tenure and establishing continuity of management for those lands specifically identified for retention.

# A New System for Multiple Use

In one sensible stroke, the new Congress can establish a sound new system of managed public lands, end decades of uncertainty and severe deterioration and firmly establish its own place in conservation history. This approach would be an organic multiple-use omnibus act to accomplish at least the following:

1. Establish a system of national resource lands or conservation areas (comparable to the national forests) out of those public domain lands already classified for retention and multiple use under the Classification and Multiple Use Act of 1964.

2. Authorize the creation of two types of management units:

    a. Large blocks composed both of lands now predominantly federally owned, and

    b. Smaller blocked units which are intermingled lands on which consolidation could take place (especially small watersheds with fragile soil situations).

3. Provide for consolidation of blocks by exchange and direct acquisition of lands classified for retention. Establish special fund from lands sold for purchase of tracts within blocked units.

4. Follow the Public Land Law Review Commission's recommendations by repealing the Homestead, Desert Land, Small Tract and a variety of outdated disposal laws. The Taylor Grazing Act should be amended to provide for multiple-use advisory boards.

5. In addition, repeal the unadministerable and environmentally devastating Mining Act of 1872 and place all "hard rock" minerals under the Mineral Leasing Act of 1920. (Preference rights should not be given to holders of exploration permits.) Amend the royalty

allocations for oil shale to place full revenue in the
federal treasury. (Under the present law 52½ percent
of the revenue from the Mineral Leasing Act goes into
the reclamation fund.) An estimated $300 billion worth
of oil shale lies up the Colorado Green River Basin.
That formula would provide enough money to build a dam
in every gulch in the West. And don't think this is a
significant national priority. It is unfortunate that
the Public Land Law Review Commission failed to recognize or mention this fact. The Congress needs to recognize it and to act quite rapidly on a revision of this
formula before any oil shale is leased under either the
proposal of the commission or any other.

6. Amend all existing revenue allocation provisions
by eliminating all earmarking and special funding; put
all revenue into the federal treasury and provide for
payments by the federal government to local governments
in lieu of property taxes. This seems particularly urgent because of the grossly distorted oil shale situation.

7. For lands classified for disposal, enact legislation to give priority to public uses such as open
space and public buildings, and require that a complete
land use plan backed up by zoning ordinances be fully
in effect before any federal lands are disposed of. A
reversion clause is needed for enforcement.

8. Oil shale--To protect environmental quality of
upper Colorado watershed, prohibit development of oil
shale on federal lands until an underground (in situ)
process has been developed as a substitute for the
environmentally damaging strip mining-retort methods.

## Ending Uncertainty

These positive measures will put an end to the
nagging uncertainty that has inhibited effective and
stable conservation of the public domain and provide the
continuity of tenure necessary to guarantee stability

of management. Without stability of tenure, continuity
of public management is threatened regularly by nagging
raids of commercial promoters actively supported by
their captive political pressure groups.

Some of these suggestions are contained in the
report of the commission. What I have tried to do here
is to gather up those which tend to advance the long-term
public interest by getting these lands secured, and to
clear up hoary obstructions and point them toward a goal
in a cohesive, systematic manner, so as to make them
add up to a total advance. This procedure is an effort
to use the mistakes and successes of the past in charting
more effective administration and management of the public lands into the future.

Once the jumble of conflicting laws and policies
has been cleared away and a new system of blocked public
lands created, we turn to the major task of developing
an effective means of administering policies and managing
the resources effectively under these policies.

## THE RELATIONSHIP OF ORGANIZATIONAL
## STRUCTURE TO ADMINISTRATION

Policy goals stated in the law can be attained on
millions of acres only with the organized teamwork of
large numbers of trained people applying the most
advanced resource management techniques. Up to this
point in time the only effective way to harness the
team has been through the establishment of an administrative organization--a bureaucracy, if you will.
Some severe criticisms have been made about large
organizations--and many of them are true--but no one
has come up with a better substitute.

It might be useful to dwell for a few moments on
some of these shortcomings and criticisms because they
directly affect the quality of resource management on
public lands.

Unfortunately, despite the criticism of larger organizations, public administration and political science
thinkers have given precious little thought to the role
of structure--and the anatomy and physiology of the larg
organizations--in the accomplishment of our policy obje
tives. In a society which has depended upon large publi
and private bureaucracies to carry out social reform leg
islation and to produce the material things in the private sector, the functioning of large aggregations of
people into specialized segments deserves far greater
consideration. The facts that so many of our federal
agencies seem to fall far short of their goals or seem
too easily pressured in directions away from the public
interest are a few of the symptoms that all is not well

## Phenomena of Aged Agencies

With the expansion of government, including the
creation of large numbers of agencies established to
perform functions or solve problems defined in the law,
two phenomena seem to develop with age:

1. The assumptions may have changed, with respect
to the nature of the problem upon which the agency's
original program was based.

2. The distance between the agency and the citizen
at large becomes so wide that the only contact with the
political decision-making process is with the chairman
of its congressional committee and the lobbyists from
the special-interest groups that feed on its largesse.

Both situations are unhealthy. One continues
useless programs and agencies which should have long
ago been abolished while the other leads to a self-
perpetuating "professionalism" that insulates the
bureaucracy from public opinion and the democratic
political process. The military, the Atomic Energy
Commission and the federal highway program are our
most egregious examples today. Many others come
readily to mind.

## Bureaucratic Responsiveness

With the maturation of the large administrative agency, a number of fairly standard phenomena begin to appear. I mentioned several specific things here.

But the lack of responsiveness by public agencies to demonstrable public concern--as in the cases of the AEC with nuclear power emission standards, the United States Department of Agriculture with DDT, the U.S. Geological Survey with its lax supervision of oil exploration and extraction--is well known. And the corollary to this, the responsiveness of public agencies to the needs of economic users and powerful pressure groups has been the subject of major and generally valid criticisms which have been supported by considerable telling evidence.

William H. Whyte in *The Organization Man*, threw much insight into the general field, as did Herbert Kaufman in *The Forest Ranger*, Ashley L. Schiff in *Fire and Water*, and Charles A. Reich in *Bureaucracy and the Forests*. There are far too few such studies. But even those we have seem to make few waves of reform.

## Characteristic Problems

It would be interesting to dwell at much greater length on the characteristics of the modern organization, but I fear we would stray too far from the subject at hand. For lack of time, I will briefly touch on a few of these aspects which directly influence land and resource management. Two deserve special mention.

One is the absence of personal responsibility for decisions on policy application and the shifting of blame to the central office or to the "regulations;" a second is the frequent transfer of key field resource managers. Both are related; the second makes possible the first, and also results in undermining continuity of management, which is a basic element in resource con- servation. Frequent transfers of land managers robs

them of the sense of personal husbandry which we need
very badly on our land today.

And finally, one of the most difficult problems is
the internecine competition which exists between agencies
of comparable missions.

## NEEDED STRUCTURAL CHANGES

I have deliberately made these observations on the
general nature of large organizations because the Public
Land Law Review Commission report exhibits a degree of
frustration over existing agency arrangements and suggests significant changes.  The commission wisely
observes that any "organization must be viewed in terms
of how well it serves the public, rather than how well
it serves the agencies."

At this point an enumeration of the key reasons for
a reorganization of resource agencies is appropriate.
Present divisions have no logical justification, and I
am just going to skim them.

Lacking any central responsibility at the cabinet
level for resources policy and management, the Bureau
of the Budget has assumed the role of coordinator and
arbiter between the various agencies.  Probably in no
other area of federal government does the Bureau of the
Budget possess as much power as in the natural resources
field.

## Federal Organization of Resource Activities

Federal organization of resource activities is in
sharp contrast to the organization of those states with
well-coordinated conservation programs.  There are successful organizational structures at the state level
where this consolidation has taken place.  I say "successful" where there's accountability, the governor has
policy control and there's coordination between the

specialized segments that can't be attained by having
the functional agencies divided up and scattered around
in the government.

Federal organization of resource activities is
also in sharp contrast to the organization of other
major federal programs. Every other sector of federal
responsibility, e.g., labor, agriculture, commerce,
health, welfare, foreign affairs, is assigned to a
single governmental department, which is publicly understood to have central accountability. These unified
centers of authority can give citizens a sense of where
responsibility lies and a central focus for citizen support or effort. Present complexity leaves the knowledge
of where these agencies are and what they do to only a
few experts and lobbyists who have mastered the laby-
rinth.

## Proposal for Change

The Public Land Law Review Commission makes a
number of suggestions for organizational and structural
change. The most significant: transfer the Forest Service to the U.S. Department of the Interior and convert
the combination into a Department of Natural Resources.
This is a beginning.

Solid reasons are given by the commission in support
of this proposal which has been floating around in one
way or another since the days of Harold Ickes and the
first Hoover Commission on reorganization of the executive branch. Although centralizing responsibilities for
resources policy under one cabinet secretary brings many
advantages, merger must be supplemented with internal
revisions to result in improved land management. Unfortunately, specific internal rearrangements (such as
transfer of the U.S. Geological Survey's conservation
division to the Bureau of Land Management) are not proposed, nor are any leads given as to what direction they
might take, except for suggesting consolidated regional

administration. Specific internal structural reorganization must be focused on goal accomplishment if administration and management programs are to effectively
fulfill the new responsibilities being placed upon them.

## RESOURCES MANAGEMENT FUNCTIONS

Until now we have dealt with the preliminaries
leading up to the administration of resources management functions, our assigned topic.

In the past, reorganization has tended to involve
juggling of functions without adequate attention to the
basic goal of coordinated land-resource management. We
have unsystematically carved up the landscape--in which
there is ecological unity--among disunified agencies and
with specialized goals such as recreation, wildlife or
forestry.

## A Unified Management Plan

Any effort to combine land management agencies
should be accompanied by a unified management plan for
a unit of geography as it is found in nature--a watershed, for example. Then and only then can a rational
administrative situation be built to carry out an effective management plan. Specialized goals and values can
be recognized in the management plan for portions of the
area, such as outstanding scenery, key wildlife habitat,
watershed yields, timber output--in other words, multiple
values but not necessarily multiple uses on each acre.
Nor should dominant, exclusive, dedicated uses be or-
dained either, except where a human developmental activity, such as a new town, would alter irrevocably the
natural quality of the landscape.

The main value found in a comprehensive resource
management plan is that it can provide a common focus
and a common denominator for all the appropriate

specialized professionals, specialized agencies and specialized uses. Agency jurisdictional lines will not be completely erased, but their management will fit into the ecological system along natural lines rather than artificial lines. Each discipline can make its appropriate contribution in consonance with all of the others, rather than through its special set of blinders. Thus foresters must practice forestry which does not disturb watershed cover or offend scenic quality, but does improve wildlife habitat. Mineral exploration and development will minimize damage and restore surface disturbances which affect the quality of the watersheds. Outdoor recreation planners will reserve some natural areas undisturbed from intensive human trampling by *not* building campgrounds.

Many other examples suggest themselves, if the area to be planned is objectively examined--not for what goods and services can be gouged out of it, but, rather, for conserving the basic resource productivity and natural quality while fitting man's uses into it, without damaging impacts. By this procedure, genuine interagency and interdisciplinary planning can be substituted for the existing "boundary wars" and "bargain table" negotiations which describe current interagency relationships.

## Unnecessary Problems

With the proper application of scientifically developed technology to forests, soils, wildlife and fish, scenic and recreational resources and to mineral extraction, there need not be any major environmental problems in the management of our natural resources. If there are, it is because we've consciously failed to use known methodology in order to increase private profits or federal revenues--an unnecessary function for public lands.

Public outcry over clear-cutting in national forests, overgrazing in the public domain and damaging

surface mining developments present widespread evidence
that we are not applying what we know to be technically
possible, nor are we practicing true multiple-use management. Public resource managers are accused of yielding
to the pressures of user groups who say sophisticated
conservation techniques are economically impracticable.

A highly valuable and most revealing contribution
of the Public Land Law Review Commission could have been
a qualitative and quantitative probe into the extent of
resource overexploitation. This was not done, nor was
the adequacy of presently used conservation practices
evaluated, despite the fact that there are serious publi(
criticisms abroad in the land and lawsuits under way in
the courts. Fortunately, at the last minute the commission did contract a special environmental impact study
which documented in chart form the many kinds of use
impacts on the public lands and the corrective measures
needed to mitigate them.

Effective application  of conservation measures on
the public lands not only requires technological practices for control of uses, but substantial capital investments to restore overgrazed range lands, eroded frai
watershed lands, unstocked and understocked forest areas
and land damaged by the mining and petroleum industry.
Several billion dollars would only begin to build back
destroyed productivity, and I am pleased to see that the
Public Land Law Review Commission did recognize this nee(
for capital investment.

## Why Have We Failed?

But this is only a part of the problem.  Another
deficiency lies in our failure to apply what those men
already knew.  Public forests, range lands, mineral
developments should be models in resource management
that should and can be the unified goal toward which we
should rededicate our public land management efforts.
Where and why have we fallen so far below our ideal
model?  That we have done so, there can be little doubt:

Santa Barbara oil spills, overgrazed range, slashing road systems, extensive clear-cuttings, pipeline and strip mine damage to watersheds, are all too common environmental "crunches" under present management-- and all are receiving heavy public criticism.

Yet the average American citizen has come to expect that the integration and application of these techniques would be of the highest order on federal lands. Much research and experimentation has gone into their perfection. The federal lands are assumed to be free of the economic pressures--property taxes, interest on mortgages, and other overhead costs--which often press private owners into resource exploitation. We have the knowledge to use but we are not translating it into action on the ground.

There are very clear reasons for this. I will skip over them, but they also lie in organized administrative structures. We really haven't organized our administrative and planning functions in our agencies to bring about a full balance of various disciplines that really are necessary in order to bring to bear the techniques that we have on the public lands.

For example, the engineers and timber management people have to have power in deciding what a timber contract will be. The watershed and recreation staff don't get into the act except in a peripheral way. This has led to a considerable part of the trouble. Also, pressure groups exert every effort to ease up on conservation requirements. This is a major problem, because they will not stop at some of the ordinary techniques of direct confrontation, but use many kinds of round-about Machiavellian political techniques to get their way.

## Public Involvement

Earlier in this paper I referred to the widening gap between the public and the administrative agency

with the Congress as the only effective bridge between
the two. To be sure, we have advisory boards in confusing abundance. The Public Land Law Review Commission
could well have devoted much more attention than it did
to advisory boards in particular and public participation
in general. Guidelines are needed for making more effective citizen advice available in place of special-
interest pressure groups.

## ADVISORY BOARDS AS ADMINISTRATIVE ADJUNCTS

I should like to conclude this paper with some suggestions for closing the widening breach between federal
resource agencies and the public. The Public Land Law
Review Commission went into considerable detail in
describing six various "publics" interested in federal
lands; these were: national public; regional public;
federal government as sovereign; federal government as
proprietor; state and local government; and users of
public lands. Each group is described in some detail
except that the latter group is not clearly shown to
be divided between those with a commodity-exploitive
interest and those concerned with conservation of
natural values.

The report makes some interesting suggestions for
improving the advisory board structure as the principal
institution for providing an input into the decision-
making process from the several interested publics--
the central point being the need for broader representation on such boards. There are, however, large questions
over the present structure of these boards which the
commission left unanswered. Yet effective revision of
such boards is essential if they are to escape the charge
of having authority and responsiblity without accountability, or if they are to become truly constructive
sources of public interest input into policymaking, or
if they are to avoid becoming the instrument of special
interests in obtaining their own goals. It will pay to
examine the situation within the Department of the
Interior and review proposals for revision particularly

if major reorganization into a Department of Natural
Resources is to come about.


## SINGLE-INTEREST COMMITTEES

The Department of the Interior is penetrated to a
considerable degree with representatives of groups
whose interests are or may be affected by policies of
the department.  It has been termed a captive of these
groups by some observers.  Probably this is most marked
in the minerals area, particularly in the petroleum
field, but it is by no means confined to minerals.  One
of the forms this penetration takes is in the formation
of advisory committees, of which, compared with other
departments, interior has a large number.  So little
is known about these committees that even their exact
number is uncertain, but there are surely no less than
35 of them in the department.

Most of these advisory committees have members
drawn predominantly or entirely from single-interest
groups.  The National Petroleum Council, for instance,
is composed entirely of oil and gas industry members.
Although the National Advisory Board Council (public
lands) was broadened to include additional members not
directly representative of the livestock industry, this
industry still provides most of the members, and there
is no assurance that many of the new members will take
a point of view different from that of the livestock
industry.  Even such a committee as the Advisory Board
on National Parks, Historic Sites, Buildings and Monuments tends to represent a particular point of view,
although the members have a variety of occupations.

Most of the committees work largely with bureau
officials, although some, especially in the minerals
field, appear to work at the assistant secretarial
level.  The terms of reference of some committees provide that the secretary convene their meetings and that
they advise him.  This seems to be largely a formal
matter, however, since the initiative in calling

meetings and setting the agenda lies with assistant
secretaries or bureau officials, and they handle most
of the working relationships with the committees.

## Relationships Between the Advisory
## Committees and Officials

One of the purposes of these committees is to
foster good relationships between the groups represented
in the committees and officials of the government. To
the extent that this purpose is achieved, family relationships tend to develop between the advisory committees
and the officials with whom they work. Officials inevitably become sensitive to the needs of the groups represented in their advisory committees, and the interest
groups, in turn, support the bureaus in Congress and
within the department. A result is a tendency for
bureau policies to show high regard for special interests
and for bureaus and their special-interest clienteles
to stand together against "outsiders," among whom, on
occasion, may be the secretary himself.

Single-interest advisory committees are simply not
equipped to bring into policy discussions all the considerations that ought to be taken into account. Indeed,
it is their business only to express the point of view
of the interests they represent. Ideally, their advice
should be taken by the officials concerned merely as one
piece of information to be considered along with others
in deciding policy. But probably what actually happens
in most cases is that officials discuss policy with their
advisory committees and reach agreement with them. Such
an agreement, because it was negotiated with some difficulty, constitutes a hardened position not easily changed
from outside without resentment by the parties to the
agreement.

All this is not to say that we can or should dispense with these committees, although there may be a
question as to whether so many separate, specialized
ones are actually required. On the contrary, advisory

committees provide technical information and information on the attitudes of affected groups that is essential to the formulation of policy in a democratic government.

The trick is to use the committees so as to minimize their tendencies to reinforce bureau separatism and harden inadequately considered policy positions and, at the same time, to maximize their contributions to development of policies reflecting a broad public interest.

## Defense Department Approach

This is easier to say than it is to do, but one step that could be taken immediately would be to supplement the existing congeries of single-interest advisory committees with a secretarial-level, multi-interest advisory committee to which single-interest committees might have the relationship of working subcommittees.

Something of this sort has been done in the Department of Defense which prior to 1963 had several dozens of industry advisory committees. The department set up the Defense Industry Advisory Council, composed of 21 members drawn from a variety of defense industries and having varied experience and sufficient stature to be generally recognized and respected in the industry. The aim of the council is to provide the Secretary of Defense and his immediate subordinates with advice from people who know the problems of the defense industry but who do not speak as representatives of particular segments of it.

Although the main industry relations problem of the Department of Defense lies in the relatively simple area of procurement, the advisory council idea may be adaptable to the problems of the Department of the Interior.

## A DEPARTMENTAL NATURAL RESOURCES ADVISORY COUNCIL

The multi-interest advisory council suggested above might be called the Natural Resources Advisory Council. It should be of manageable size, and it should have a membership competent to provide the secretary with advice and support in respect to any policy question he might refer to it, regardless of the question's nature.

The members of the council should not be selected with the expectation that the council will provide the secretary with expert technical advice, since that is already available from existing advisory committees. On the contrary, each council member should be selected for his knowledgeability or sophistication in a broad policy area, for his generally recognized stature in his area of competence, and for his independence of judgment. Of these qualifications, the last is probably most important.

Many of the problems referred to the council would require preliminary study by working subcommittees. Occasionally it might be necessary to set up a special subcommittee from time to time, but for the most part, the existing single-interest advisory committees could be used as working subcommittees and could report to the council through their chairmen--not to the bureaus or assistant secretaries.

## The Importance of a Staff

A staff would be necessary to the success of the council. It should not be large, but it should be large enough and capable enough to identify policy questions that could profitably be referred to the council, to keep track of subcommittee work, and to assist the council in other ways. It should be manned by men independent of economic interest groups: perhaps from university faculties and perhaps on a rotating or temporary basis.

Department regulations require (*Departmental Manual* 308.2 6D.5) that "minutes of each meeting [of an advisory committee] shall be kept which shall contain a summary of the matters discussed and the conclusions reached. The departmental representative shall certify that such minutes are accurate and make arrangements for a copy to be sent to the Office of the Secretary *files*." There is evidence that this requirement is not fully complied with, but even when minutes are filed in the Office of the Secretary, the action is inconsequential because no one has the responsibility for reading them. This is a function that might profitably be assigned to the council staff and if properly carried out might provide a useful instrument for increasing secretarial control of the department.

## Results of a Properly Staffed Council

If a Natural Resources Advisory Council were set up with a small staff, the secretary and the department would have (1) in the beginning, at least, the same advisory committees that exist now; (2) a connection between these committees and the secretary provided by the council staff and by the employment of single-interest advisory committees as working subcommittees of the council; and (3) a broad-gauge council to which the secretary could go for advice and support on matters falling in all the main policy areas of the department.

## CONCLUSION

This paper has been an effort to cover some aspects of public land administration which appear to me to be important but are perhaps not treated elsewhere. It is my feeling that an earth with defined limits and with a fragile ecosystem requires that we make great haste in applying our great choices of technology--not for exploitation--but for careful husbandry of the great public land resource still remaining in our federal custodianship. Adaptation of man's technology to our natural ecosystem calls for an ecotechnology to replace frontier exploitation.

To do this, I am suggesting how we might mold our institutions into more effective relationships between the people in those institutions created for resource administration, the citizens of the United States to whom these lands belong and the natural systems which in the final analysis govern their long-term destruction or conservation.

# PANEL DISCUSSION ON
# THE ADMINISTRATION OF THE PUBLIC LANDS

Moderator:   Ira M. Heyman
             *Professor of Law and City and Regional*
             *Planning*
             *University of California, Berkeley*

Panelists:   Theodore Conn
             *Attorney*
             *Lakeview, Oregon*

             Jeanne O. Nienaber
             *Graduate Student*
             *Department of Political Science*
             *University of California, Berkeley*

             Robert H. Twiss
             *Professor of Environmental Planning*
             *University of California, Berkeley*


*Heyman:*  Our first panelist is an attorney from Lakeview, Oregon, who has been most involved with public land problems--Mr. Theodore Conn.

*Conn:*  I want you to watch this glass of water that I am setting on the lectern.  I am going to talk about it in a minute.  Keep your eyes on it because it's probably the most important thing there is on the face of the earth.


## MULTIPLE USE OR DOMINANT USE

Just a few comments in support of Chuck Stoddard and his discussion of multiple use as it relates to the dominant-use theory.  I think probably there is no other language in the Land Law Review Commission

263

report that has caused as much consternation among lay
people as the words "dominant use." It scares everybody
to death. It scares the recreationists, it scares the
timber people, it scares the folks that are here. And
I am not quite sure that the people who used the language had the background to determine exactly what they
meant by "dominant use," even though they accused those
of us who used "multiple use" down through the years as
being indefinite and uncertain and providing various
meanings to various people.

The multiple-use program was sold to the people
of the western United States after considerable effort.
It certainly didn't mean that you had to apply multiple
use on every acre of land, certainly not in the usual
multiple-use concept that the lay people understood.
They recognized that some areas would be set aside for
parks, some for wildlife reserves, some for wild rivers,
and this didn't do violence to the multiple-use theory.

## Importance of Multiple Use

Actually, there is a great mass of public lands upon
which multiple use, of necessity, is important. We know
that some particular land is watershed land, whether
it's in a national park or wildlife refuge or on the
wild rivers. And it must be managed for that purpose
so that we can continue to live and enjoy our drinks.

There must be flexibility in land management use.
Let's take the illustration of a grove of Douglas fir
timber. Certainly the taking of that wood from that
section of land to build houses is important and will
be done. And at the time the logging operation is
being conducted, certainly there is somewhat of a
single use upon that land. But that lasts only a
relatively short time; the Almighty also put on that
ground some excellent browse for wildlife or livestock,
and certainly they should use it too. If there are
recreation values there, the recreationists should use
it too. By zoning lands into dominant uses and getting

away from this multiple-use idea, it seems to me that
we are very definitely trying to limit these lands and
their uses.

## Taking Water for Granted

Now, there hasn't been enough said about water,
in my opinion, at this conference. The 11 western
states are semiarid areas. Sixty percent of all the
runoff of water occurs in this region, according to
the Land Law Review Commission's report. Billions
of dollars have been spent in developing water for
irrigation, for domestic use and for hydroelectric
power. Yet each of us takes these things for granted.
The Water Conservation Commission, as Mr. Pearl pointed
out, has the very difficult job of considering the
issues relating to that water.

But the doctrine of implied reservation is one of
very grave concern to people who use water for recreation, irrigation, power production, for any number of
reasons.

The commission recognizes that this is a problem.
And they have a recommendation that I think is very
important and should be talked about. This is Recommendation 56. It appears on page 146, and it says:

> The implied reservation doctrine of
> water rights for federally reserved
> lands should be clarified and limited
> by Congress in at least four ways:
> (a) amounts of water claimed, both
> surface and underground, should be
> formally established;

(In other words, what is the government's right? Now,
all the laws of the United States in regard to desert
land and reclamation encourage and, in fact, recognize
as the procedure the prior appropriation doctrine: The
guy that put the waters to beneficial use has the first
right.)

(b) procedures for contesting each
claim should be provided;

(This is public involvement. This is important. This
water is for the people and they should have a right
to examine the claims.)

(c) water requirements for future
reservations should be expressly
reserved; and

(And I think this, again, should be subject to public
examination.)

(d) compensation should be awarded
where interference results with
claims valid under state law before
the decision in *Arizona v. California*.
[which was 1963]

(In other words, at least everybody up until that
time recognized a property right in water, just like
an interest in real property and the right to put it
to an additional use in a good many ways.)

I think these rights are very important to the 11
western states. They should be determined immediately.

*Heyman:* Our second panelist is Jeanne Nienaber, who is
a consultant to the Public Land Law Review Commission,
but her better claim for being here, it seems to me,
is that she is a graduate student in political science
at the University of California at Berkeley, and she
is presently involved in finishing a thesis relevant
to public land management problems.


STUDENT CONCERN FOR THE NATURAL ENVIRONMENT

*Nienaber:* Let me preface my remarks today by saying
that it is indeed a nerve-racking pleasure to appear
before you. It's not often that a student has the

opportunity to address such a distinguished audience, and I appreciate this opportunity. While I claim no special expertise in many of these questions, my comments today will, hopefully, be representative of the under-30 generation which displays great concern for the natural environment. In fact, I don't think it would be an overstatement to say that it is *the* concern of today's student generation. We are genuinely worried about the future of this country and believe we are living on borrowed time.

## The Commodity Orientation

Before addressing myself to the particular area of concern of this panel, which is the administration of the public lands, I would like to say a word about the commission report itself. I was fortunate to have worked closely with the Public Land Law Review Commission, as Professor Heyman mentioned, on the contractual studies, and I wish to acknowledge here that the hard work and dedication that went into the writing of the final report is indeed monumental and sincerely motivated.

But I must say I am in serious disagreement with many of the general assumptions that underlie the report and provide the basis for most of the recommendations. These assumptions were eloquently stated yesterday by Mr. Borbridge and Professor Rogers on the Alaska panel in particular. And I only want to add my voice to their criticism of the commodity orientation that runs through the entire report.

I cannot, for instance, agree that all uses of the public lands be viewed in terms of commodities, or that in most instances use is to be preferred over nonuse. As an aside, I think it's a curious mentality that believes natural areas are not being used if they are not being exploited economically, or that "mineral exploration and development should have a preference over some or all other uses on much of the public

lands." Or, finally, that preservation of the environment in its least disruptive state is an interest that
simply has to be balanced and weighed or bargained over
like any other economic interest on the public lands.
I would submit, rather, that a livable and healthy envi
ronment be accorded the same status as a truly national
or public interest.

## Administration and Management

This question of the public interest, which the report raises but does not satisfactorily resolve, brings
me to comment more specifically on administrative and
management practices on the public lands. The report's
observations in this area include some of the following

First, that, in general, land use planning by feder
al agencies has been rather deficient and haphazard. I
seeks to remedy this unhappy condition principally by
introducing a dominant-use principle to land management
And this dominant-use principle we have talked about a
lot. It's to be applied particularly to national forests and Bureau of Land Management lands.

I don't see any great gains with the dominant-use
principle over a multiple-use concept. It appears to m
to be a rather artificial dichotomy, a cutting up of th
land that is very unnatural and which, according to one
critic, would lead to the lumber interests getting the
timber, the cattlemen getting the grazing land, the oil
industries getting the oil and the general public getting nothing.

Then there is the concept of land use planning,
which the commission says hasn't been used enough in
the federal agencies. I am most familiar with the
Forest Service and the National Park Service, and I
don't think their deficiency is a lack of land use
planning. Plans are abundant in these agencies.

Actually, most of the plans are sabotaged by external circumstances: a lack of appropriation, lack of funds or actions that take place in the private sector over which the agencies have no control. It's really not a question of planning, and it's not a question of dominant use.

## Congressional Control

The second point I'd like to address is a corollary to the first. The report recommends that greater congressional control be introduced in land use planning decisions. Previously certain agencies, notably the Forest Service and the Bureau of Land Management, have enjoyed a rather considerable degree of flexibility and autonomy in deciding how to use the land under their jurisdiction. The report recommends that this autonomy be circumscribed and that Congress--meaning certain committees in Congress--have a greater responsibility in deciding these matters.

I would just like to throw out the question--and this is a political scientist's question: Has Congress had any better record on land management than have the agencies themselves?

## Agency Reorganization

Third, the commission also recommends that a new Department of Natural Resources be created which would merge the Forest Service with the existing agencies within the Interior Department. I'd like to comment on this question of agency reorganization before returning to a brief discussion of the problem of administrative determination of the public interest, inasmuch as I think the final report is very deficient on this question and inasmuch as I think it's a central question.

Mr. Stoddard mentioned in his thought-provoking paper that he favors creation of a new Department of Natural Resources. The report also recommends this as a means for achieving a greater "coordination" of administrative policies. I tend to disagree with this recommendation because I think reorganization schemes are illusory and normally they do not produce any significant changes in policy direction. It looks as though a great deal is going on whereas, in fact, nothing happens.

Moreover, I take rather seriously the argument that limited competition among federal agencies engaged in roughly similar activities is, in fact, a more healthy and genuinely pluralistic condition than any resulting in a merger of functions within a single department.

In other words, while it may appear to many as inherently illogical or untidy that the Forest Service be housed in another department, in actuality I think it results in greater diversity, more opportunity for access and a wider audience for land management questions. Different departments are involved, different congressional committees are likewise involved and, accordingly, somewhat different clienteles are built up around it. To many of us far away from the seat of power in Washington, the federal government already appears far too monolithic, uniform and centralized to take seriously a recommendation for further centralization, or, as it is called in the report, coordination. Coordination is one of those tantalizing phrases like "land use planning," which need only to be voiced to have us nod our heads in agreement. When people talk about these things, they normally don't mean what the words intend. Coordination really means control and centralization of functions, and, incidentally, on this question of reorganization I wonder why the Corps of Engineers, that *bête noire* of federal bureaucracy, was left out of the new Department of Natural Resources. If it is really a question of coordination, I think that many other agencies should be included in this department.

# The Public Interest:   Economic Uses?

In actuality, then, the question of reorganization is rather beside the point in my estimation. The central problem having to do with the administration of federal lands involves policy choices, and I think it can be simply stated:   How can these lands best be administered so they truly serve the public interest and not just local, sectional, narrow or purely economic interests?

While the commission report speaks the language of the public interest, it never rises above the assumption that generally a mix of economic uses on the federal lands is, in fact, in the public interest. Unfortunately, both agencies and Congress have excessively shared this view and pursued policies accordingly. Few people of my generation feel that this is in the public interest or that this is the best way to manage the public lands.

The public interest relates to policies that serve the majority of the people of this country in the long run.   I would never submit that it is an easy matter to determine what is in the public's best interest, or that it would be easy to follow when it's known.   The pressures for opting for a policy of short-run material prosperity are simply too great, and yet, if the administration of the public lands is ever to serve as a model of good management--and that's what we are talking about here today--we have to recognize that the easiest way isn't always the best way.   Therefore, if one takes seriously the environmental crisis which presently faces us, and likewise the concern of the student generation over this crisis, the beginning of a rational land management policy is the realization that one's first concern should be with preserving and not exploiting the environment.

First and foremost in the minds of administrators ought to be:   "Does this policy ultimately endanger the natural balance or natural ecosystem?"   Let me hasten to add that I realize any human use of the land will result in some change or disturbance of the environment. 1 am not arguing that all uses be prohibited on the federal lands, or that they be locked up forever. What I am saying is that I don't think it is beyond our human intelligence to recognize certain limits of disturbance and disruption and manage accordingly.

## Outrageous Policies

Perhaps by citing just a few examples of outrageous land use policy, I can clarify this concept of limits. First, I was recently told by a Park Service official that the Everglades National Park is hanging by a thread, and that where once there were millions of species, there now are thousands. This has nothing to do with mismanagement or lack of planning on the part of the National Park Service. It has to do with the Corps of Engineers scheming together with real estate interests and agricultural interests in the State of Florida to build a canal through central Florida, thereby cutting off the water supply of the park. Talk about land use planning in this sense is irrelevant, because it's really external circumstances out of the control of the Park Service.

Second, the practice of clear-cutting on the national forests, which has been brought up in this conference, is also to be seriously questioned insofar as it destroys watershed, violates scenic beauty and disrupts wildlife habitat. Incidentally, when we were talking about timber cutting yesterday, Mr. Pearl, I believe, said that we have to allow for some resources to come from the public lands. I agree with that, but I don't think it would have been out of place to put in a recommendation that perhaps the resources coming from the public lands should be earmarked for low-income groups or for rebuilding the ghettos. If we are really talking about social goals, a recommendation of that sort would have been very progressive.

Third, the apparent compulsion on the part of land managing agencies to accommodate every type of recreational and economic activity on the public lands ought not to be tolerated. Some uses cannot be tolerated precisely because they result in serious and irreparable damage to the environment.

As I was talking with a forest official the other day, he was concerned with the motorcycle clubs that might want trails in the national forests, and he envisioned the day that there would be problems with having helicopter landing fields on these lands. The problem of limits is real, but I think we have to recognize that in good management there are always limits and that the first and foremost question in management's mind should be the natural environmental system.

*Heyman:* Well, we have a panelist who is going to turn to that. He is Professor Robert Twiss from the University of California at Berkeley, who is a professor in landscape architecture, has done considerable work with the Forest Service in the past, and it was a great pleasure to work with him on the consultant report to the commission on environmental management problems.

## ENVIRONMENTAL MANAGEMENT

*Twiss:* My comments deal with getting on with the job of environmental management and protection of public lands. I think we are all well aware that logging, grazing, highways, home subdivisions on interspersed lands all have environmental impact on our public lands and that things aren't going as well as they ought to. And we would agree that to preserve the environment, we have to get on with the job of environmental management.

## Some Beginnings

The BLM has a brand new planning system which, indeed, enforces the consideration of environmental data at many steps in the planning process. It's a well-designed system, but it must have additional funds and skilled technicians and scientists to implement it, or it's going to be unworkable.

The Forest Service has the largest cadre of scientists and professionals, but they are still generally weak in many environmental fields--engineering, geology, hydrology, soils and plants, community ecology.

There is some cause for optimism. The National Park Service has some natural resource management and protection programs which are excellent, but these are not yet prepared for most of the parks. The BLM has a major proposal for studying the California desert. The Forest Service, which is doing regional planning work in the Lake Tahoe Basin, has taken a further step by calling a moratorium on special-use permits until the regional environmental plan is completed.

Such a moratorium really puts planning into the decision-making process. It supports the concept of the "environmental imperative," which says that when the data are lacking and we are not sure what the environmental effects may be, let's wait until we have adequate studies and planning, and then make rational decisions.

## Recommendations for Goals and Criteria

A number of recommendations of the Public Land Law Review Commission deal with administration of public lands vis-à-vis the environment. But I have seldom heard them discussed in the criticisms of the commission's work or in discussions at this conference thus far. Recommendation 17, dealing with the environmental management, treats the problems of standards. For example, all of the public land management agencies have expressed the goal of maintaining environmental quality. But if the goals are not supported by measurable criteria and standards, then environmental management will likely suffer.

Now, in Recommendation 18 the commission proposes a classification system that is based on environmental capabilities. I think this recognizes the point that land use decisions don't necessarily reflect environmental sensitivity. The system proposed in the report is just another way of trying to assure that environmental sensitivity is included in all major decisions, and if it takes a special classification system to do this, then let us proceed.

Recommendation 20 deals with impact studies and the expectation that the public land agencies will set high standards for "Section 102 statements" under the Environmental Policy Act. The question of whether these statements should become public is certainly in the public eye at this point in time, with the President's decision to withhold impact studies from the public until the decisions are made. That is certainly not the thrust of public involvement in environment management that I would hope for. We need new attempts to bring the public into the process of determining the significance of environmental impacts.

## Needed Research

Recommendation 21 deals with research needed for environmental management. You are probably aware that the geologic surveys were in many instances done years ago for essentially mining purposes. The timber and the vegetation surveys were done primarily for commercial timber management purposes. Soil reports were done for agriculture. The early versions of the National Environmental Policy Act contained a section dealing with a "national environment inventory" but that was deleted prior to enactment. Today we are making million-dollar decisions with two-bit data. We do need better environmental data. The Forest Service, the National Park Service and others have research branches, but these need to be made more environmental in emphasis and to be coordinated on a regional basis. There is very little coordination between the U.S.G.S., Soil Conservation Service and Forest Service inventory programs.

In summary I would point out that, although it may not be necessary to legislate action on all the above points, some progress should be sought. The commission's recommendations in the environmental field are to be well taken and studied by all concerned.

## DISCUSSION WITH THE AUDIENCE

*Heyman:* All right, let's start out. We have our first question. Let me introduce Frank Barry, who is now a professor of law at the University of Oregon and who used to be a solicitor in the Department of the Interior.

*Barry:* I would like to say a word on the position that Miss Nienaber took with respect to the merger of the Forest Service and the Interior Department. We don't hear a great deal about it, although the points that she raised are very important. I am speaking from eight years of work in the Interior Department. Let me give you some examples of what I mean.

### AGENCY COMPETITION

For instance, in the grazing feed area, I am sure in my heart that the issue of gross undervaluation would not have been raised in the public's mind, if it hadn't been for the fact that the Forest Service charge nearly twice as much for an AUM (animal unit per month) as the Department of the Interior did. That discrepanc was obvious to the public and the public knew that

somebody was either getting overcharged or somebody
was getting undercharged.

Another example occurred while we were administering the provisions of the Colorado River storage
project in the upper part of the Colorado River. There
was a provision in the original authorizing legislation
that the Secretary of the Interior was required to
build structures to prevent the flow of water from
Lake Powell into the Rainbow Bridge National Monument.
The Department of the Interior included both the Bureau
of Reclamation and the Park Service. The Park Service
had its own ideas about this, but the decision was
made in private, not in public. Indeed, there couldn't
be any opposition by the Park Service once the Secretary
of the Interior made up his mind. You know, you have
to play on the team.

Now, if the Park Service had been in another agency,
another cabinet member would have been on the firing
line. The fact that the Corps of Engineers was the
outfit that was trying to wreck the Everglades and the
fact that it was in a different department was the
reason that the Interior Department was active in
a public way, so that the public interest was preserved
and a cabinet member was pleading the case to preserve
the Everglades against the interests that the Corps of
Engineers were serving.

It seems to me that this competition is excellent.
I think it's a great idea to have an environmental protection agency but I think it's a big mistake to put
it into a secondary sort of administration where it is
not headed by a cabinet member and is separated from
the decisionmakers. Somebody who is an agency administrator is going to be the one that will make the
trouble, but somebody in the government ought always
to be around to call a halt to some move that is
against the public interest.

I think this is an extremely healthy thing, and I really believe that I come down on the other side of the issue that was presented by Mr. Stoddard. I think it would be a good idea to diversify as much as we can, so that there will be more and more public debate and consideration of issues that have such an important impact on all of us.

*Heyman:* It seems to me there are three issues.

One is that if you have responsibilities in different agencies, then they might well conflict, for instance with respect to a particular development proposal and having both agencies at cabinet level makes for a much more effective debate.

*Barry:* Well, it becomes a public debate. The Park Service didn't have a word to say about the dams in the Grand Canyon except for the Secretary of the Interior. When he heard the argument and made up his mind that there would be dams in the Grand Canyon, the only reason it got stopped was that the Sierra Club had enough gumption to get in and move its exemption.

*Heyman:* Okay, that is one issue. The second one, that Jeanne Nienaber did get to a little bit, is that competition in resource management is a good idea in itself--having two different agencies trying to act effectively. There is some competition between them, and one learns from the other.

The third issue that Jeanne mentioned was that simple reorganization creates a pattern and a set of expectations that our problem has been solved, although it might not be solved at all. I would like Chuck Stoddard to speak to this.

## THE CHAOS OF PLURALISM

*Stoddard:* You haven't convinced me a darn bit. I have
seen the chaos of the so-called pluralism and it "don't
work." Let me say a couple of things.

Frank Barry talked about the public exposure that
competition brings out; this is what you get when you
have a sloppy system of organization and there is no
other way the public can find out. Why not run our
decision-making process so that it is exposed in every
step to the public, rather than run to the Secretary
of the Interior about a dam in the lower Colorado,
and have somebody in the Sierra Club find out about
it at the last minute?

The point is that the American public does not know
where the decisions are made now. They are buried in
the Corps of Engineers or the Federal Power Commission.
This is one of the major problems that the American
public has.

There is no secretary who is a part of the administration or the cabinet who has the responsibility for
coordinating and directing resources policy. Consequently, these agencies can keep hiding from the public,
and all you get is a little bit of internecine warfare,
which is destructive and really doesn't effectively
bring out the public consideration.

Was there another question?

*Barry:* You just asked one. Do I get to answer it?

*Stoddard:* Sure. You've got your last chance.

*Barry:* I don't like smooth-running machines in government. I think there ought to be a lot of monkey
wrenches thrown in the works all the time. I never
saw an instance yet, where when somebody brought things
to a halt that there wasn't an improvement when he got
through. And I think the important issues ought to be

decided on the President's desk, even though every administrator would like to get them delegated down below so that everything runs smoothly and no one ever hears about all the problems that go on about the birds and bees down in the Everglades.

*Stoddard:* I wasn't arguing for decisions; I was arguing for a point of responsibility that the public could go to. And I am arguing that, as decisions are made, they should be exposed to the public at various stages in the process, through hearings, through local advisory boards, through various processes, but not through the endless internecine war which takes place between bureaucracies today.

*Heyman:* Let me say that it's the classic debate between the lawyer with the conflict model and the resource manager with the planning model.

## CLIENTS AND ADMINISTRATORS

*Wood:* My name is Sam Wood. I think that what we need is not necessarily a great monolithic centralization of funding, but rather the same rules of the game affecting all the agencies in the field so that they have to toe the line. But I think that one of the basic problems is that even with consolidation you are not going to cure the client-administrative relationship to which you can credit most of the problems in the field of the environment.

Basically, the administrators of the public lands and the Forest Service are stumping people. They were graduated from the same universities as the timber man. They sympathize and relate to these guys. They want their clients to be successful, the same as the railroad commission wants the railroads to be successful. And being successful means an awful lot of stumping.

And as long as you have that sort of administrative client marriage, you are going to have real problems

with the environment. I think that if there is one
question here that hasn't been faced up to, it is this:
How do you break the dominance of these administrative
agencies by the clients that they serve?

*Heyman:* One of the few ways that I have thought about
is that you urge your students, if you are in the
teaching world, to get to these agencies.

## A Seductive Illusion About Agencies

*Herbert:* I'm Frank Herbert from Seattle. I think a
point that we all ought to address ourselves to in considering the commission's report rests in the seductive
illusion that the appointment of an agency will solve
a problem. And the best way I can describe this is to
tell you something we all know. The worst air pollution
increments added to the lethal atmosphere in the Los
Angeles Basin came during a period when the Los Angeles
Basin had an air pollution control agency.

The presence of an agency with a directive in its
title or in its description implies that something is
"being done about it" and tends to lull a great many
people into the belief that something is actually being
done. It also tends to keep people's attention away
from this arena of activity. Therefore, we need to
discourage the idea that the organization of a super-
agency with great efficiency can solve these monumental
problems while we turn our backs and go about our business. This is a very seductive concept, but very illu-
sionary.

## Endangered Species

*Edmisten:* I am Buela Edmisten from Los Angeles. I was
glad that Professor Twiss brought up the question of
standards. I have been itching to hear some comment
on page 47 of the report. It gives us three possible
standards. Only one seems at all possible to me:

that we should choose the uses of the public lands or the standards of the public lands with the least environmental degradation.

Yesterday I mentioned a criticism of this report. This morning I would like to say there is one point I think is highly significant:  the need to halt this thing called predator control and to give concern for the saving of rare and endangered species on the public land.

And then I'd like to ask a question of Dr. Stoddard. How do we go about getting this ecological input to make it significant?

## WAITING FOR ECOLOGICAL INFORMATION

*Stoddard:*  Well, one of the reasons we have got into the ecological trouble we are in is that we have made decisions for development before we knew what the effect would be.  And I think Bob Twiss's point was that we had better know the effect before we make the decisions. And if we don't know the effect, then we should put off making the decision until we do.  If the decision is such that the development can't be fitted into the needs of the environment, then we had better call the whole thing off.

This, hopefully, is what the Council on Environmental Quality, in their five-point statements, would do.  But there is a question of whether there is going to be enough public exposure.  Now, whether this is outside of the Department of Natural Resources or anywhere else, it really demands public exposure of the decision-making process, and apparently we are not going to get this on these five-point environmental impact statements until the appropriation goes through and then the damage will start.

*Heyman:*  It seems to me that the way you make the kind of principle you are interested in operative is not

just by stating it. I am not criticizing your saying
it, but just saying it isn't enough, and that really
is your point. My own view is that we have to start
building more theory than we have presently with respect
to, if you will, ecological change. What happens if you
do this? What will be the effects? What are the probabilities of effects that are created by doing this kind
of a development at this site, or within this area?

But that is a tremendously expensive job, and we
don't have the science yet. The science is just being
built. We have a little of it, but we really don't have
it in depth; it's very necessary to expend a lot of
money, it seems to me, to build that science.

## Making Information Public

But it also seems to me that once you get that
science you start to integrate your analysis into the
decision-making process. Then allow the fruits of that
analysis to become public so that conservation organizations and the like have real access to that information
in an administrative process. Then at last you can
start to build a case publicly that has real sex appeal.
Because if you can say, here are the probabilities with
respect to the impacts that are going to occur if we do
X, then you really have something to sell. My own view
is that the public will respond affirmatively to that
kind of information packaged well. I think there is a
lot of group activity in the United States that is prepared, and will be more prepared in the future, to take
advantage of that kind of information.

In my view, the commission's recommendation with
respect to decision-making systems really goes a long
way toward saying, "This is what we have got to build."
In terms of whatever activity I might participate in in
the future with respect to legislation, I will try as
effectively as I can to urge the timely support of the

recommendations and to make very sure that those recommendations aren't lost in the legislative process.
Because I really think there is a lot of salvation in
those recommendations.

*Edmisten:* All of them?

*Heyman:* No, I am talking about the ones with respect to
the environmental information and management systems.
I don't want to be Pollyannish about this, but if those
get adequate funding my prediction is that the kind of
process that I indicate will ensue.

## Planning Management Systems

*Twiss:* Just a very brief comment on the planning management systems. As you probably know, most of the planning that now goes on is what I call functional planning: transportation planning to get cars from here to
there, recreation planning to locate campgrounds, hiking
trails, and so on. But it's not very often that these
plans get double-checked on their environmental impacts.

Now, in terms of research on the environment, it
tends to be problem oriented. There are studies on
specific subjects such as the ecology of the polar
bears, which is the way research has to be carried on.
But somehow over the years we have lost an ability to
understand the land parts of land management whenever
we make these functional decisions.

Timber is a case in point where allowable cuts are
set in Washington and parceled out. There *is* an attempt
to comprehend the environmental impacts of these things,
but it's an extremely difficult job.

Dr. Stoddard made reference to some solutions. He
mentioned the idea of regional organization or a comprehensive resource management plan on the basis of a
natural plan unit, such as watershed. Now, this would

help. You could have actual data brought together.
BLM's planning system doesn't include all the unit
resource analyses, which are a compilation of the
geologic soil, hydrologic, vegetation map, wildlife
habitats, and so on. It's a straightforward process
of amassing data, bringing it together and making it
physically available to the decisionmakers when a
problem is at hand.

## Analysis Paralysis

In my teaching university students to do environmental management, we try to teach how to synthesize
these environmental factors. But sometimes you reach
what we call "analysis paralysis." You get all these
things together and you can't put a road here because
of the landslides, and you can't put it down there
because of the drainage problem and you can't put it
up on the ridge because it is too windy and it will
blow the Volkswagens off. You know so much that you
are almost frozen and petrified by the amount of information you have got.

In order to get out of that and into design solutions, you have got to have a lot more information so
that you don't have these vague fears.

What are the probabilities? What is the range of
evidence here? To be constructive and solve the problem, you have to have even more information and this
is costly. At Tahoe we have committees on every one
of these subjects. We've got computer data banks that
will produce quickly environmental capability maps on
all these subjects. We used to make decisions very
cheaply, sort of by the seat of the pants. Now we make
what we call rational, comprehensive decisions based on
data. The cost today may be eight or ten times as much,
but you get acceptable decisions instead of the old
kind which aren't doing very well.

*Nienaber:* I just have one short comment on this planning question. You know, I am for planning; I think it has a limited value and a limited utility, but you can have all the plans in the world and still not get anywhere. You have to take into account the political realities of the situation, and the political realities have been that the government has opted for short-term prosperity and development. So we are going to have to realize that plans are fine, but we still have to cut down on consumption and on population growth and face the other innumerable problems that we all know about.

## POLICY DECISIONS NEEDED

*Heyman:* Please identify yourself loud and clear.

*Scott:* Tom Scott. I am a student of yours.

*Heyman:* Oh. It's only my bad eyesight.

*Scott:* I have listened to this conference. I have read this report, and it strikes me that the main thing the commission has done is to tidy up organizational charts when it was really asked to make some basic policy suggestions to Congress. It seems to me that the scope has been very, very limited and that the commission has refused to do what it was told to do. And I wonder when we consider the public lands and what they are--a source of resources, both renewable and nonrenewable. We look at the state of the United States and admit that our resources, both renewable and nonrenewable, are running frighteningly low, if we continue without a policy decision.

Maybe with certain of these resources we intend to lock them up. What would this effect? Maybe it would effect some recycling of our present resources. Maybe it would recycle some of the waste that we are up to our necks in, and bring it back to be used for other purposes. Now, this would be a policy tool that we could use our public lands for. The timber, perhaps, that is being used now for pulp purposes could be locked up. Maybe we still have to use some of the timber for building purposes, but that doesn't mean we have to give everything we've got.

As for the oil wells, the government could buy them, cap them, open up the import quotas and let oil in from other sources. Maybe the industry wouldn't like this, but maybe, for the general public good, it should be done.

## NONGROWTH POLICIES AND PROBLEMS

*Heyman:* Well, let me be pedagogic for a second and say that with respect to those kinds of goals, the question more at issue is how do you get the political structure to support that change? That seems to me to be the level that we are working for.

*Twiss:* I think the criticism was made yesterday, too, that there should have been a nongrowth strategy proposed in the commission report. One way to handle this is to chart the effects of a no-growth policy and no increase in resource production from the public land, and then run it through the planning machinery and find out what it would mean to society. Then let's also take a full-speed-ahead, damn-the-environment, get-out-the-cellulose-and-the-minerals approach and let's look at likely effects of that. Give the public a range of alternatives, so that we have some understanding of what we mean when we say what we say.

*Lee:* This is Eugene Lee. I'd like to remind the audience of Mr. Pearl's remark of yesterday: Even if we were to adopt a viable no-growth policy tomorrow--with every family now of childbearing age having only two children--we still would have a substantial population growth in this country, which we would be unwise not to plan for.

## Unworkable Mining Laws

*Hatch:* My name is Richard Hatch, and I represent mining interests as a provider of professional mining counsel. We have had a no-growth policy for some time. Our mining laws are 100 years old, and yet more than half of our western states are still public domain. Far less than one percent of the western states has ever been touched with mining.

I have a question for Dr. Stoddard. In your talk you mentioned the devastating, unworkable mining laws we have had for 100 years that have built the greatest industrial nation the world has ever seen.

*Stoddard:* Do you say there is a cause and effect relationship there?

*Hatch:* I would like you to back up your statement with some facts, and I would like to give you my card and have you send me those facts showing that we have unworkable mining laws that have devastated our land.

## The Mining Act of 1872

*Stoddard:* Well, I asked you whether there is a cause and effect relationship between our industrial growth and the Mining Act of 1872. The mining industry itself in all its meetings tears it apart. The bigger companies would like to see the doggone thing abolished. They would just as soon pay the royalty, but it's the old image of the guy with the pick and donkey going out and finding a little mining claim and making a fortune that keeps this antiquated thing on the books. It's too bad that the Public Land Law Review Commission didn't just wipe it off.

I know what the problems are: the vested interests of the lawyers and some of the other people who insist on keeping this thing intact. But there is a whale of a lot of damage all over the public lands, and why should the mining industry have any special right? That act gives the mining industry a special right over and above anybody else. We are suggesting simply that they compete on an equal basis.

I will write this letter, if you write yours.

## LIMITATION OF TITLE

*Williamson:* I am John Williamson. The commission's report suggests that, as the result of a change in the withdrawal policy, there will be land available for agricultural use and other uses, whereas it has not been in the past. Many states are faced with the problem now of a disappearance of agricultural land, largely land upon which large public expenditures are made for water, for soil conservation and for flood control--land that is now being taken out of agricultural production and used for other purposes.

Did the commission consider the possibility, in its recommendations for the disposal of land for agricultural purposes, of putting actual limitations in the title as to what this land was going to be used for in the future?

Recommendation 24 suggests that restrictive covenants be placed upon the land. I would like to ask a further question of Mr. Heyman: What are the relative merits--from the standpoint of success in exercising future control on use of land--between a restrictive covenant and a less-than-fee-interest in the title?

*Heyman:* I was very pleased with the commission's recommendation with respect to disposal (Recommendation 24), which says that the agency that disposes ought to have the power to protect public land environment by imposing protective covenants in disposals of public lands and by acquiring easements on nonfederal lands adjacent to public lands.

## The Use of Covenants

Now, John Williamson, who as many of you know is
the author of the Open Space Act in California and has
been probably the most important fellow in terms of
its implementation, really asks a kind of legal question
with respect to "What about covenants as compared with
other devices?" For instance, suppose the federal
government gave certain development rights but kept
some portion of the title or some other legal arrangement.

First of all, I am not sure that the commission
in using the phrase "imposing protective covenants"
did not really mean it as a term of choice. This
recommendation might well, as I believe it does, say
to essentially use the best technique under the circumstances; that was my understanding. But if it did mean
use restrictive covenants in themselves, that's a pretty
good technique, although there in some situations I
would prefer to see an agency keep a fee title, say on
a long-term lease, and thus recapture, or at least have
the possibility of recapturing, the fee at the end of
that lease and have the ability to determine what it
wants to do with that land.

But, as I say, it is my understanding that the term
"covenant" was used kind of generically.

## Land Disposal

*Pearl:* I wanted to answer the other part of the question
that was raised. First of all, the commission's recommendation with regard to sales of any land is that the
lands must be classified as being chiefly valuable for
that purpose re the public interest test first. And
the commission, of course, right on page 1, says that it
it anticipates that there will only be modest disposals
for any purpose.

But as I said yesterday, if you don't agree that any land should be disposed of, you can't agree with the idea of having procedures set up by which lands can be disposed of or sold.

Now, if you are going to have a public interest test to determine which land should be sold or disposed of, then you will have to have some procedures by which to do it. The commission then spells out for agricultural lands its idea of what those procedures should be. But you have to meet the public interest test first through a planning process in which everyone is involved before any decisions are made, before any plans are laid out by the management agency. It starts right from the beginning.

## PROMOTING MIGRATION AND MANAGING LAND USERS

*Heyman:* We are going to be going for only five more minutes, and there was a gentleman I recognized here.

*Weber:* I'm John Weber, representing the livestock industry. Talking about the public lands, I think maybe you ought to think about the thousands of communities in the western states that depend on the lands for their economy. If you are going to lock these lands up, what are the communities going to do?

We are driving our people to the cities, where we are getting a concentration polluting the air and burning fuel. This is the concern of our area, to keep these people in the country. What you are talking about is going to promote this migration.

*Blum:* My name is Joseph Blum, from Alaska, and I would like to question a couple of points on the dominant-use theory.

What you have done is to violate the precept that Mr. Pearl brought out yesterday. You should look at the commission report as a whole. What you seem to have done is isolated the dominant-use theory and left it standing alone. But if you take the other parts, why won't dominant use work?

*Stoddard:* In nature your land has various combinations of resources; and that governs use right there.

*Blum:* If I can interrupt at this point: the report doesn't simply say dominant use; it says dominant and compatible. Isn't this recognizing more than one use?

*Stoddard:* It recognizes it, but you have got the real practical problem of how to manage it and how to manage the users that are using that land. The problem came up in the discussion a little bit earlier. You build many a clientele with a dominant use and, boy, they fix on an agency like a bloodsucker if you try to get a change in allowable cut, in grazing fees or in mineral rights. You have a built-in pressure group with all the political pressures lined up and with the budget all lined up with the major amount going to that environmental use. This is going on in some agencies right now, and this is one of the reasons they are in trouble.

Now setting this all up with a cute little special dominant-use budget practically amounts to providing private rights in public lands, without paying any taxes or a darn thing on them. And I don't think this is what we want, because it closes in our whole chance of making some independent decisions, of having some flexibility and the ability to make changes as we go along.

*Heyman:* Do you want to say anything with respect to this use on dominant versus multiple?

*Pearl:* It is not dominant versus multiple use; it is commercial use. The commission is in favor of multiple use and merely offers this as an extension of multiple-use operation.

*Heyman:* Well, I am going to close this panel now.

It was entitled "Administration of the Public Lands." Perhaps it should have been entitled "Environment on the Public Lands."

# PART SIX

# Politics and the Public Lands

# POLITICS AND PUBLIC LAND POLICY

Lynton K. Caldwell

*Professor of Political Science and Government
University of Indiana*

Any treatment of public land policy is invariably
influenced by the premises upon which it is based.

## SOME UNDERLYING PREMISES

The basic proposition underlying this paper is that
there can be no public land policy apart from a national
policy for land generally. The national policy may be
tacit or implicit, as it has been throughout most of our
national history, or it may be explicit, as it will need
to be in the future. Public land policy is not an end
in itself; the complex issue of precedent, practice and
legislation that we sum up under the heading "public
land policy" may not reflect an underlying national
policy in any coherent sense. Consistency and coherence
are not essential characteristics of any aspect of public
policy; yet this complexity and confusion reinforce the
point that land policy (public or otherwise) is seldom
an end in itself and is most commonly a means to a
variety of objectives, most of which are economic. This
relationship between public land policy and a general
policy for land is implicit in many of the sections and
recommendations of the report of the Public Land Law
Review Commission--particularly those dealing with the
interface between publicly owned and privately owned
land.[1]

An additional premise underlying this paper has to
do with the value of experience. Practical politicians

are reputed to place great faith in practical expe-
rience--their experience. All recollected experience
(ours and others) is the substance of history; history
being the recorded and analyzed experience of many persons extended beyond the lifetimes of single individuals.
Contrary to the cynical disclaimers of Georg Wilhelm,
Friedrich Hegel and Oscar Wilde, history and experience
may afford reliable guidance, but there is also abundant
evidence to indicate that history misinterpreted may mis-
lead. For example, the history of American attitudes
toward the land and toward public policy for land helps
us to understand how this nation arrived at its present
posture in relation to public land policy.[2] However, if
we ask what action should be taken now and in the foreseeable future in relation to national land policy and
the public lands, it might be a serious error to base
our judgments upon past or even present public attitudes.
For this purpose the most pertinent question we might ask
in relation to the past is: Do the factors that prompted
prior attitudes and actions still hold? If past attitudes still persist while the motivating and extenuating
factors are disappearing, will we find present attitudes
(supported mainly by inertia and tradition) reliable in-
dicators of future trends in politics?

## THE CONTINGENT NATURE OF PUBLIC LAND QUESTIONS

Where one comes out in consideration of any public
issue may depend upon where one enters the forum of discussion. It is, of course, possible to reach conclusions
that are at variance with initial premises, but this requires a reconsideration of the issues and a shifting of
position during the course of deliberation or debate. It
is seldom easy for a public figure, particularly an
elected representative of the people to change his mind
publicly. There appears to be a compulsion in public
life to be consistent, and while the record shows that
inconsistency is the more common characteristic of
political behavior, successful politicians often develop
remarkable skills in rationalizing incongruities in the
policies they support. Nevertheless, the assumptions

and premises underlying political attitudes can have a powerful channeling effect upon reasoning and logic. For example, attitudes on public land policy may be strongly influenced by the assumptions one brings to the questions at issue on such matters as federal-state relations, taxation, priority of private rights versus public interest, economic as distinguished from ecological considerations and the weighting one gives to the opinions of people in contradistinction to the findings of science.

## Choices Among Alternatives

The report of the Public Land Law Review Commission contains many explicit and more implicit assumptions regarding all and more of the preceding factors, but it may be significant that the commission did not consider whether the public lands of the United States ought to be increased; whether large areas of land now in private holdings should, by some appropriate means, be acquired by government to be managed in the public interest. A study of public policy that is premised on the continuation of things as they are (or have been) assuming only relatively minor changes in the character of the political and economic systems has, in fact, elected to base its deliberations on only one of a much larger number of alternative propositions. Lest the basically conventional and conservative premises of the commission's report be, therefore, taken as "practical," one should consider whether such an approach is realistic in a world characterized by rapid, widespread and frequently violent change.

It would not be difficult to show that the political assumptions of the commission were generally consistent with widely prevailing attitudes among the American people toward public land questions. The report, however, turned out to be a less conservative document than many of its more skeptical critics had expected. It recognized the force of the environmental quality movement and the growth of public concern for open space, natural area preservation and the use of public lands for recreation. It is doubtful that had this same commission reported five to ten years earlier, it would have taken cognizance of these interests and values, for although these concerns could have been found among the citizenry of 1960 and 1965, they were then far more in the minority than in 1970.

To the extent that the commission reflected a shift in popular values in relation to land, its action illustrates our contention that decisions on public land questions share the contingent character of public policy decisions generally, and that if basic principles and assumptions change, the basis for public land decisions also changes and new policies reflecting new outlooks may be anticipated.

## Unreliable Guides to Public Opinion

One could cite a long list of political commentators to the effect that public opinion is a chancy thing Techniques of opinion sampling have been refined to a degree that encourages the belief that public attitudes and reactions can be more reliably analyzed and predicted today than at any prior period of time. But opinion samples could be unreliable guides to future opinions and behaviors.

It is readily apparent that large numbers of people hold a variety of mutually incompatible opinions. Any given opinion sample or questionnaire may reveal some of these while missing others. Which of a variety of opinions an individual will act upon may depend upon circumstances that cannot be foreseen. Especially unreliable are those opinions that persist only because of habit, social convention or apathy. These are opinions from which the supporting understructure of fact or of logic has been weakened or even cut away. Nevertheless the opinion, in the absence of competing doctrines, survives. Like the character in the animated cartoon who runs over the edge of a cliff and continues to run through thin air until he discovers there is nothing beneath him and then suddenly falls, a social convention or idea may enjoy general public and political support so long as not too many people notice that the proposition lacks support in fact. The resulting crash of institutions or ideas is what is known in the vernacular as "falling under its own weight."

When long-standing doctrines or institutions collapse or are threatened with collapse, the practical need for their replacement arises--necessity is the mother of political innovation. This aphorism is not quite a cliché, because the circumstances that we call "necessities" almost always involve contingencies. In relatively small countries such as Switzerland or the Netherlands necessities in regard to land are more readily demonstrable and the parameters of choice obviously less than in nations of continental proportions such as the United States. In the U.S.A. or U.S.S.R. there remain vast areas of uncommitted land and correspondingly wide ranges of choice in many land use decisions. But even in America, the amount of land and more particularly the amount of given kinds of land is fixed, and the expectations and values held by people in relation to the land are not unlimited. In some sense, therefore, the politician and the public administrator are confronted to a degree with necessities in dealing with public land questions. It is the margins of choice in dealing with these necessities that provide the challenges, the difficulties and the opportunities that public land policy in the United States presents.


SOCIAL CHANGES AFFECTING THE POLITICS OF LAND

It is axiomatic to say that we live in a period of accelerated change. The effect of nearly every one of our major social changes is to alter radically the circumstances under which our policy for lands, including public lands, develops. These changes are not necessarily consistent with one another, although they have

some causal factors in common. Collectively the changes
are largely inconsistent with the circumstances that have
gone before them. We have no suitable word to describe
the political syndrome of our times, but terms such as
urbanism, scientism, technology, cosmopolitanism and
futurism suggest some of its elements.

## Population Dynamics

Social changes affecting the politics of land may
be grouped into three categories. The first of these
is population dynamics: numbers of people and what
they do. The tremendous increase in the numbers of
people is an obvious factor, but numbers alone do not
fully explain the impact of people upon land. Where
and how people live are significant factors, and the
increasing concentration of population in large sprawl-
ing urban areas is one of the most obvious social phenomena of our times.

Some geographically large areas of the country have
in fact been losing population, and although the metropolitan population is diffused over extended areas by a
culture of individual homeownership and the automobile,
the affluence of American society and its extraordinary
mobility makes the "crowding" effect of these concentrations as pronounced as in areas in which there are actually more people but less money and mobility. The largely unregulated private development of land has responded
to the population explosion and to the automobile by creating patterns of settlement that are extremely ineffi-
cient for the administration of public services and in-
terpersonal communications. The wasteful, profit-
dominated, short-sighted and irresponsible exploitation
of land in America's metropolitan areas has tended to
accentuate public pressures on the land, particularly
for purposes of outdoor recreation.

Obviously, it is not mere numbers of people that
account for their pressure on the land; what they are
doing on and to the land is equally significant. Within

the past quarter century, technological innovation has sharply accentuated the trends which were observable throughout the earlier decades of this century. For example, managers of public lands now must contend with the demands of the operators of snowmobiles, dune buggies, motorcycles for trailing, and small airplanes, all of which intensify human impact upon the land, often at points far removed from concentrations of population.

Other aspects of technology work to reduce the number of people earning their living on the land. In agriculture, mining and forestry, mechanization has reduced the need for production workers. These new technologies, however, become economical when employed on a large scale; it is not feasible, for example, to employ many of them on the traditional family-sized farm woodlot. Modern mechanized science-based forest practices can be applied only when large acreages of land are brought under common planning and management. Although the family farm or woodlot could theoretically be well managed and, by cooperative systems of harvesting and marketing, could afford a base adequate to meet a large part of the nation's timber needs, the social structure and behavior patterns of the American people make it unlikely that such a system could ever be developed.

## Diminishing Chances for Work on the Land

All of the preceding factors relating to population dynamics accentuate in one way or another the problems of the poor and the inept among the American people. Work on the land has for ages been the most obvious source of sustenance for those lacking the skills, temperament or perhaps even the type of mentality required for industrial and urbanized civilization. The population explosion has increased the absolute numbers of such people in modern society, even though affluence and public education may have reduced their relative numbers. But psychologically and politically, they present more difficult social and political problems than

did their counterparts in traditional societies. The
commitment of the United States to full employment as
well as to social welfare doctrines has led to expectations not only among the poor, but among society generally which that same society has been unable to bring to
realization. This circumstance is not peculiar to the
United States, as it is found in nearly all industrialized countries in the modern world where there has been
a widespread indigent rural population.

If it is not readily apparent how this sociological
problem affects public land policy, it should be recalled
that as the migration of rural poor into the metropolitan
areas continues, as potentially more productive areas of
the country are losing population, as the size, complexity and disorganization of the metropolitan areas
approaches a condition sometimes described as "ungovern-
able," arguments for the establishment of new towns and
for a redistribution of population are being heard. The
Public Land Law Review Commission took cognizance of
these circumstances, suggesting the possible availability
of publicly owned lands for the location of some of these
new population centers.[3] The possible consequences of
these population trends should not be overlooked. While
large corporations and wealthy individuals have been buying up land as a hedge against inflation and for speculative profits, similar opportunities for most individuals
have rapidly diminished.

Very large numbers of Americans, particularly in
the lower income groups in the urban centers, own no
land at all. In the more affluent suburbs the only
land owned by most individuals is a private homestead.
Affluence and urban discomforts have stimulated the
building of second or weekend houses not only in this
country, but even in such ostensibly contrasting economies as those of Czechoslovakia and Sweden. The popu-
larity of the weekend house, especially the demand of
citizens from the more influential sectors of society
that public lands be made available for weekend house
construction, is productive of a substantial list of
land use and public land problems. A clash of interests

readily develops among the would-be weekend house
builders, the lovers of untrammeled nature, the professional foresters, the wildlife managers and local populations in or adjacent to the areas where weekend housing
has become popular.

## LAND HUNGER AND THE TERRITORIAL IMPERATIVE

A second social change affecting the politics of
the land may be described as intellectual or conceptual. This has to do with what people value, but beneath
cultural attitudes may or may not lie an inherent biological urge to acquire and maintain a personal "territory." Whether man as an animal shares with certain
other species an innate tendency to establish personal
territory is a question that has not been answered with
certainty.

Robert Ardrey has written a well-known exposition
of the evidence in support of human territoriality.[4]
Although Ardrey's thesis has been criticized by a number
of social scientists (not always for reasons relevant to
the argument) there is an undeniable amount of empirical
evidence to indicate that land hunger has been a widespread human trait. The territorial imperative may not
necessarily be confined to land in the conventional
sense, nor to private landownership of the type established through legal conventions in the United States
today.

Ecological psychologists have been interested in
the "space needs" of human individuals. Kurt Lewin, who
was perhaps the founder of ecological psychology,[5] and
Edward T. Hall in *The Hidden Dimension*,[6] appear to have
shown that, whatever its genetic base, there are ascer-
tainable cultural factors involved in the attitudes of
people with respect to their needs for personal space,
for privacy and for control of their immediate personal
environment.

One may question in what way personal space needs
relate  to public land policy, but as we have already
observed, where you come out in considering the public
issue depends very much upon where you came in.  The
urbanized Puerto Rican accustomed to "physical" crowding,
to minimal privacy and to a very high degree of inter-
personal interaction would enter the arena of public
land policy from a door far removed from the Montana
rancher whose nearest neighbor may be 10 miles away,
where privacy is inherent in the environmental circumstances, and where personal interaction is sufficiently
infrequent that one does not take it as routine.  Obviously these two types represent extremes in the spectrum
of American society, but under the federal system of
representative government, these extremes may be more
significant than they would be in a wholly majoritarian
political system.

## The Influential Sector

It would be reasonable to suppose that the single
most influential sector of American society with respect
to any public policy (including policy for public land)
would be the middle- to upper-income sector of the
society--that sector which collectively has the highest
degree of education, is best informed, is most cognizant
of social, economic and technological trends and which
occupies the largest number of professional, technical
and administrative positions in the society.  Inasmuch
as this sector of the population in effect "runs" the
society, very few of its members see themselves (or the
sector as a whole) as posing any sociological problem.
Although presently the target of polemical attack from
the so-called "new left" and "militant Blacks," the
upper-middle class while receiving some attention from
sociologists has received relatively little truly per-
ceptive or objective behavioral study.  It is questionable, to say the least, whether the Lynds' study of
*Middletown*[7] would be a reliable guide to predicting the
political behavior of America's upper-middle class in
the decade of the seventies.

The greatly increased and increasing role of information and information technology systems, computerization, and science-based analysis generally represents an influence vastly disproportionate to the number of individuals directly engaged in the activities that these terms represent. Mass opinion over time has historically tended to be influenced by the thinking of creative minorities, and when that thinking links controlling factors in the industrial and economic systems with a perception of the natural world and its parameters, the ingredients of a powerful and unifying concept of man in relation to his environment are present.

## Emergence of an Ecological Ideology

Conjecturing as to the intellectual and conceptual trends in this critical sector of society, I risk a hypothesis suggested by mounting empirical evidence: the proposition that we are seeing the emergence of a comprehensive and relatively coherent "ideology" among the more highly educated and science-oriented sectors of modern societies everywhere--and especially in the United States. I do not suggest that this group shares a common doctrine nor, on a large variety of issues, even a common viewpoint, but rather a set of basic assumptions about the world (and man in relation to it) which could be fundamental in relation to opinions on certain political issues. The group in question sees the world as described by contemporary physical and biological science, but sees it holistically. To most members of this group, no explanation would be required for such words as ecology, ecosystem, biosphere, chain reaction, critical mass, exponential growth, time lag effects, energy cycles and systems theory. If the reader understands these terms or has a general sense of their interrelated meanings, he belongs to what has elsewhere been described as "the scientific supercul-ture."[8]

The general viewpoint characterizing this culture may be summarized by the term "ecological," and it leads to conclusions differing materially from traditional American attitudes toward land. Hitherto prevailing modes of thought in America considered land primarily as property. Subsequently it was seen as a natural resource. Now increasingly it is viewed as an essential element of the biosphere. The boundaries or subdivisions of land viewed as most important in these respective modes of thought reveal their differing emphases. From the property point of view, the legally established boundaries for purposes of title transfer and taxation are of foremost importance; from a resource point of view, the economic capability of defined sectors of land is primary; from the ecological point of view, natural ecosystems (usually modified by man) are the most significant boundary criteria. These respective modes of measurement or evaluation are not necessarily contradictory; it is the judgment as to which of them is most important that is politically significant.

## USE v. OWNERSHIP

In a society in which innovation and its corollary, obsolescence, have become dominating conditions of life, the use to which any material substance may be put becomes more important than the mere fact of ownership. Thus there is the tendency in the industrial world to lease machinery, plant space and human talent in the form of specialized consulting and technical services, and the tendency among affluent individuals who can afford to own almost anything to lease their automobiles and condominiums, avoiding direct ownership of material things other than those of an essentially personal nature. The wealth of nations is increasingly seen to depend upon effective utilization of intellectual and physical energy rather than upon mere possession of natural wealth. The histories of Indonesia and Japan illustrate the point.

Although the acquisition of great fortunes in America has historically depended heavily upon the ownership of land, it is questionable whether this

circumstance could be safely projected as a probable
condition of the future.  If wealth in land depends primarily upon the use to which the land is put and that
use is increasingly seen as relating to complex natural
and man-made systems involving the public welfare and
survival, the free and unrestricted private use of land
becomes increasingly improbable.  If, for example, there
were no possibilities for speculative profits in land
transactions and if the responsibilities of landownership were greatly increased while the freedom of choice
available to landowners were sharply reduced, the
attractiveness of landownership would be diminished.
Its security value might remain, but relative to other
investment possibilities it would lose much of its
traditional advantage.  To the extent that such developments, in fact, took place there would be diminished
resistance in society to the extension of public landownership and to an increased public role in specific
decisions regarding the use of privately owned land.
Under these circumstances, the prevailing distinction
between national land policy and public land policy
would lose much of its raison d'être, and the management
of land as a natural resource would become a major aspect
of public policy and administration.

## Institutional Stress

A third area in which social change may affect the
politics of land is that of institutional stress.  The
strains of accelerating change have been increasingly
evident upon all social structures, including arrangements affecting the land and its ownership and use.
This stress is obvious upon the legal and judicial
system and upon the structure of government, especially
at its local level.  It is difficult to demonstrate the
extent to which existing institutions of government in
the United States are failing adequately to serve the
public needs.

It is also difficult to determine the extent to
which such inadequacies are inherent in the structure

of government and the law, which are the result of
defects of the political party system, or which reflect
the attitudes and behaviors of electorates. While the
kind of proof that a scientist may call adequate is not
available, there is nevertheless a widespread conviction
that relative to the present and emerging needs of our
society, the laws, the courts of justice and the traditional structures of government--particularly of state
and local government--are inadequate to a degree that
may be fairly described as "critical."

## A Matrix of Complexity and Confusion

If one considers questions of the public lands
exclusively (which is not the way to consider them
realistically) the institutional problem is ostensibly
less critical because of the common jurisdiction of the
federal government. But the Public Land Law Review Commission found that the only thing common with respect to
federal jurisdiction was its mere fact. Beneath this
fact was revealed a multiplicity of specific forms of
ownership and jurisdiction; a multiplicity of redundant,
incongruent and conflicting laws and regulations; and
underlying all of these, widely differing assumptions
in philosophies with respect to Uncle Sam as a landowner.

If one adds to this matrix of complexity and confusion the circumstances governing public landownership
among the states and their subdivisions, and in addition
considers the regulatory powers of federal, state and
local government over privately owned land, one finds
himself in a seemingly incomprehensible wilderness of
jurisdictions, doctrines and procedures that make the
expressions "public land policy" or "public policies for
land" wholly abstract and theoretical. Accumulative and
reinforcing effects of these social changes, however,
contrast so sharply with the circumstances that have
hitherto prevailed in America as to make it highly questionable whether the new circumstances afford a basis
upon which traditional doctrines and practices can long
continue to rest. Because no pronounced change in public

attitudes and demands regarding land policy seems imminent, it does not therefore follow that one can safely
conclude that the status quo will continue to prevail.

It has been observed repeatedly by students of
social change that the processes leading to fundamental
restructuring of society often occur so quietly, so
gradually and so pervasively that they are discounted
or overlooked by those who might be expected to be most
affected by them. This curious imperceptibility of
maturing social change was described by Alexis de
Tocqueville in his analysis of conditions preceding
the French Revolution. "Never," he wrote, "were there
events more important, longer in ripening, more fully
prepared, or less foreseen."[9] If the political institutions of our times are more flexible, alert and more
responsive than were those of the France of the old
regime, the changes affecting society are of orders of
magnitude greater. Thus, we have a question of the
*relative* fitness of institutions for the social challenges that confront them, and it does not follow that
the more responsive institutions of our time are better
able to handle the circumstances facing them than were
those of the France of Louis XVI to handle the social
changes maturing on the eve of the French Revolution.

## EMERGENT ISSUES AND PROSPECTIVE
## PROBLEMS OF POLICY

The implication of the changes and trends just
delineated is that new land policy issues will arise
and certain old ones will become accentuated. The
most important and fundamental of these issues is that
of a national policy for land generally. It is a basic
premise of this paper that we cannot have an effective
policy for public land apart from a national policy for
land generally. It could be demonstrated that one of
the reasons for the chaotic and inconsistent conglomera-
tion of policies affecting public lands in the United
States is a consequence of lawmaking on an ad hoc basis
without the benefit of adequate guiding principles and

without adequate consideration for what was happening on privately owned land in relation to the use of land in public ownership. Many of the specific issues of resource development on the public lands, notably in forestry, mining, grazing and generation of electric power, can only be properly assessed in relation to the status of these activities on privately owned lands.

In addition to the question of a national policy for land one may identify at least three other major areas for political action. These are, in the order of importance that I would attach to them: (1) ecological and environmental considerations, (2) technoeconomic considerations and (3) rights and responsibilities--social and individual. In all of these areas basic human needs and welfare are involved; abstract categorical terminology ought not obscure the issues of human life and conditions underlying the terms.

## A National Policy for Land

In his message to the Congress transmitting the first annual report of the Council on Environmental Quality (August 1970) President Richard Nixon endorsed the concept of a national policy for land, declaring:

> I believe that the problems of urbanization which I have described, of resource management, and land and water use generally can only be met by comprehensive approaches which take into account the widest range of social, economic, and ecological concerns. I believe we must work toward development of a National Land Use Policy to be carried out by an effective partnership of Federal, State, and local governments together, and where appropriate, with new regional institutional arrangements.[10]

By way of background to this statement the President observed that: "Throughout the Nation there is critical need for more effective land use, and for better controls over the use of land and living systems that depend upon it....The time has come when we must accept the idea that none of us has a right to abuse the land, and that on the contrary society as a whole has a legitimate interest in proper land use. There is a national interest in effective land use planning all across the Nation."[11]

Legislation to create such a national land use policy was introduced into the second session of the 91st Congress by Senator Henry M. Jackson of Washington and was referred to the Senate Committee on Interior and Insular Affairs. Hearings on S. 3354, to amend the Water Resources Planning Act (79 Stat. 244) to provide for a national land use policy were begun on March 24, 1970 and continued on April 28 and 29.[12] The Council on Environmental Quality has endorsed the concept of a national land use policy and has identified a 10-point strategy for immediate action coterminous with reforms in government needed to institute effective land use decisions. Foremost among these is the necessity "to determine which levels of government must assume which specific responsibilities, and to identify the appropriate mechanism at each level to achieve such a policy."[13]

Senate bill 3354 would approach this problem by establishing a nationwide system of planning grants from the federal government to the states, and to interstate agencies authorized by federal law or state compact, to plan and regulate land use development. The act would be administered under guidelines and requirements established through a national land and water resources planning council. It would provide for federal-state interchange of information on land use plans and would undertake to assure state compliance with the intentions of Congress, as expressed in the act, through federal funding to assist compliance and reduction of certain federal grants and the denial of certain forms of access to the public domain and other federal lands in the event of the failure of a state to comply. Details and implications of S. 3354 extend beyond the scope of this present essay, but if enacted it would be certain to affect the use of the public lands particularly in relation to state and local governments.

## Politics of the Environment

The need for a national land policy and for a new approach to questions involving the public lands has been given emphasis by an emerging politics of the environment. Ecology has joined civil rights, full employment, peace and prosperity as a talisman of vote-getting in politics. More than this, the man-environment relationship is or may become an effective organizing and coordinative concept in a way never possible to the traditional categorization of the environment into natural resources.

Environment as a focus for public policy is displacing resources only in the order of priority. The environmental concept is the more fundamental, and resources (basically an economic concept) can now be placed in proper context--a major economic aspect of man-environment relationships. Natural resources will remain a factor in public and environmental policy as long as men must eat, be clothed and be sheltered. But natural resources, as a concept, does not lead toward organizing or coordinative policies or structures in government. A century of repetitive efforts to coordinate natural resources policy in the United States has uniformly ended in failure.

Competition among resource uses has historically been a kind of political and economic trial by combat, but the presence of a governing body of ecological or environmental policy could provide the basis for the allocation of priorities and the resolution of conflict with respect to the exploitation or conservation of specific natural resources at specific times and places.

For example, the multiple-use concept, which has been
strongly urged by the Public Land Law Review Commission
and adopted by several of the federal agencies, is difficult to apply if administered solely on the basis of
competition among resource uses without regard to the
larger environmental and ecological implications of
the action under consideration.

The concepts of ecological viability and environmental quality add new and frequently decisive factors
to otherwise insoluble disputes. To the extent that
environmental quality and the maintenance of a regenerative capacity of ecosystems become factors in a decision,
it becomes more difficult to argue that because of demonstrated national needs regardless of other considerations, a specific local piece of the public domain should
be devoted to a particular resource use. The multiple-
use concept is consistent with the public welfare and
the ecological facts of life only when applied in broad
context that includes all opportunities for the land
uses in question regardless of the incidental fact of
legal ownership.

## Politics of Values

There are those who view advocates of the new environmental emphasis and the politics of ecology as merely
a new interest group joining those that have traditionally battled over the allocation of the resource potential of the public lands. But it can be argued (and
I think rightly argued) that the politics of ecology and
environment is of a different conceptual mode or order
than the traditional politics of natural resources--
including much of traditional politics of conservation.
The politics of natural resources has largely been a
politics of interest, specifically economic interest,
whereas the politics of ecology is a politics of values
and is more akin to an ideology than to customary interest group politics.

The idea of a politics of values has been baffling to some politicians and to not a few political scientists. Ecology is not the only focus for a politics of values that has emerged in this and other countries during the past decade. In some respects, it qualitatively resembles more the politics of race and religion than the politics of forestry versus mass recreation, or of wildlife versus the grazing of domestic livestock.

Resource politics, whatever its ultimate justification by way of public needs, tends to be locally based, whereas the political arguments of ecologists and environmentalists tend to be influenced by broad ecological considerations sometimes embracing the biosphere or the planet itself.

## THE POLITICS OF ECOLOGY AND LAND USE DECISIONS

Among the specific conceptual elements in the politics of ecology that bear upon land use decisions are the following: (1) the importance of maintaining the regenerative capacity of natural systems, (2) the optimal utilization of natural energetics as opposed to unnecessary reliance upon man-managed systems, (3) the desirability of managing the environment where necessary through ecologically compatible methods of control (e.g., biological control of so-called insect "pests" in contradistinction to the use of chemical biocides), and (4) a more sophisticated interpretation of the multiple-use concept. Implicit in each of these factors is focus on the ecosystem as a criterion in land use decisions.

From an ecologically oriented viewpoint, distinctions between public lands and other lands are merely matters of temporary legal arrangements. From an ecological viewpoint, the distinction between public and private landownership, real enough in the world of law and economics, is not relevant to the conditions

and necessities of the biophysical world. Policies
regarding the use of land must, therefore, consider all
available land in relation to the policy and not merely
that land which is conveniently available under present
legal arrangements.

## Technoeconomic Considerations

Other papers in this symposium have considered economic and technological aspects of public land policy.
It will suffice, therefore, merely to point out some of
the political problems that grow out of the interaction
of economics and technology in the use of land. It is,
however, necessary to understand that technology and
economics are inextricably linked in most ecological
natural resource aspects of land use policy today.

For example, technology in the forest products industries may develop toward a variety of dissimilar out-
comes affecting demands upon forest production on the
public lands. Forest industry technology is most economical when organized on a large scale. The more sophisticated machinery for the harvesting of trees is economically out of reach to any but large corporate enterprises and could not be efficiently employed on small
farm woodlots; hence, there is an understandable preference in the forest products industries for access to the
large unobstructed stands of timber on the public lands.

There are extensive areas of the United States capable of producing merchantable timber but the potential
for forest industries cannot be realized without changes
in the patterns of land tenure, taxation and distribution of populations. The forest products industries
would be unequal to the political, economic and sociological task of reorganizing the economies of substantial areas in Appalachia, in the Ohio Valley and in
some parts of the upper Midwest and New England where
most forest land is in small private holdings. A

national policy that would change the prospect for forestry on private lands in these areas could substantially lessen the pressure of the forest products industry on the public lands.

## The Factor of Certainty

An important aspect of the economics of land policy in relation to natural resources has to do with the factor of certainty. Growing conflicts over land use have threatened the resource base of a large number of the extractive and other natural resource industries. Spokesmen for the forest products industries may be regarded as generally representative of the natural resources industries as a whole in their plea for a greater degree of stability and certainty respecting the resource base.

Uncertainties of the market are congenital to most, or at least many, forms of business enterprise. Resource industry spokesmen, however, contend that it would be easier to live with the certainty of a predictable diminished resource base rather than with the condition of extreme uncertainty prevailing since the rise of mass outdoor recreation and the environmental quality movement. The politics of ecology has proven to be a more effective adversary in political contests than the old conservation movement ever was.

It seems improbable, however, that resource bases could be stabilized solely on the basis of public land policies whether in relation to forests, to mineral deposits, to grazing lands or to recreational areas. Sound public decisions cannot be taken unless the entire universe of the issue is brought into view. This necessity is most forcibly evident in the case of the taxation of land. The notorious dependence of local government both upon taxes on land and improvements on land lies at the root of many of America's political and environmental difficulties at local levels.

## The Politics of Revenue and Taxation

But the problems of land use policy growing out of public fiscal needs are not confined to local levels. Indeed, many ecologically disastrous decisions--not the least of which was the decision to lease mineral rights on public lands underlying the Santa Barbara Channel--may be traced back to the politics of public revenues and taxation. To the ecologically oriented and the future-oriented, a large part of the structure of taxation in America is archaic and destructive. For example, a major source of pressure to "reclaim" San Francisco Bay has come from the anxiety of local officials to add assessable properties to the tax rolls.

The Public Land Law Review Commission gave extended consideration to the effect of federal land holdings on the local tax base, and proposed a variety of remedial measures.[14] But the commission was taking a "practical man's" view of the problem--which may not represent a practical analysis if measured by consequences and compared with alternatives that are at least theoretically possible (such as a shift from taxation on land to greater reliance on other revenue sources). The land tax, of course, has been the mainstay of the independence of local government, and virtually every kind of alternative revenue source implies a transfer of taxing power to the state governments or, more likely, to the nation as a whole. It has always been true, as Alexander Hamilton averred, that the "power which holds the purse strings absolutely, must rule."[15]

If, however, one assumes (as I do) that local government in the traditional American sense has long been outmoded and that an entirely new kind of structure of government at local levels is needed, the elimination of the land tax as the fiscal mainstay of local government should not be viewed as either impractical or undesirable. The notion that local units of government in

America are inherently most responsible to the people
as a whole and most representative of the public interest has been repeatedly demonstrated to be one of the
more fraudulent propositions of our public life. One
can, of course, find examples of responsive and responsible local governments, but it is more valid in America
today to generalize on the shortcomings rather than the
virtues of local government. It is doubtful if an
effective national policy for land could be administered
through the prevailing institutions of local government,
and there is urgent need for constructive, creative
thought concerning alternative new institutions for
revitalizing this level of our civic life.

## Rights and Responsibilities:
## Societal and Individual

Questions over use of the public lands and their
resources invariably involve the respective rights of
society and of the individual. Concepts of ownership
and usufruct underlie many of the more specific legal
doctrines and arrangements invoked in the political
controversy over use of the public lands. To the
extent that the rights of individuals or corporations
with respect to privately owned lands are modified by
law, there may be a corresponding implication regarding
the rights or privileges that they may reasonably expect
to enjoy on the public lands. If one accepts the asser-
tion of President Nixon that "none of us has a right to
abuse the land," and that "...society as a whole has a
legitimate interest in proper land use,"[16] a major aspect
of land policy would be the determination of what does in
fact constitute abuse of the land.

Legislative bodies have shown an increasing willingness to become more specific in the prescription of
standards of land use and of criteria for identifying

abuse. Nevertheless, only a few states and municipalities have taken effective legislative action and protection against land abuse still lies largely in dependence upon the uncertain willingness of the courts to apply the doctrines of public nuisance in any particular case.[17] Public ownership of land tends to shift the locus of authority from judicial to administrative decisionmakers. Ostensibly this permits the tests of truth in any controversy over the use of land and its resources to be based on scientific evidence rather than upon legal prescriptions and technicalities. But of course, over the years, various interest groups (among which mining interests afford the clearest example) have managed to obtain prescriptive rights on the public lands.

Accumulative efforts to establish private rights on the public lands have been successful to such an extent that the administration of these lands has been greatly complicated. The report of the Public Land Law Review Commission and its several task forces has documented this complexity, and a redefinition of these legally prescribed rights would be undeniably in the public interest. However, if one views land as an indispensable and by no means fully renewable component of the ecosphere, and if one believes that the welfare of all humanity and indeed of the living world depends upon ecologically wise use of the land, the question of rights and privileges regarding land use should be considered quite apart from any question of legal jurisdiction or ownership.

To cite once more one of America's most thoughtful analysts on the relationship among political stability, the public welfare and property rights, Alexander Hamilton observed that "wherever, indeed, a right of property is infringed for the general good, if the nature of the case admits of compensation, it ought to be made; but if compensation is impractical, that impracticality ought not to be an obstacle to a clearly essential reform."[18]

## Rules for Private and Public Ownership

In cases in which and to the extent that science affords the test of truth, there is no justification for having one set of rules that apply to land in private ownership and another set where ownership is public. From an ecological point of view, government is just one more "owner" who may be no more wise and no more foolish, no more far sighted and no more responsible than an individual private or corporate owner. It could be persuasively argued that many if not most of the "rights" and advantages that individuals seek in the private ownership of land are not well protected by existing conventional legal arrangements. Under the law as interpreted in most states, many values that a private owner may wish to protect in his land can be ruined with impunity by his neighbor. An effective public environmental policy superseding the traditional right of owners to use their land as they please might afford a much greater protection for the vast majority of individual landowners.

This problem of the freedom of a landowner to use of his own land in ways that inflict damage upon his neighbors has been notably acute at the interface between publicly and privately owned land, especially in areas peripheral to national parks, monuments and military establishments. The Public Land Law Review Commission, taking cognizance of this difficulty, proposed that the federal government be empowered to establish regulations over the use of peripheral lands.[19] This type of regulation has usually been opposed by the land owning and commercial interests adjacent to federal installations. Yet business interests whose haphazard, self-centered and indiscriminate growth create serious economic, esthetic and health and safety problems in the areas adjacent to public parks and other public establishments, owe their very existence and profits to the public investment on publicly owned lands.

Once again we confront the impracticality of separating public land policy from land policy generally.

The nation clearly needs a revised set of policies for the future use and administration of its public lands, but it needs even more a revised set of policies governing the use of land generally.

## A NATIONAL LAND USE PLANNING SYSTEM

Establishment of a national land use planning system ought logically to be the number one environmental priority in the United States at the present time. It is a priority that I would rate even higher than the necessity for bringing environmental pollution under control, for it is probable that control of environmental pollution cannot be made fully effective without a national land use policy. The greater part of air and water pollution originates on the land and in relation to the use of the land. But the legal and political circumstances involved in land use policy are vastly more complicated than those affecting the water and the air.

The complexities of the law affecting privately owned land in the United States present extremely difficult obstacles to the effective implementation of environmental planning. Batteries of legal devices, such as development rights and scenic easements, have been assembled to provide some measure of publicly sponsored control over the use of the land while preserving rights of private ownership. If the nation is to bring the development of its environment under responsible and rational control, these devices should be refined and extended, but they may not be extensible to all cases wherein a major long-range public interest is involved.

I would therefore argue that the public lands of the United States should not be stabilized at their present acreage, but should be extended--possibly by as much as one-third. Given the fractional, incongruent and widely ineffective structure of local government in the United States, and the reluctance of most states to act in opposition to private land speculation and

development, I see no agent for the extension of public
landownership other than the federal government or
regional agents of its creation.

## Extending Public Lands

The extension of public lands should occur primarily
in two types of areas. The first type of area includes
those natural areas and ecosystems now in unprotected
or precariously protected private ownership. The Public
Land Law Review Commission has endorsed a national system
of natural areas and this recommendation can most readily
be realized through public acquisition.[20] The establishment of a grasslands national park on the western prairie
and public purchase of coastal and estuarial lands would
be responsive to this type of need. The other areas for
extensions of public ownership are peripheral to the
large urban concentrations.

It seems probable that recreational pressures on
the national parks (particularly the large primeval
parks, such as Yellowstone, Yosemite and the Grand
Canyon) can be alleviated only if areas suitable for
outdoor recreation can be provided much closer to the
places where people live. Particularly for the urban
areas east of the Mississippi, metropolitan sprawl and
unplanned development have not only deprived the urban
population of sufficient nearby areas for open space
recreation, but have complicated and encumbered the
use of such areas as do exist.

In the far West, in areas adjacent to the metropolitan centers of Seattle, San Francisco and Los Angeles,
there remain large areas of open, unspoiled space, most
of which is, in fact, under public ownership. Its utilization and enjoyment has been diminished and frustrated
by developments occurring on privately owned lands adjacent to them and between them and the metropolitan centers.

## CONCLUSIONS AND PROJECTIONS

The politics of land, including public land, can only be understood if viewed in historical perspective. The land hunger and land possessiveness that characterized the past behavior of Americans has well-established historical roots both in the conditions prevailing in Europe at the time of colonization and in the economic opportunities presented by the settlement and exploitation of the North American continent. But that is past history and it would be unrealistic to extrapolate past attitudes and behaviors indefinitely into the future. As we have noted, far-reaching and fundamental changes have occurred in the composition, distribution and economic condition of the American people. Looking to the future there are reasons to believe that the following changes in our public attitudes toward land may be anticipated.

## Anticipating Attitudes of the Future

We may anticipate a time when the private ownership of land will not be viewed as inherently more virtuous than public ownership; when social sanction and the law are as concerned with the social and ecological responsibilities of the owner of land as they are with his right to use the land for his personal economic advantage. There may be a time when private landowners become more sophisticated about those aspects of the law that protect their real needs and values in contrast to those that merely appear to do so but in fact do not and when the motivation of public officials for "getting land on the taxrolls" would be removed by more rational systems of public revenue. We may anticipate that our present ecologically damaging practices of property tax administration will be relegated to the museum of historical curiosities along with quit rents and indentured servitude; and the politics and administration of the public lands be viewed generally as the politics and administration of a public trust. There is a strong ethical undercurrent in much of the polemical or policy-oriented

literature on land use. David Lowenthal declares "a
new religion is in the making."[21] But the idea of a
land ethic or a theology of the earth is not new.[22]
The circumstances of our times give it renewed perti-
nence.

These conjectural propositions and the changes they
imply go far beyond the deliberations and recommendations of the Public Land Law Review Commission. I do
not argue that the commission was wrong in its failure
to consider them. But I believe that any adequate
critique of the Public Land Law Review Commission's
report *must* consider them, because they represent the
issues to be confronted if we are to create a rational
and coherent public policy for public land.

## Not Visions But Projections

There can be no adequate policy for public lands
that is not a part of a larger policy for land as an
essential element in a life-support base for the nation.
This being so, it follows that the policy changes which
have been conjectured in this paper are neither visionary
nor idealistic, but are the projections of trends already
evident in society. Our focus in these papers is upon
the public lands, but we cannot obtain that focus, we
cannot be sure that it is accurate and complete, unless
we relate to the larger field of vision which includes
all of the land constituting the nation. For these
lands, although not by law but in a more fundamental,
ecological and historical sense, *are* our public lands.

# NOTES

[1] See U.S. Public Land Law Review Commission, *One Third of the Nation's Land: A Report...* (Washington, D.C.: 1970), Recommendations 23 and 24, pp. 81-83. All subsequent references to the report will be cited by recommendation number only.

[2] For historical background see the following: Frank E. Smith, "The Development of Public Land Policy," pp. 3-22 and Norman Wengert, "The Political Context of Public Land Policy," pp. 23-42 in Philip O. Foss, ed., *Public Land Policy: Proceedings of the Western Resources Conference, Fort Collins, Colorado, 1968* (Boulder: Colorado Associated University Press, 1970). See also Vernon Carstensen, ed., *The Public Land: Studies in the History of the Public Domain* (Madison: University of Wisconsin Press, 1963), and Howard W. Ottoson, ed., *Land Use Policy and Problems in the United States* (Lincoln: University of Nebraska Press, 1963).

[3] Recommendation 97, pp. 226-228.

[4] Robert Ardrey, *The Territorial Imperative: A Personal Inquiry into the Animal Origins of Property and Nations* (New York: Atheneum, 1966).

[5] Kurt Lewin, *Field Theory in Social Science: Selected Theoretical Papers*, ed. Dorwin Cartwright (New York: Harper, 1951).

[6] (Garden City, New York: Doubleday, 1966).

[7] Robert S. and Helen M. Lynd, *Middletown* (New York: Harcourt, Brace, 1929).

[8] See Lynton K. Caldwell, "Managing the Scientific Super-Culture: The Task of Educational Preparation," *Public Administration Review*, 27(2): 128-133 (1967).

[9] *On The State of Society in France before the Revolution of 1789*, third edition (London: John Murray Publisher, 1888), p. 1.

[10] U.S. Council on Environmental Quality, *Environmental Quality: The First Annual Report* (Washington, D.C.: 1970), p. xiii.

[11] Ibid., pp. xii-xiii.

[12] See *National Land Use Policy*, Hearings before the Committee on Interior and Insular Affairs, United States Senate, 91st Cong., 2nd sess. on S. 3354, To Amend the Water Resources Planning Act (79 Stat. 244) To Provide for for a National Land Use Policy, Part I, March 24, April 28 and 29, 1970 (Washington, D.C.: 1970).

[13] *Environmental Quality*, p. 192. See note 10 above.

[14] Recommendations 101, 102, 103, and pp. 235-237.

[15] Letter to James Duane, September 3, 1780, in Henry Cabot Lodge, ed., *The Works of Alexander Hamilton* (New York: G.P. Putnam's Sons, 1885), Vol. I, pp. 1, 218-219.

[16] *Environmental Quality*, pp. xii-xiii.

[17] See Joseph L. Sax, "Environment in the Courtroom," *Saturday Review*, 53(40): 55-57 (October 3, 1970).

[18] "Vindication of the Funding System, No. III" (1791), *Works*, Vol. III, p. 16.

[19] Recommendation 24: "Federal land administering agencies should be authorized to protect the public land environment by (1) imposing protective covenants in disposals of public lands, and (2) acquiring easements on non-Federal lands adjacent to public lands," p. 82.

[20] Recommendation 27: "Congress should provide for the creation and preservation of a natural area system for scientific and educational purposes."

[21] "Is Wilderness 'Paradise Enow'? Images of Nature in America," *Columbia University Forum*, 7(2): 34-40 (Spring 1964).

[22]Note for example Liberty Hyde Bailey, *The Holy Earth* (New York: The Scribner Press, 1915) and René Dubos, "A Theology of the Earth"--a lecture delivered on October 2, 1969 at the Smithsonian Institution in Washington, D.C. under the sponsorship of the Smithsonian Office of Environmental Sciences.

# PANEL DISCUSSION ON
# POLITICS AND THE PUBLIC LANDS

Moderator:   Grant McConnell
             *Professor of Politics*
             *University of California, Santa Cruz*

Panelists:   Luther Carter
             *Science Magazine*
             *Washington, D.C.*

             George A. Craig
             *Western Lumber Manufacturers, Inc.*

             Michael McCloskey
             *Sierra Club, San Francisco*

             Geoffrey Wandesforde-Smith
             *Professor of Political Science*
             *University of California, Davis*

*McConnell:*  We turn now to our commentators on Lynton
Caldwell's policy paper.  I intend to take the people
at this table in alphabetical order and will call on
Luther Carter first.  Mr. Carter is one of the key
staff members of *Science,* a magazine to which I think
a great many of us here are deeply indebted for weekly
information.

## EXPANSION:  PUBLIC OWNERSHIP
## OR CONSERVATION EASEMENTS

*Carter:*  I think the thrust of what I have to say is
that Dr. Caldwell's propositions are, in fact, based
in realistic assessment.  I was struck yesterday by
Mr. Pearl's emphasis on population and economic growth
projections as being part of the rationale of the

commission's report. I was also struck by the fact
that the report contemplated no large increases in
public land acquisitions, despite the fact that only
a very small part of the existing public lands are in
the eastern half of the United States where most of
the people live.

## How Much Expansion?

Dr. Caldwell suggested that perhaps a one-third
expansion in the public land holdings is in order.
Well, now, is this possible? Here, I would say paren-
thetically that when I speak of adding to the public
lands, I am thinking of state as well as federal
acquisitions, and also of putting land under conservation easements, which would accomplish some of
the same objectives as bringing land into public
ownership.

Dr. Caldwell brought out very well the tremendous
need that exists for additional land under public
ownership or control. I would just like to note that
more than half of the land in the State of Maine is
owned by paper companies. Some of those lands, I am
sure, are much better cared for than others. But a
friend of mine recently visited a small trout stream
that he used to fish, and found that the upper reaches
of it had completely disappeared--the watershed had
been so altered by destructive logging practices.

Here in the West some of your tree farms are larger
than some of the national parks we have in the East.
Smoky Mountains National Park in the southern Appala-
chians has about 500 thousand acres. Sometime ago in
the State of Washington, I visited Weyerhaeuser's St.
Helen's Tree Farm, which covers more than a half million
acres. Companies that own such extensive lands realize
that they can't keep them to themselves and do with
them just what they please. They stress the fact that
these lands are open to recreation, open to hunting,
and so on. So, already, these properties have some
of the attributes of publicly held lands.

## More Public Controls

Well, I think the logic of this should be imposed. I was told during a visit to the Gifford Pinchot National Forest in the State of Washington that current practice is to limit clear-cuts to no more than 40 acres. Now, if this is good for the national forests, I wonder why it wouldn't be good for Weyerhaeuser. When I went to St. Helen's Tree Farm, I was shown a clear-cut of nearly an entire section of 640 acres.

Dr. Caldwell mentioned a great need for more open space in urban areas. To that, I would like to add that more of the few remaining undeveloped areas along our coasts--the barrier islands of eastern shore Virginia, for example--belong in public ownership. It seems to me that the flood plains, the green sheaths along a great many small rivers and even some of the larger rivers should be brought under public control, either through public ownership or conservation easements. This would make great sense ecologically, for these bottomlands are havens for many kinds of fish and wildlife and they provide recreation of a very high quality. I can tell you that as a confirmed canoeist.

In the past the wild and scenic rivers concept has been one of picking out only the most choice streams for preservation. The concept should, I think, be extended beyond that. There are many streams that are not of outstanding scenic quality, but nevertheless are worth preserving.

### A MILLION-DOLLAR PROFIT

Now, to bring more land under public ownership or control is certainly going to be fiercely resisted by many interests. Just the raising of money to pay for these properties will be enormously difficult, and as long as land speculators are allowed to play the game the way they see it, I think it will be manifestly impossible.

Recently, there was a 600-acre wooded tract along the Potomac that Fairfax County in Virginia bought for, I think, about $3 or $3.5 million. This land was purchased from some real estate operators who had bought it the year before for about $2.5 million. The company turned a profit of $1 million by keeping the land one year. I am scandalized by that. I don't see how we can permit this kind of thing to go on. Perhaps increasing the capital gains tax on the sale of undeveloped land would be one way of getting at the problem. Maybe in the same way, some of the revenues could be raised that are needed for conservation easements and public acquisition of land.

## Changing Attitudes

Even though there will be tremendous opposition to enlarging the public lands, I think that there is some reason for optimism. To political conservatives, the idea of extensive land use planning and controls has always been abhorrent. This has been an obstacle, but when you look at the fortunes of the national land use policy bill which Professor Caldwell mentioned, you find evidence of changing attitudes. Gordon Allott of Colorado, the ranking Republican of the Senate Interior Committee, has endorsed this bill. Len Jordan of Idaho, another conservative, has endorsed it. Rogers Morton, now the Secretary-designate of the Interior Department, testified before Senator Jackson's Interior Committee and gave a ringing endorsement to this bill, stressing particularly the need for such legislation in the eastern states.

Now, it is also well to point out that the Department of the Interior that Hickel has left is not the same department he came to two years ago. The Water Quality Administration, which commanded the largest budget of any unit in the department, has now become a part of the Environmental Protection Agency. The Bureau of Commercial Fisheries and the maritime mining program is a part of the new Oceanographic and Atmospheric Agency.

This is a department in decline. If it's going to be important and cut a figure in the Nixon administration, it's going to have to stress the land use issue. Morton is, I think, the first easterner to head this department. He apparently wanted the job very much, and he must certainly have in mind to address himself to the land use question.

## Some Legislative Proposals

Congressman Morris Udall of Arizona who could very well be the next majority leader, told me last week that he intends to sponsor the land use bill in the House. He, incidentally, is looking to environmentalists, to conservationists, to support him in his bid for the majority leadership.

Udall is very much concerned about what is happening in Arizona, where only 12 percent of the land is in private ownership. Large blocks of land are being bought up by speculators and sold in small parcels. Many of the speculators who are doing this have operated previously in Florida. Udall thinks that so much time may have been lost that it may be necessary to go back to Senator Jackson's original formulation of his bill, which was not only to require states to adopt a land use plan as a condition for receiving full federal support for programs that have an environmental impact, but also to make all these plans subject to federal approval.

Senator Muskie has a power plant siting bill which, in effect, is a land use measure, and this is a bill that points up the fact that meeting air and water quality standards may really depend on land use control. Pollution control technology alone is unlikely to suffice.

## Building Momentum

Very hurriedly, I want to mention, as all of you know, the defeat of the SST appropriation last Wednesday [December 1970]. Earlier, the Clean Air Bill was passed 73 to 0. Of Environmental Action's Dirty Dozen, 7 out of 12 of these incumbent House members were defeated. All are indications of the powerful momentum that the environmental movement now has assumed, and the influence of the new youth culture is likely to add to that momentum.

I will close with a final observation. As Dr. Caldwell pointed out, President Nixon spoke in favor of land use policy. He has also spoken in favor of developing a national growth policy. With Senator Muskie the front runner for the Democratic nomination, President Nixon will be under increasing pressure to take advanced positions on environmental questions. For these various reasons I hold some hope that the nation's stake in its public lands will be well protected and enhanced.

*McConnell:* Thank you very much.

Our next speaker is Mr. George A. Craig, secretary and manager of Western Lumber Manufacturers, and a very eloquent spokesman, as we heard yesterday when he spoke from the floor.


## POLITICAL POLLUTION AND PUBLIC LAND POLICY

*Craig:* I did not indicate yesterday that I am a professional forester, but I did indicate that I represent people who buy timber from the government. From much of what has been said here in the last two days, it's evident that at least some of the audience might view such a person with suspicion. I want you to know that I have four grandchildren, I never beat my wife, I pay my debts and, in my view, I am otherwise honest.

I think that we are here today really to try to stimulate thought. We were told in our letter of invitation that we were to be provocative. I am sure that I am going to be that. I hope that I will provoke some thought, as well as some emotion, and I hope that you will evaluate what I say and then consider the source, not the other way around.

I chose as a general topic, "Political Pollution and Public Land Policy." Public land policy will come to us to a large extent on the continuing stream of public opinion, as Professor Caldwell suggests. I believe that the source of this stream should be a watershed as broad as the nation itself and its quality should be the best possible. We must receive inputs from all sources, not just the "scientific superculture," which has its own set of biases coloring the stream. Further, we must avoid the erosion of ignorance, the lack of clarity that comes from poor communications, and the muddy effects caused by deliberate distortion.

Major elements of the general public do not appear to be represented here today. Where are the opinion leaders of labor? I notice two people in the list of those attending who may be associated with labor; none on any of the panels. How about the urban poor who comprise most of the 55 million Americans living at the poverty level? Why were not the governmental agencies dealing with labor and the underprivileged asked to participate? There can be no doubt about their stake in "the people's land." We need the opinions of such thoughtful and informed men as Mr. Whitney Young of the National Urban League or Mr. Robert Pitts, the regional administrator of the Department of Housing and Urban Development. They could offer guidance regarding the needs of great segments of our society for food, fiber, shelter and recreation.

## Understanding Public Needs

There is not general understanding of such needs and the potential for their partial satisfaction from the public lands. Most people don't even know that the national forests were established so that they could be improved and protected for the production of wood and water to meet the needs of the nation. The Forest Service has reported that domestic consumption of industrial roundwood, that is, all products except fuelwood, had risen by 23 percent between 1950 and 1968.

Housing needs alone will require much greater increases in supply in 10 years, if the current needs are to be met. The public generally doesn't know that it is being cheated of the annual production of enough additional wood on the national forests to build 700 thousand new homes each year, because sound practices of forest culture have not been financed for selected areas. People are not aware of the need to plant nearly 5 million acres of national forest and thin another 13 million acres with the effect of enhancing much of the forest for other uses. Care would be exercised to protect the environment in all such activities. Failure to do these things is increasing the cost of homes.

## What Words Mean

Another problem is that of poor communications compounded by the tendency of people to use words improperly. A prime example that has been illustrated over and over again here is the word "ecology." We hear of "ecological integrity," for example. Since "ecology" is a body of knowledge about the relationships between living organisms and their environment, the intent of the word "integrity" is not clear. According to some, there can be "damage to the ecology." Others would not include man as a part of such knowledge. It is hard to communicate ideas when such language is used. Other examples include the use of the word "economic" in such a way as to mean only values that can be measured in dollars and cents. To others, it means the allocation of resources of any type to meet human needs. If, as Alice said in *Through the Looking Glass*, "Words mean whatever I say they mean," we are in trouble when trying to establish good policy.

Finally, the worst pollution of the streams of public opinion comes with the deliberate distortion of data to achieve special objectives--"the end justifies the means" approach. A destructive example is the printed statement used by opponents of timber supply legislation in the last Congress.

Incidentally, the other night I mentioned timber supply legislation and I got an actual physical reaction from a young man in the group who was a member of the Sierra Club--it was a conditioned reflex. He is an intelligent man. He tried to learn what he could about this important public issue, and he reacted in response to what he heard. The executive director of the Sierra Club wrote: "Disaster for our national forests.... Surviving virgin timber in all other locations will be quickly liquidated too.... Logging will be officially enthroned as the main use on the 97 million acres of forest land, supporting merchantable timber that belongs to every one of us." [Brock Evans yesterday spoke of 47 or 45 million acres.] "On that land 'multiple use' will be no more than a hollow phrase. The unstable, and relatively sterile, ecology of mass tree farming"--there is the misuse of that word again--"will supplant a more or less natural forest."

## More Misleading Statements

The timber supply bill was improperly described as a land classification act. Quotations from it left out the words "subject to the provisions of the Act of June 12, 1960," which is the Multiple Use Act. Mr. McCloskey said, "Four billion board feet are being exported in 1969, and the rate has been doubling in recent years..." The facts are that in 1969 exports were below the 1968 export total and well below the 4 billion board foot figure. Mr. McCloskey failed to mention that the United States is a net importer of wood by a substantial amount.

Among other misleading statements, the Sierra Club's release quoted Secretary of Agriculture Hardin and Forest Service Chief Cliff regarding an earlier bill and failed to note that it had been modified in accord with recommendations of these gentlemen. The club material recommended the showing of its film "The Wasted Woods," which the president of the Society of American Foresters (Philip Briegleb, a respected scientist) had recommended be withdrawn because it was "full of errors and distortions of the true situation."

In the light of this, it was rather ironical to hear Mr. Evans say yesterday that the club "takes care not to misrepresent the position of others." While he claimed that the commission's director, Milton Pearl, had set up a straw man in respect to the club's opposition to the commission's report, this is not borne out by the facts. The club's president, Mr. Berry, stated in the October 1970 *Sierra Club Bulletin*: "The basic premises and assumptions of the report are wrong.... The specific deficiencies of the report are numerous." That certainly was not an endorsement.

In conclusion, this problem of political pollution is a serious one because it is wasteful and damaging. It deserves careful examination by you political scientists, because perhaps you can suggest what must be done to prevent further degradation of our political process, so that we can have a public land policy based on consideration of factual data.

*McConnell:* Thank you.

After having heard the mention of Mike McCloskey, I will call on Mike McCloskey.

EVALUATING THE REPORT

*McCloskey:* Well, having sat through Mr. Craig's presentation, I am wondering really whether I should ask for another conference to debate the timber supply bill. George and I have done that in the past, and I would be quite interested in doing it again.

In characterizing that legislation, we persuaded the people of the United States and the Congress of the United States that we were not lying, that we were accurately representing things. The Congress accepted our word. The people accepted it. The only people that haven't done so are those of the lumber industry. So I think it would be appropriate to abide by that decision, though I am quite willing to defend all of the things we have said. I think they are accurate in the context in which they were said.

## Two Different Directions

This issue does indicate, though, the difficulties of addressing yourself to the subject matter. The diversions are many, and this brings us to our subject of the public lands and the Public Land Law Review Commission report. Professor Caldwell's presentation was in marked contrast to the thrust of the report itself. In contrast to the report, it is notable that he recommended acquiring more public lands, substantially more, and setting forth a national framework for planning what happens to all lands, to thus increase the national input and direction for decisionmaking, and to emphasize the ecological factors in that decisionmaking.

The Public Land Law Review Commission report really goes in quite a different direction, as has been brought out at a number of points in this conference. Despite that fact, an effort is afoot, through these many conferences, to create the impression that the report is actually a balanced document. Throughout the report various references are made to the environment, and you have seen the staff director attempt to assume a posture of being in the middle. And, indeed, one can selectively cite the references to environmental recommendations in the report; there is almost a constant gesture that is made in that direction, to sort of cover rhetorical ground. Yet, if one looks at the actual recommendations themselves and the patterns they assume, in toto, in context, it's not at all a balanced report. In fact, the pattern is one of preserving maximum advantage for western commercial interests, to the extent that it may still be politically feasible to do so in the remaining one-third of the twentieth century.

## Looking Backward

You see a holding on, a backward look rather than a forward look, with the exception of a forward look based upon assumptions of continued population growth and continued economic growth. As a parenthetical statement--to pick up one of the things that George Craig said, it's interesting to note that the economic contributions of the various commodity interests on the public lands are in a posture, in many cases, of just holding on, particularly the timber industry which likes to always assert it has a bright future, that it is going to sell a great deal more and build more and more homes. But it is simultaneously worried about holding onto its markets in the face of all sorts of substitute products. The industry is schizophrenic about what its real concern is.

Similarly with respect to people in the grazing industry, they worry about the importation of wool from Australia and beef from South America and Australia. The reclamation groups are having a harder and harder time economically justifying their projects.

I think it's quite plausible that the future of the commodity industries on public lands is a failing

future; it's not a future tied in any sense to any
rising demand of the American people. I think it's
an entirely different question as to what the real
needs of the American people are to be in the future.

In the Sierra Club article that George Craig
referred to, I summarized the findings of the commission
in these terms:

> Under their recommendations a majority
> of the public lands would be retained,
> but an old set of disposal laws would
> be replaced by a new set; and most
> prospective takers of these public
> lands would be indulged if they would
> pay fair market value. Even that is
> compromised in many places. The ad-
> ministration of public lands would
> be tidied up to some extent, but
> management would put a premium on
> product output. The miners would
> have to operate under somewhat more
> restrictive rules, but more areas
> would be open to them.
>
> Supposedly, conservationists would
> get their choice areas protected,
> but nothing is promised beyond inven-
> tories and short-term withdrawals.
> Conservationists could also try to
> perfect environmental classification
> systems, but intensified commodity
> programs would go into operation at
> once. The balance is not one to in-
> spire much hope. Environmentalists
> will be looking for a better blue-
> print for the future of public lands.

# FUNCTIONAL OMISSION OF ECOLOGY

If you go through the report, I think you can see biases--bias after bias--which go exactly in the opposite direction from what Professor Caldwell urged. We see emphasis on benefiting commercial industries, commodity industries, toward maximizing commodity output, toward making economic factors more dominant in all decisionmaking. And while George has referred to that approach as an allocation system, the truth of the matter is that it looks toward quantifying the various competing values in dollar terms. In a sense, ecology cannot be expressed in those terms. It's functionally left out of any such equation.

The report stresses maximizing the areas that would be open to commodity production, giving preferences to certain types of commodities, such as minerals. It looks toward continuing to find ways to dispose of public lands, toward giving the commodity industries greater tenure in their operations, toward minimizing administrative flexibility in using our public lands and managing them. It looks toward increasing the role of the local interests which historically are short-sighted interests. That is the outlook of this report.

# SUPPORT FROM COMMODITY INTERESTS

Well, in looking at how people characterize and react to it, I think it's very curious that the people who are calling the report a balanced report are not people who lack self-interest. At conference after conference, it is the commodity industries, who are benefiting in these matters or would benefit from the commission's report, who come forward to claim that this is a balanced report and commend the commission profusely. You don't hear the conservationists say that. This leads to very profound skepticism about the claims for balance.

The commodity industries, however, aren't even going as far as the commission report does. In some instances they are beginning to dissent from the idea of having to pay fair market value for products, minerals, forage and timber, though the report does recommend cutting those prices in some instances. There is resistance to increasing environmental controls, resistance to acquiring more public lands and generally a holding onto the traditional stances they have taken.

## Criticism From Many Quarters

Now, I think it's also curious that the chairman of the commission is charging that the Sierra Club is alone in opposing the commission report and in criticizing it. I think any objective review of the record will indicate that that's not true, either. The conservation groups of the country are exceedingly concerned about this report, and the criticism is coming from many quarters. In fact, I would say that I doubt that there will have been one single environmental issue in the last 10 years, or in the next 10 years, that will unify conservationists as will the future of our public lands. Most of these groups belong to the Natural Resources Council of America, and it is preparing its own recommendations.

In the next Congress we will see recommendations coming from many quarters. We will see the commission's bills. We will see the conservationists with their bills. We will see the Nixon administration with its bill. We will see the bills of people like Senator Jackson and we will see positions of the various commodity industries, too. I think that there will be immense confusion on this issue and a stand-off for a good many years as these positions are sorted out. In the end, as Professor Caldwell stated, and Professor McConnell too, the forces that represent the new winds that are blowing in this country will prevail. They will have to prevail in whatever is finally enacted.

*McConnell:*  Thank you.

Our last panelist is Professor Geoffrey Wandesforde-Smith, who is a political scientist and has a joint appointment in the environmental program at the University of California at Davis.

## A POLITICAL DOCUMENT

*Wandesforde-Smith:*  The report of the Public Land Law Review Commission is, above all, a political document. It has been described by the Sierra Club and others as a document that is designed to perpetuate and reaffirm the hold exercised over federal public lands by western and commercial interests. It has also been described, partly in jest but with more than a grain of truth, as one of the best reports ever written during the 1950s. The report has much in common with another massive report that was begun in the last year of the 1950s, the report of the Senate Select Committee on National Water Resources.

Among the similarities between these two reports is their association with a powerful congressional figure. In the case of the Senate Select Committee on National Water Resources, this was the late Senator Robert Kerr of Oklahoma. In the case of the Public Land Law Review Commission, it is Congressman Wayne Aspinall of Colorado, a gentleman whose name has been conspicuously absent from most of the speeches and comments made at this conference. A much more important but related aspect of each report is the extent to which it maintains the exclusivity of a significant area of public policy. It excludes from the political process of determining that policy a wider range of interests that has traditionally been involved in decisions about the use, management and disposition of the nation's land and water resources.

## Points of Concern

Yesterday Professor Crutchfield expressed dismay and concern about the treatment afforded in the Public Land Law Review Commission's report to certain economic concepts and the results of economic research, particularly in water resources management. Professor Rogers hinted at, but unfortunately did not have time to develop comments about a similar point concerning political concepts and the fruits of political science research.

The point at which the commission's report reveals its ignorance of political research--perhaps a willful disregard rather than ignorance--is to be found in Chapter Two, the chapter in which the commission's somewhat strange formula for determining public interest is outlined. Professor Rogers has dealt very well in his paper with the concept of the public interest advanced by the commission. To my satisfaction he has demolished it. Professor Caldwell has dealt it an equally devastating, if more restrained, death blow, emphasizing the fundamental point that in a holistic sense all of the lands in the United States are public lands, and that the time-honored distinction between federal lands and other lands is simply inapplicable for the purposes of long-range planning and policy development in the 1970s and beyond.

I should like to comment briefly on one specific aspect of the report that was touched upon this morning, but which seems to me to deserve greater attention: namely, the question of administrative reorganization or, as I prefer to call it, administrative gadgetry.

## Failure to Deal with Political Consequences

Among the many recommendations in the report there are three pertaining to administrative gadgetry that deserve special mention because they demonstrate the almost total failure of the commission to deal explicitly, seriously and in depth with the political consequences of the subject at hand. These are, first, the recommendation for the creation of a Department of Natural Resources to replace the Department of the Interior. Secondly, there is the endorsement of a bill offered by Senator Henry Jackson that would convert the Water Resources Council into a Land and Water Resources Council and also convert the several water resources planning commissions into entities for land and water resources planning. Third, there is the recommendation for a new federal-state planning commission for Alaska that will presumably replace the present federal Field Committee for Development Planning in Alaska.

All of these recommendations surely must be rejected or at least viewed with extreme suspicion. It was implicit in the discussion this morning that administrative reorganization is itself a fundamental political issue, and the bureaucratic reshuffling that the commission recommends will do very little to bring about a basic change in the politics of land use and management. There are several reasons for this, and I will only mention one.

## NEEDED: A BROADER VIEW OF PUBLIC INTEREST

Perhaps the most telling and significant reason is to be found in the absence in the commission's report of any suggestions that institutional arrangements be modified in a way that would strengthen or add to the mechanisms that support a broader view of the public interest. And by "a broader view," I mean one that would embrace the holistic philosophy of Professor Caldwell and one that would go beyond the miners, lumbermen, cattlemen, and sheepmen and the oil and gasmen to embrace the Indians, the Blacks, the young and many other segments of society for whom the future of one-third of the nation's land has so far held very little hope, promise or significance. If we are

talking about the future of the nation's land, we are
talking also about a set of policy decisions that are
of consequence to a national constituency. The dis-
tinguishing feature of past and present land policy is
the remarkable and unacceptable degree to which decisions about the federal public lands have been appropriated by private, narrowly economic and essentially
local interests.

This development is not illogical, as Mr. Stoddard
suggested this morning; it is both logical and highly
rational within very clearly marked limits and to a
very narrowly defined constituency.

## Political Mythology of Pluralism

We know, for example, that existing political and
administrative arrangements for making policy with
respect to both land and water confer benefits upon
interests that are not only specialized, but also
highly *organized*. The mythology of American politics
teaches us that the public interest is determined by
the conflict and competition among interest groups.
Political scientists have come to refer to this as
interest group pluralism.

The report of the commission proposes to legitimize
this political theory by placing it on a scientific or
mechanistic base that will have all the appearances
of a political process from which no relevant interest
or public is excluded. Yet we have already seen--
thanks to the acumen and courage of John Borbridge--
that one vitally important group has been excluded
through the artifice of an analytical definition which
takes no account of the direct and indirect interests
of the American Indians in the federal public lands
off the reservations.

## Massive Confusion

In response to Grant McConnell's urgings, let me conclude by asking a question. Consider the relationship between the Public Land Law Review Commission's report and the general public. It is abundantly evident from this conference, and the comments that it has occasioned, that this massive report has created considerable confusion.

Take, for example, the concept of dominant use which appears to some to be a mirror image of and largely indistinguishable in practice from the concept of multiple use. Only a limited, organized set of interests are really equipped to evaluate the full report in an effort to find the real meaning of dominant use. Groups such as the forest products industry, represented by my colleague, Mr. Craig, and the Sierra Club, represented by Mr. McCloskey, have the money and manpower to try to meet Director Pearl and his staff on their own ground. University professors may have a similar advantage. But what about the great majority of landowners I referred to earlier? Can they rely upon Mr. Craig and Mr. McCloskey or myself to represent preferences and viewpoints, or must they purchase and wade through the Public Land Law Review Commission's report and related documents one by one? It seems to me a major failing of the Public Land Law Review Commission's report in terms of political and administrative arrangements that it does not consider any real institutional innovations that might help us determine a public interest in the public lands that is much broader than that we have seen in the past.

## INSTITUTIONALIZING PUBLIC CRITICISM

Clearly, any system of representation is imperfect in the sense that individual preferences must be aggregated, evaluated and to some extent compromised. However, it is not at all clear that interest, expression and reconciliation must take place in a setting where

information costs are very high for the public at large.
We are indebted to the commission for its views, to
Mr. Craig for his, and to the Sierra Club and Mr.
McCloskey for theirs. But what if we are still dissat-
isfied and interested in a more detached, straightforward and relatively brief critique of the report? In
other words, what about the possibility of institution-
alizing public criticism of public policy proposals
through an organization responsible to the broadest
possible national constituency?

This idea does not apply only to land policy but
to a great variety of policy areas. I am not sure
what precise form it might take in terms of funding
and personnel, for example. Perhaps an institutional-
ized Nader's Raiders would be appropriate. Perhaps
the universities can serve to a greater extent as
advocates of the public interest, although this carries
some serious risks. Whatever format is adopted, it
seems reasonably clear that the new politics gaining
support in this country will not much longer tolerate
the maintenance of what our chairman referred to in
his writing as a politics of preemption with respect
to land and water resources. I notice that the commission ignored his work on this subject.

Innovative institutional arrangements will be
needed to shift the focus of our concerns, and especially those of political and administrative decisionmakers, away from land as primarily a commodity and a
source of material benefits, and toward those social
and political values, including that of widespread
participation in government, that *together with* ecological values add to the quality of life in America.
Let it be noted that, if new institutions are employed
to help clean up what Mr. Craig calls political pollution, both Mr. Craig and Mr. McCloskey may have to be
more accommodating to the power and preferences of the
people who own one-third of the nation's land.

## DISCUSSION WITH THE AUDIENCE

*McConnell:*   Thank you.

In turning this over to questions from the floor,
I wish to exercise one prerogative.  Mr. Craig noted
the absence of any representative from organized labor
here.  With your indulgence, I might ask the gentleman
whom I see in the front row if he will be willing to
speak, since he is with the AFL-CIO--Dr. Paul Taylor.

### ACREAGE LIMITATIONS AND WATER GRANTS

*Taylor:*   The Public Land Law Review Commission's report
emphasizes the retention of management and disposal of
land.  It says very little about acquisition of the
land by the public.  It says, "Let us maximize public
benefit."  And certainly that is an essential principle
to guide us.

## A Matter of 900,000 Acres

I want to speak for just a moment about a specific
case where I think the public can and should acquire
new private lands and so maximize the public benefit.
I want to speak about what might be called a case study.
To give you a little idea of the extent, I am talking
about something like 900 thousand acres in the State
of California alone.  I don't know what the acreage is
in the 17 western states, but it's very large.  Those
900 thousand acres receive or are about to receive,
public water, publicly subsidized under reclamation
law.

Now, the present law says the owner of more than
160 acres about to receive water shall agree, by
recordable legal contract, to dispose of the excess
of 160 acres at the prewater price.  That is present
law.  The Public Land Law Review Commission apparently

is opposed to that. Certainly its chairman, as a congressman and chairman of the House Interior Committee,
has a distinguished record in opposition to acreage
limitation as a control over monopoly and speculation.

## Acquiring Lands at Prewater Prices

Now we start with the present law which requires
the owners of excess lands to agree to their disposal
at the prewater price. My proposal is that we add to
the present reclamation law a provision that shall
authorize the government to acquire those lands which
are about to be disposed of at the prewater price.

When I speak of 900 thousand acres in California,
I am talking about an area larger than the State of
Rhode Island, some of it presently in agriculture,
some of it presently in cities. Now, how will public
acquisition of these lands, if the government acquires
them, maximize public benefit? Let me indicate as
specifically and briefly as I can.

First, it will put money in the public treasury.
Secretary of the Interior Harold L. Ickes stated it
very pithily when he said, "It is the age-old battle
over who is to cash in on the unearned increment in
land values created by a public investment," in this
case the public investment in reclamation, the public
gift of public water.

Second, it will enable the government to gain title
to the land, to attach land use regulations and permit
the preservation of open spaces. The ability of the
public to plan its future is at stake.

## Water Grants for Education

Third, we can apply the revenues to public purposes,
such as grants for education. Abraham Lincoln and
Thomas Jefferson gave land grants when we gave away

the public land for education. Let us now give away
a portion of those revenues that we might call water
grants for education.

## AN INDIAN VIEW OF THE CONFERENCE

*McConnell:* There's a gentleman back there and I recognize him first.

*A Member of the Audience:* I am a Sioux Indian from South
Dakota. I'm president of a national Indian organization. I found out about this meeting through reading
a newspaper, about how an Indian woman came here yesterday and had to criticize the people to get some
news in the papers so Indians could find out you had
a meeting here to discuss public lands.

As Mr. Craig up here has said, public lands belong
to everybody; they belong to Indians and Blacks and
everybody else. Well, public lands essentially belong
to Indian people and, in many cases, like the State
of California, the Indians have never been paid by
the State of California, and the land still legally
belongs to them.

You are holding public land meetings here and you
don't invite the Indian people, even though the land
still legally belongs to them. You don't even notify
us so we can come and listen, even if we are not going
to be able to speak. There is not one Indian speaker
listed on this whole thing. I think this is the most
hypocritical damn meeting I have ever been to. Not
one Indian on this thing. A bunch of political scientists and ecology professors, and what-have-you.

*McConnell:* I beg your pardon, sir. There were a number
of Indians...

*A Member of the Audience:* Speakers, I am talking about.
[Simultaneous audience reaction]

*McConnell:* There was one speaker.

*A Member of the Audience:* Well, it's nice you did have one speaker. I'm sorry. I didn't know you had any. But the fact is you should have Indians on this panel. In fact, every panel should have had one, and it's a sad thing when you have got to find out about a meeting by reading the newspaper.

I think I've about said what I wanted. I think this meeting is really a farce.

## Economics of 1906

*Kiml:* My name is Larry Kiml. I represent all interests in the consumer field and probably some in the commercial field--the California Chamber of Commerce.

I wasn't going to speak at this meeting, but since Paul Taylor saw fit to raise the acreage limitation issue, I felt compelled to set the record straight. We are talking about a law enacted in 1906 that had its antecedents in legislation that was intended to encourage the settlement of the West, the very type of law the Land Law Review Commission is trying to modernize and bring up to date.

I just want to raise one point. Can you farm with two mules on 160 acres in today's economy? Are we forever saying that the poor guy that has to have the water for federal projects is forced to a quality of life, a living standard and environment, if you will, based on 1906 economics?

*Taylor:* I was talking about agribusiness and the big landowners, not about the small farmers.

## REAL NEEDS OF THE URBAN POOR

*Emerson:* I'm Pat Emerson of Seattle.

I find that I must agree with Mr. Craig in his comment that there are many segments of the public who are not represented here as well as those he specifically mentioned. But I want further to say that I would be most distressed to find that anyone would be using the very real and overwhelming and pressing needs of the urban poor or of the rural poor to further any particular interest in the formulation or the implementation of public land policies.

*McConnell:* Would you comment on that?

*Craig:* I agree with you. Our problem in setting any policy should be to establish objectives, and the only way we are going to establish objectives in the public resource field is to determine needs. One of the major needs of our urban people is housing.

It disturbs me to hear these statements about the emphasis on timber production. In 1959 the Eisenhower administration came out with a program for the national forests. The Kennedy administration, in the next year, came out with a development program for the national forests. It outlined specific goals for management of these lands. These objectives were approved by the Congress. They called for a variety of input in the way of budget, investment, and one of these had to do with the production of wood to meet the anticipated urban needs. But the budgets were not provided.

## Obligations for Housing

This was a way of finally attempting to wake up the Congress and the conscience of America to its obligations and its opportunities. And this is the reason why I specifically refer to this need of the

urban poor, and the fact is that even if wood goes into
the more luxurious home of the nonurban poor, the net
effect is that the urban poor are improved in their
lot, and we have an opportunity here.

It won't take all the national forests; it is an
objective which has been put out in a program in a
balanced form, and we need the budgets to do it.

*Emerson:* Mr. Craig, let me point out that when I say
"anyone," I mean anyone. And I was not referring only
to your comment; I am referring to the fact that no
one, whatever his point of view, should use those needs
to further that point of view. I wasn't referring to
timber.

## Another Indian View

*McConnell:* I recognize the gentleman in the rear--
Michael Rogers.

*Rogers:* First of all, I would like to extend my appreciation as an Indian for the opportunity to be able to
meet with you and for the privilege of discussing the
ideals and the concepts of Indian people. We realize
that there is much confusion in the country, and of
course we are part of that confusion because we are the
human element.

This conference has been one that I can say that I
have been truly proud to have attended and participated
in, and I think that the staff and the University of
California at Berkeley have done a tremendous job in
getting the people who have participated here.

I think one thing that the report has done, it has
awakened many people. It is stimulating, and I think
that we are going to have more concern about what
America really is and to promote the democracy that
we have a right to protect.

## LOOKING FOR OTHER MATERIALS

I do have a question for Mr. Craig in regard to the logging industry. I have spent several years in the logging field myself, and the question I'd like to address to him is: Now that there are almost no more public lands or private logging areas left, what happens when the public land timber is gone? Then where do we look to? We look to other materials. Housing is important, but there are other materials and we should take more interest in them instead of merely using up the timber resources as quickly as possible.

The practices that have been used in public logging have created much erosion, much waste, and nobody can tell me any different because I have been part of it. There is need, yes, for reform and because the public lands are the last lands left with timber on them, we must move with caution.

## A Good Investment

*Craig:* Very briefly, in California approximately three-fifths of the commercial timber harvest comes from the private lands. Now, there are reasons why the private lands were cut first. They were, obviously, those most accessible, and they were taken up in part for that purpose.

It's also true that because of population growth and other demands, the economy of forest production is such that firms are acquiring forest lands in order to provide a continuous source of wood for their plants. It's a good investment today and it will be growing wood.

With the tax burdens that exist, they can't afford not to. In the interim, in many areas the least accessible public lands are now filling the need for which they were originally established.

## NO BLACK LEADERS

*McConnell:* The lady in the rear has been standing there patiently.

*A Member of the Audience:* I, too, am one of the persons who learned about the conference through reading it in the newspaper. I have been a school teacher for the past two years, very involved in many political groups, and I have attended some conferences that are dealing with the problem of ecology and the environment.

I was rather disappointed that throughout the conference I didn't see any of the Black leaders or persons who are employed in high offices here within this area being utilized in your conference. I know that so many times we hear references to persons such as Whitney Young who are world renowned, but there are persons who are located more in our immediate area, who are of such standards and status and have equal background that can be utilized and be of value in a conference such as this. This is my one criticism that I have here.

But I am appreciative to have been able to attend, and I have learned a great deal.

## WHY ACQUIRE MORE LAND?

*Hill:* My name is Clair Hill. I was interested in discussion concerning the goal of several of the panel members to acquire a great deal more public land. I am very puzzled as to what the goal is. Will it raise more game, more fish, more timber? I don't understand the big emphasis on acquiring more public lands.

*Caldwell:* Well, if I may react to the question, I suggested that there be a fairly substantial addition to the public lands of the United States, but I suggested that this be distributed over quite a variety

of areas. I mentioned specifically coastal areas, estuarial lands partly submerged. I referred to certain in-
holding problems in which there may well be exchange of
land, but in which the sale of land by the United States
government and the subsequent purchase of land by the
United States government may be involved.

I particularly directed attention to the needs of
the large urban areas and the problems of open space,
public housing, recreation. The acquisition of these
lands was not intended primarily in the urban areas
for hunting and fishing, but for the daily lives of
people.

Moreover, although I suggested that the funds for
these purchases would probably have to come from the
federal treasury, it does not necessarily follow that
they would be administered by the federal government.
That is another question.

Quite conceivably, they could be administered by
the municipalities, by states or regional organizations in the area where they were purchased.

## PLACER MINING AND TRESPASSING

*McConnell:* Just one last question. This gentleman
near the rail.

*Adams:* Alonzo Adams. I represent the Adams Placer
Mining Claims. These mining claims had their origin
back in 1915 when an old prospector or miner went into
Charlie Canyon in Los Angeles County in 1914 and re-
turned in 1915 after he had discovered gold and other
precious minerals. He worked these mining claims for
years. I joined him in 1928. He died in 1937.

At that time I put together all the loose ends
of all these many properties and I became the sole

owner of Adams Placer. In 1951 I applied to the government to patent 450 acres of my excess of 2,000 acres. After 11-and-a-half years in federal court my government confiscated those 450 acres, and in doing that, the courts also confiscated the balance of the 2,000 acres along with the 450 acres, which balance is not included in the suit in the court.

Now, I won't go into detail on the Department of the Interior's innovations and intentions to dispossess me, deprive me and confiscate my mining claims, but I will say that that Bill of Rights states nowhere that the government can confiscate private property without compensation. I was not only not compensated, but I was kicked out for trespassing.

Now, I notice that both speakers here have touched on this subject...

*McConnell:* I am sorry, sir. Our time is very limited.

*Adams:* No one has said to me or to any member here what the Public Land Law Review report will do to my 2,000 acres.

*McConnell:* Our time has run out. Many of us have not only promises to keep, but planes to catch.


A CLOSING WORD

*Lee:* Before you adjourn, may I have one last word?

I want to thank you, but I want to also do something else on your behalf and on my behalf. We have spent two days here analyzing and criticizing the commission's report, and I want you to know you have done this at the invitation--and at no small expense--of the federal government, more specifically the commission itself. And I think it is something very remarkable, for I have never been party before to an enterprise where an organization has delivered a public report and then gone out to seek criticism of that report. I think we owe a great debt of gratitude to the commission and specifically to Milton Pearl, the director, for inviting what I think has been very constructive and creative, but also incisive and tough criticism.

I want to thank you for being one of the most attentive and hard-working audiences that it has ever been my pleasure to work with.

# Appendix

# SUMMARY OF COMMISSION RECOMMENDATIONS AS LISTED IN
## *ONE THIRD OF THE NATION'S LAND:*
*A REPORT TO THE PRESIDENT AND THE CONGRESS BY THE*
*PUBLIC LAND LAW REVIEW COMMISSION*

## Chapter Three (Planning Future Public Land Use)

1. Goals should be established by statute for a continuing, dynamic program of land use planning. These should include:

Use of all public lands in a manner that will result in a maximum net public benefit.

Disposal of those lands identified in land use plans as being able to maximize net public benefit only if they are transferred to private or state or local governmental ownership, as specified in other Commission recommendations.

Management of primary use lands for secondary uses where they are compatible with the primary purpose for which the lands were designated.

Management of all lands not having a statutory primary use for such uses as they are capable of sustaining.

Disposition or retention and management of public lands in a manner that complements uses and patterns of use on other ownership in the locality and the region.

2. Public land agencies should be required to plan land uses to obtain the greatest net public benefit. Congress should specify the factors to be considered by the agencies in making these determinations, and an analytical system should be developed for their application.

3. Public lands should be classified for transfer from Federal ownership when net public benefits would be maximized by disposal.

4. Management of public lands should recognize the highest and best use of particular areas of land as dominant over other authorized uses.

5. All public land agencies should be required to formulate long range, comprehensive land use plans for each state or region, relating such plans not only to internal agency programs but also to land use plans and attendant management programs of other agencies. Specific findings should be provided in their plans, indicating how various factors were taken into account.

6. As an essential first step to the planning system we recommend, Congress should provide for a careful review of (1) all Executive withdrawals and reservations, and (2) BLM retention and disposal classifications under the Classification and Multiple Use Act of 1964.

7. Congress should provide authority to classify national forest and BLM lands, including the authority to suspend or limit the operation of any public land laws in specified areas. Withdrawal authority should no longer be used for such purpose.

8. Large scale, limited or single use withdrawals of a permanent or indefinite term should be accomplished only by act of Congress. All other withdrawal authority should be expressly delegated with statutory guidelines to insure proper justification for proposed withdrawals, provide for public participation in their consideration, and establish criteria for executive action.

9. Congress should establish a formal program by which withdrawals would be periodically reviewed and either rejustified or modified.

10. All Executive withdrawal authority, without limitation, should be delegated to the Secretary of the

Interior, subject to the continuing limitation of existing law that the Secretary cannot redelegate to anyone other than an official of the Department appointed by the President, thereby making the exercise of this authority wholly independent of public land management operating agency heads.

11. Provision should be made for public participation in land use planning, including public hearings on proposed Federal land use plans, as an initial step in a regional coordination process.

12. Land use planning among Federal agencies should be systematically coordinated.

13. State and local governments should be given an effective role in Federal agency land use planning. Federal land use plans should be developed in consultation with these governments, circulated to them for comments, and should conform to state or local zoning to the maximum extent feasible. As a general rule, no use of public land should be permitted which is prohibited by state or local zoning.

14. Congress should provide additional financial assistance to public land states to facilitate better and more comprehensive land use planning.

15. Comprehensive land use planning should be encouraged through regional commissions along the lines of the river basin commissions created under the Water Resources Planning Act of 1965. Such commissions should come into existence only with the consent of the states involved, with regional coordination being initiated when possible within the context of existing state and local political boundaries.

## Chapter Four (Public Land Policy and the Environment)

16. Environmental quality should be recognized by law as an important objective of public land management,

and public land policy should be designed to enhance and maintain a high quality environment both on and off the public lands.

17. Federal standards for environmental quality should be established for public lands to the extent possible, except that, where state standards have been adopted under Federal law, state standards should be utilized.

18. Congress should require classification of the public lands for environmental quality and enhancement and maintenance.

19. Congress should specify the kinds of environmental factors to be considered in land use planning and decisionmaking, and require the agencies to indicate clearly how they were taken into account.

20. Congress should provide for greater use of studies of environmental impacts as a precondition to certain kinds of uses.

21. Existing research programs related to the public lands should be expanded for greater emphasis on environmental quality.

22. Public hearings with respect to environmental considerations should be mandatory on proposed public land projects or decisions when requested by the states or by the Council on Environmental Quality.

23. Congress should authorize and require the public land agencies to condition the granting of rights or privileges to the public lands or their resources on compliance with applicable environmental control measures governing operations off public lands which are closely related to the right or privilege granted.

24. Federal land administering agencies should be authorized to protect the public land environment by (1) imposing protective covenants in disposals of public

lands, and (2) acquiring easements on non-Federal lands adjacent to public lands.

25. Those who use the public lands and resources should, in each instance, be required by statute to conduct their activities in a manner that avoids or minimizes adverse environmental impacts, and should be responsible for restoring areas to an acceptable standard where their use has an adverse impact on the environment.

26. Public land areas in need of environmental rehabilitation should be inventoried and the Federal Government should undertake such rehabilitation. Funds should be appropriated as soon as practical for environmental management and rehabilitation research.

27. Congress should provide for the creation and preservation of a natural area system for scientific and educational purposes.

## Chapter Five (Timber Resources)

28. There should be a statutory requirement that those public lands that are highly productive for timber be classified for commercial timber production as the dominant use, consistent with the Commission's concept of how multiple use should be applied in practice.

29. Federal programs on timber production units should be financed by appropriations from a revolving fund made up of receipts from timber sales on these units. Financing for development and use of public forest lands, other than those classified for timber production as the dominant use, would be by appropriation of funds unrelated to receipts from the sale of timber.

30. Dominant timber production units should be managed primarily on the basis of economic factors so as to maximize net returns to the Federal Treasury. Such factors should also play an important but not primary role in timber management on other public lands.

31. Major timber management decisions, including allowable-cut determinations, should include specific consideration of economic factors.

32. Timber sales procedures should be simplified wherever possible.

33. There should be an accelerated program of timber access road construction.

34. Communities and firms dependent on public land timber should be given consideration in the management and disposal of public land timber.

35. Timber production should not be used as a justification for acquisition or disposition of Federal public lands.

36. Controls to assure that timber harvesting is conducted so as to minimize adverse impacts on the environment on and off the public lands must be imposed.

## Chapter Six (Range Resources)

37. Public land forage policies should be flexible, designed to attain maximum economic efficiency in the production and use of forage from the public land, and to support regional economic growth.

38. The grazing of domestic livestock on the public lands should be consistent with the productivity of those lands.

39. Existing eligibility requirements should be retained for the allocation of grazing privileges up to recent levels of forage use. Increases in forage production above recent levels should be allocated by public auction among qualified applicants.

40. Private grazing on public land should be pursuant to a permit that is issued for a fixed statutory

term and spells out in detail the conditions and obligations of both the Federal Government and the permittee, including provisions for compensation for termination prior to the end of the term.

41. Funds should be invested under statutory guidelines in deteriorated public grazing lands retained in Federal ownership to protect them against further deterioration and to rehabilitate them where possible. On all other retained grazing lands, investments to improve grazing should generally be controlled by economic guidelines promulgated under statutory requirements.

42. Public lands, including those in national forests and land utilization projects should be reviewed and those chiefly valuable for the grazing of domestic livestock identified. Some such public lands should, when important public values will not be lost, be offered for sale at market value with grazing permittees given a preference to buy them. Domestic livestock grazing should be declared as the dominant use on retained lands where appropriate.

43. Control should be asserted over public access to and use of retained public grazing lands for nongrazing uses in order to avoid unreasonable interference with authorized livestock use.

44. Fair-market value, taking into consideration factors in each area of the lands involved, should be established by law as a basis for grazing fees.

45. Policies applicable to the use of public lands for grazing purposes generally should be uniform for all classes of public lands.

## Chapter Seven (Mineral Resources)

46. Congress should continue to exclude some classes of public lands from future mineral development.

47. Existing Federal systems for exploration, development, and production of mineral resources on the public lands should be modified.

48. Whether a prospector has done preliminary exploration work or not, he should, by giving written notice to the appropriate Federal land management agency, obtain an exclusive right to explore a claim of sufficient size to permit the use of advanced methods of exploration. As a means of assuring exploration, reasonable rentals should be charged for such claims, but actual expenditures for exploration and development work should be credited against the rentals.

Upon receipt of the notice of location, a permit should be issued to the claimholder, including measures specifically authorized by statute necessary to maintain the quality of the environment, together with the type of rehabilitation that is required.

When the claimholder is satisfied that he has discovered a commercially mineable deposit, he should obtain firm development and production rights by entering into a contract with the United States to satisfy specified work or investment requirements over a reasonable period of time.

When a claimholder begins to produce and market minerals, he should have the right to obtain a patent only to the mineral deposit, along with the right to utilize surface for production. He should have the option of acquiring title or lease to surface upon payment of market value.

Patent fees should be increased and equitable royalties should be paid to the United States on all minerals produced and marketed whether before or after patent.

49. Competitive sale of exploration permits or leases should be held whenever competitive interest can reasonably be expected.

50. Statutory provision should be made to permit
hobby collecting of minerals on the unappropriated public
domain and the Secretary of the Interior should be
required to promulgate regulations in accordance with
statutory guidelines applicable to these activities.

51. Legislation should be enacted which would
authorize legal actions by the Government to acquire
outstanding claims or interests in public land oil shale
subject to judicial determination of value.

52. Some oil shale public lands should be made
available now for experimental commercial development
by private industry with the cooperation of the Federal
Government in some aspects of the development.

53. Restrictions on public land mineral activity
that are no longer relevant to existing conditions
should be eliminated so as to encourage mineral exploration and development and long standing claims should be
disposed of expeditiously.

54. The Department of the Interior should continue
to have sole responsibility for administering mineral
activities on all public lands, subject to consultation
with the department having management functions for
other uses.

55. In future disposals of public lands for nonmin-
eral purposes, all mineral interests known to be of
value should be reserved with exploration and development discretionary in the Federal Government and a
uniform policy adopted relative to all reserved mineral
interests.

Chapter Eight (Water Resources):

56. The implied reservation doctrine of water
rights for federally reserved lands should be clarified and limited by Congress in at least four ways:

(a) amounts of water claimed, both surface and underground, should be formally established; (b) procedures for contesting each claim should be provided; (c) water requirements for future reservations should be expressly reserved; and (d) compensation should be awarded where interference results with claims valid under state law before the decision in *Arizona v. California*.

57. Congress should require the public land management agencies to submit a comprehensive report describing: (1) the objectives of current watershed protection and management programs; (2) the actual practices carried on under these programs; (3) the demonstrated effect of such practices on the program objectives. Based on such information, Congress should establish specific goals for watershed protection and management, provide for preference among them, and commit adequate funds to achieve them.

58. "Watershed protection" should in specified, limited cases be: (1) a reason for retaining lands in Federal ownership; and (2) justification for land acquisition.

59. Congress should require federally authorized water development projects on public lands to be planned and managed to give due regard to other values of the public lands.

## Chapter Nine (Fish and Wildlife Resources):

60. Federal officials should be given clear statutory authority for final land use decisions that affect fish and wildlife habitat or populations on the public lands. But they should not take action inconsistent with state harvesting regulations, except upon a finding of overriding national need after adequate notice to, and full consultation with, the states.

61. Formal statewide cooperative agreements should be used to coordinate public land fish and wildlife programs with the states.

62. The objectives to be served in the management of fish and resident wildlife resources, and providing for their use on all classes of Federal public lands, should be clearly defined by statute.

63. Statutory guidelines are required for minimizing conflicts between fish and wildlife and other public land uses and values.

64. Public lands should be reviewed and key fish and wildlife habitat zones identified and formally designated for such dominant use.

65. A Federal land use fee should be charged for hunting and fishing on all public lands open for such purposes.

66. The states and the Federal Government should share on an equitable basis in financing fish and wildlife programs on public lands.

67. State policies which unduly discriminate against nonresident hunters and fishermen in the use of public lands through license fee differentials and various forms of nonfee regulations should be discouraged.

## Chapter Ten (Intensive Agriculture):

68. The homestead laws and the Desert Land Act should be repealed and replaced with statutory authority for the sale of public lands for intensive agriculture when that is the highest and best use of the land.

69. Public lands should be sold for agricultural purposes at market value in response to normal market demand. Unreserved public domain lands and lands in

land utilization projects should be considered for disposal for intensive agriculture purposes.

70. The states should be given a greater role in
the determination of which public lands should be sold
for intensive agricultural purposes. The state governments should be given the right to certify or veto the
potential agricultural use of public lands but only
according to the availability of state water rights.
Consideration should also be given to consistency of
use with state or local economic development plans
and zoning regulations.

71. The allocation of public lands to agricultural
use should not be burdened by artificial and obsolete
restraints such as acreage limitations on individual
holdings, farm residency requirements, and the exclu-
sions of corporations as eligible applicants.

Chapter Eleven (The Outer Continental Shelf):

72. Complete authority over all activities on the
Outer Continental Shelf should continue to be vested by
statute in the Federal Government. Moreover, all Federal
functions pertaining to that authority, including navi-
gational safety, safety on or about structures and
islands used for mineral activities, pollution control
and supervision, mapping and charting, oceanographic
and other scientific research, preservation and protection of the living resources of the sea, and occupancy
uses of the Outer Continental Shelf, should be consolidated within the Government to the greatest possible
degree.

73. Protection of the environment from adverse
effects of activities on the Federal Outer Continental
Shelf is a matter of national concern and is a responsibility of the Federal Government. The Commission's
recommendations concerning improved protection and
enhancement of the environment generally require separate
recognition in connection with activities on the Shelf,

and agencies having resource management responsibility
on the Shelf should be required by statute to review
practices periodically and consider recommendations from
all interested sources, including the Council on Environmental Quality.

In addition, there must be a continuing statutory
liability upon lessees for the cleanup of oil spills
occasioned from drilling or production activities on
Federal Outer Continental Shelf leases.

74. Proposals to open areas of the Outer Continental
Shelf to leasing, including both the call for nomination
of tracts and the invitation to bid, as well as operational orders and waivers of order requirements should
be published in at least one newspaper of general circu-
lation in each state adjacent to the area proposed for
leasing or for which orders are promulgated.

Where a state, on the recommendation of local interests or otherwise, believes that Outer Continental
Shelf leasing may create environmental hazards, or that
necessary precautionary measures may not be provided,
or that natural preservation of an area is in the best
interest of the public, then, at the state's request,
a public hearing should be held and specific findings
issued concerning the objections raised.

75. The Outer Continental Shelf Lands Act should
be amended to give the Secretary of the Interior authority for utilizing flexible methods of competitive sale.
Flexible methods of pricing should be encouraged, rather
than the present exclusive reliance on bonus bidding,
plus a fixed royalty. In addition, the timing and size
of lease sales, both of which are presently irregular,
should be regularized. Furthermore, while discretion to
reject bids should remain with the Secretary, this authority should be qualified to require that he state his
reasons for rejection.

76. To the extent that adjacent states can prove net burdens resulting from onshore or offshore operations, in connection with Federal mineral leases on the Outer Continental Shelf, compensatory impact payments should be authorized and negotiated.

77. The Federal Government should undertake an expanded offshore program of collection and dissemination of basic geological and geophysical data.

As part of that program, information developed under exploration permits should be fully disclosed to the Government in advance of Outer Continental Shelf lease sales. However, industry evaluations of raw data should be treated as proprietary and excluded from mandatory disclosure.

## Chapter Twelve (Outdoor Recreation):

78. An immediate effort should be undertaken to identify and protect those unique areas of national significance that exist on the public lands.

79. Recreation policies and programs on those public lands of less than national significance should be designed to meet needs identified by statewide recreation plans.

80. The Bureau of Outdoor Recreation should be directed to review, and empowered to disapprove, recreation proposals for public lands administered under general multiple-use policy if they are not in general conformity with statewide recreation plans.

81. A general recreation land use fee, collected through sale of annual permits, should be required of all public land recreation users and, where feasible, additional fees should be charged for use of facilities constructed at Federal expense.

82. Statutory guidelines should be established for resolving and minimizing conflicts among recreation uses and between outdoor recreation and other uses of public lands.

83. The Federal role in assuming responsibility for public accommodations in areas of national significance should be expanded. The Federal Government should, in some instances, finance and construct adequate facilities with operation and maintenance left to concessioners. The security of investment afforded National Park Service concessioners by the Concessioner Act of 1965 should be extended to concessioners operating under comparable conditions elsewhere on the Federal public lands.

84. Private enterprise should be encouraged to play a greater role in the development and management of intensive recreation use areas on those public lands not designated by statute for concessioner development.

85. Congress should provide guidelines for developing and managing the public land resources for outdoor recreation. The system of recreation land classification recommended by the Outdoor Recreation Resources Review Commission should be refined and adopted as a statutory guide to be applied to all public lands.

86. Congress should authorize a program for acquiring and developing reasonable rights-of-way across private lands to provide a more extensive system of access for outdoor recreation and other uses of the public lands.

87. The direct Federal acquisition of land for recreation purposes should be restricted primarily to support the Federal role in acquiring and preserving areas of unique national significance; acquisitions of additions to Federal multiple use lands for recreation purposes should be limited to inholdings only.

88. The Land and Water Conservation Fund Act should be amended to improve financing of public land outdoor

recreation programs. During the interim period until the recreation land use fee we recommend is adopted, the Golden Eagle Program should be continued. After essential acquisitions have been completed, the Land and Water Conservation Fund should be available for development of Federal public land areas.

## Chapter Thirteen (Occupancy Uses):

89. Congress should consolidate and clarify in a single statute the policies relating to the occupancy purposes for which public lands may be made available.

90. Where practicable, planning and advanced classification of public lands for specific occupancy uses should be required.

91. Public land should be allocated to occupancy uses only where equally suitable private land is not abundantly available.

92. All individuals and entities generally empowered under state law to exercise an authorized occupancy privilege should be eligible applicants for occupancy uses, although a showing of financial and administrative capability should be required where large investments are involved.

Lands generally should be allocated competitively where there is more than one qualified private applicant, but preference should be given to state and local governments and nonprofit organizations to obtain land for public purposes and to REA cooperatives where incidental to regular REA operations.

93. In general, disposal should be the preferred policy in meeting the need for occupancy uses that require substantial investment, materially alter the land, and are comparatively permanent in character, except where such uses are nonexclusive.

94. Where occupancy uses are authorized on retained lands by permit, lease, or otherwise, (a) the term and size of permits should be adequate to accommodate the project and the required investment; (b) compensation should be paid when the use is terminated by Federal action prior to expiration of the prescribed term; and (c) a preference right to purchase should be accorded to such users dependent on the lands if they are later offered for disposal.

95. Public lands should not hereafter be made available under lease or permit for private residential and vacation purposes, and such existing uses should be phased out.

96. Land management agencies should have the authority to require a reciprocal right-of-way on equitable terms as a condition of a grant of a right-of-way across public land.

97. A new statutory framework should be enacted to make public lands available for the expansion of existing communities and for the development of new cities and towns.

98. Whenever the Federal Government utilizes its position as landowner to accomplish, indirectly, public policy objectives unrelated to protection or development of the public lands, the purpose to be achieved and the authority therefor should be provided expressly by statute.

99. While control and administration of occupancy uses should remain with the agencies managing the lands, assistance should be obtained from agencies having technical competence in connection with specific programs.

100. The Secretary of the Interior should be authorized to approve other uses of railroad rights-of-way with the consent of the affected railroad, and persons holding defective titles from railroads to

right-of-way lands should be confirmed in their uses by the Federal Government and the affected railroads.

## Chapter Fourteen (Tax Immunity):

101. If the national interest dictates that lands should be retained in Federal ownership, it is the obligation of the United States to make certain that the burden of that policy is spread among all the people of the United States and is not borne only by those states and governments in whose area the lands are located.

Therefore, the Federal Government should make payments to compensate state and local governments for the tax immunity of Federal lands.

102. Payments in lieu of taxes should be made to state governments, but such payments should not attempt to provide full equivalency with payments that would be received if the property was in private ownership. A public benefits discount of at least 10 percent but not more than 40 percent should be applied to payments made by the Government in order to give recognition to the intangible benefits that some public lands provide, while, at the same time, recognizing the continuing burdens imposed on state and local governments through the increased use of public lands. The payments to states should be conditioned on distribution to those local units of government where the Federal lands are located, subject to criteria and formulae established by the states. Extraordinary benefits and burdens should be treated separately and payments made accordingly.

103. In a payments-in-lieu-of-taxes system, a transition period should be provided for states and counties to adjust in changing from the existing system.

## Chapter Fifteen (Land Grants to States):

104. No additonal grants should be made to any of the 50 states.

105. Within a relatively brief period, perhaps from 3 to 5 years, the Secretary of the Interior, in consultation with the involved states, should be required to classify land as suitable for state indemnity selection, in reasonably compact units, and such classifications should aggregate at least 3 or 4 times the acreage due to each state. In the event the affected states do not agree, within 2 years thereafter, to satisfy their grants from the lands so classified, the Secretary should be required to report the differences to the Congress. If no resolution, legislative or otherwise, is reached at the end of 3 years after such report, making a total of 10 years of classification, selection, and negotiation, all such grants should be terminated.

106. Limitations originally placed by the Federal Government on the use of grant lands, or funds derived from them, should be eliminated.

107. The satisfaction of Federal land grants to Alaska should be expedited with the aim of completing selection by 1984 in accordance with the Statehood Act, and selections of land under the Alaska Statehood Act should have priority over any land classification program of the Bureau of Land Management.

## Chapter Sixteen (Administrative Procedures):

108. Congress should require public land management agencies to utilize rulemaking to the fullest extent possible in interpreting statutes and exercising delegated discretion, and should provide legislative restrictions to insure compliance with this goal.

109. Congress should direct the public land agencies to restructure their adjudication organization and

procedures in order to assure: (1) procedural due process; (2) greater third party participation; (3) objective administrative review of initial decisions; and (4) more expeditious decisionmaking.

110. Judicial review of public land adjudications should be expressly provided for by Congress.

## Chapter Seventeen (Trespass and Disputed Title):

111. Statutes and administrative practices defining unauthorized use of public lands should be clarified, and remedies available to the Federal Government should be uniform among land management agencies. Where necessary, statutory authority for policing by Federal agencies should be provided.

112. An intensified survey program to locate and mark boundaries of all public lands based upon a system of priorities, over a period of years, should be undertaken as the public interest requires.

113. The doctrine of adverse possession should be made applicable against the United States with respect to the public lands where the land has been occupied in good faith. Citizens should be permitted to bring quiet title actions in which the Government could be named as defendant. The defenses of equitable estoppel and laches should be available in a suit brought by the Government for the purpose of trying title to real property or for ejectment.

In cases where questions of adverse possession, equitable estoppel, and laches do not apply, persons who claim an interest in public land based upon good faith, undisturbed, unauthorized occupancy for a substantial period of time, should be afforded an opportunity to purchase or lease such lands.

Chapter Eighteen (Disposals, Acquisitions, and Exchanges):

114. Statutory eligibility qualifications of applicants for public lands subject to disposal should generally avoid artificial restraints and promote maximum competition for such lands. Preferences for certain classes of applicants should be used sparingly.

115. Disposals in excess of a specified dollar or acreage amount should require congressional authorization.

116. Where land is disposed of at less than fair-market value, or where it is desired to assure that lands be used for the purpose disposed of for a limited period to avoid undue speculation, transfers should provide for a possibility of reverter, which should expire after a reasonable period of time.

117. Public lands generally should not be disposed of in an area unless adequate state or local zoning is in effect. In the absence of such zoning, and where disposal is otherwise desirable, covenants in Federal deeds should be used to protect public values.

118. Protective covenants should be included in Federal deeds to preserve important environmental values on public lands in certain situations, even where state or local zoning is in effect.

119. The general acquisition authority of the public land management agencies should be consistent with agency missions.

120. The general land acquisition authority of the public land management agencies should be revised to provide uniformity and comprehensiveness with respect to (1) the interests in lands which may be acquired, and (2) the techniques available to acquire them.

121. The public land management agencies should be authorized to employ a broad array of acquisition techniques on an experimental basis in order to determine which appear best adapted to meeting the problem of price escalation of lands required for Federal programs.

122. Congress should specify the general program needs for which lands may be acquired by each public land agency.

123. Justification standards for and oversight of public land acquisitions should be strengthened, and present statutory requirements for state consent to certain land acquisitions should be replaced with directives to engage in meaningful coordination of Federal acquisition programs with state and local governments.

124. General land exchange authority should be used primarily to block up existing Federal holdings or to accomplish minor land tenure adjustments in the public interest, but not for acquisition of major new Federal units.

125. Exchange authority of the public land management agencies should be made uniform to permit (1) the exchange of all classes of real property interests, and (2) cash equalization within percentage limits of the value of the transaction.

126. Generally, within each department, all federally owned lands otherwise available for disposal should be subject to exchange, regardless of agency jurisdiction and geographic limitation.

127. Public land administrators should be authorized by law to dispense with the requirement of a formal appraisal: (1) in any sale or lease where there is a formal finding that competition exists, the sale or lease will be held under competitive bidding procedures, and the property does not have a value in excess of some specified amount set forth in the statute; and (2) whenever property can be acquired

for less than some specified price set forth in the statute, provided a formal finding is made that the property to be acquired has a value at least equal to the amount the Government would be paying in either a direct purchase or exchange.

128. Administration of all land acquisition programs for Department of the Interior agencies, including performance of the appraisal function, should be consolidated within the Department. Procedures, however, should be standardized for all public land management agencies.

## Chapter Nineteen (Federal Legislative Jurisdiction)

129. Exclusive Federal legislative jurisdiction should be obtained, or retained, only in those uncommon instances where it is absolutely necessary to the Federal Government, and in such instances the United States should provide a statutory or regulatory code to govern the areas.

130. Federal departments and agencies should have the authority to retrocede exclusive Federal legislative jurisdiction to the states, with the consent of the states.

## Chapter Twenty (Organization, Administration, and Budgeting Policy):

131. The Forest Service should be merged with the Department of the Interior into a new department of natural resources.

132. Greater emphasis should be placed on regional administration of public land programs.

133. The recommended consolidation of public land programs should be accompanied by a consolidation of congressional committee jurisdiction over public land programs into a single committee in each House of Congress.

134. The President's budget should include a consolidated budget for public land programs that shows
the relationship between costs and benefits of each
program.

135. Periodic regional public land programs should
be authorized by statute as a basis for annual budgets
and for appropriation of funds.

136. There should be a uniform, statutory basis
for pricing goods and services furnished from the
public lands.

137. Statutory authority should be provided for
public land citizen advisory boards and guidelines for
their operation should be established by statute.

# Selected Reading List

# FEDERALLY OWNED LAND IN THE UNITED STATES

*The selected reading list of titles from the Institute of Governmental Studies Library collection was prepared by the Library staff.*

A lengthy bibliography is contained in the *History of Public Land Law Development*, by Paul W. Gates. It is one of the studies prepared for the Public Land Law Review Commission and published by the Government Printing Office in November 1968.

## GENERAL BACKGROUND

Aspinall, Wayne N. and others. "Symposium: Administration of Public Lands." *Natural Resources Journal*, 7(2): 149-265 (1967).

> Contents: The Public Land Law Review Commission: Origins and Goals, by Wayne N. Aspinall; Whose Public Lands? by R. Burnell Held; Strategy and Organization in Public Land Policy, by George R. Hall; The Federal Lands as Big Business, by Marion Clawson; Natural Resources Disposal Policy--Oral Auction Versus Sealed Bids, by Walter J. Mead; Administration of the Mining Laws in Areas of Conflict, by Irving Senzel; The Mining Law and Multiple Use, by Jerry A. O'Callaghan; Managing State Lands: Some Legal-Economic Considerations, by E. Boyd Wennergren and N. Keith Roberts.

Clawson, Marion and Burnell Held. *The Federal Lands: Their Use and Management.* Baltimore: Johns Hopkins Press, 1957. 501p

"Controversy Over Proposal to Establish a Wilderness Area System: Pro and Con." *Congressional Digest*, 40: 289-314 (December 1961).

Contents: How the Federal Lands were Acquired; The Policy for Disposing of Public Lands; How the Vast Federal Lands are Managed; The Present Practice of Public Land Use; Proposal for a Wilderness Area System; Pro and Con Discussion: Should Congress Approve the Bill, S.174, to Establish a Wilderness Area System?

Foss, Phillip O. *Politics and Grass: The Administration of Grazing on the Public Domain*. Seattle: University of Washington Press, 1960. 236p

"The Problem of the Public Lands." *Congressional Digest*, 32: 289-314 (December 1953).

Contents: History of the Public Domain, 1781-1952; U.S. Agencies Managing Federal Lands; The Problem in the Present Congress; Proposal for a Uniform Grazing Act; Differing Views on Final Dispositions; Pro and Con Discussion: Should Congress Enact the D'Ewart Uniform Grazing Bill?

FEDERAL GOVERNMENT

U.S. Bureau of Land Management

*Program for the Public Lands and Resources*. Washington, D.C.: 1962. 40p

This supersedes the 1960 program listed below which "is no longer consistent with

current resource conservation policies of
the Department." The target year for this
program is 1980, whereas the earlier plan
attempted to cover a 52-year span.

*Project Twenty-Twelve: A Long Range Program for Our
Public Lands.* Washington, D.C.: 1960. 63p

This is a proposed program for the Bureau of
Land Management until the year 2012 which
"represents a reasonable projection of the
future needs for the long range management
of the public lands..."

*The Public Lands: Selected Public Land Documents.*
Washington, D.C.: 1963. n.p.

These are reproductions of significant documents and papers on the public lands. The
originals are preserved in the National
Archives. The selection is aimed at showing
the contribution of the federal public lands
to the growth and development of the United
States.

U.S. Congress

House Committee on Interior and Insular Affairs.

Subcommittee on Public Lands. *Federal Land
Ownership and The Public Land Laws: Report
on Taxes and Other In-Lieu Payments on Federal Property*, prepared by the Legislative
Reference Service, Library of Congress.
(83: 2, H. Com. Print, no. 23) Washington,
D.C.: 1954. 9p

Special Subcommittee on Revision of the Public
Land Laws. *Revision of the Public Land Laws:
Report.* (82: 2, H. Rep., no. 2511) Washington,
D.C.: 1952. 9p

Senate Committee on Interior and Insular Affairs

> Subcommittee on Public Lands. *The Public Lands:*
> *Background Information on the Operation of the*
> *Present Public Land Laws.* (88: 1, S. Com. Print)
> Washington, D.C.: 1963. 129p; and *Survey of*
> *National Policies on Federal Land Ownership:*
> *with Special Reference to Studies Conducted*
> *by Committees of the Congress or Commissions*
> *of the Executive Branch of the Federal Govern-*
> *ment,* by John Kerr Rose (85: 1, S. Doc., no. 56)
> Washington, D.C.: 1957. 44p

U.S. National Resources Board

*Report on National Planning and Public Works in*
*Relation to Natural Resources and Including Land*
*Use and Water Resources with Findings and Recom-*
*mendations.* Washington, D.C.: December 1934. 455p

> Contents: Part 1--Report of the Board;
> Part 2--Report of the Land Planning Com-
> mittee; Part 3--Report of the Water Plan-
> ning Committee; Part 4--Report of the
> Planning Committee for Mineral Policy;
> Part 5--Report of the Board of Surveys
> and Maps.

## STATE GOVERNMENTS

Alaska. Legislative Council. Legislative Affairs
Agency. *Public Land in Alaska: Acquisition, Use*
*Administration and Disposition by the State.* Juneau:
1966. 37p

California. Legislature. Senate Interim Committee on
Public Lands. *Partial Report.* Sacramento: 1951. 87p

> This is largely concerned with federally
> owned land in California.

Cooley, Richard A. "State Land Policy in Alaska: Progress and Prospects." *Natural Resources Journal*, 4(3): 455-467 (1965).